VODOU NATION

Haitian Art
Music and
Cultural
Nationalism

VODOU
NATION

MICHAEL
LARGEY

The University of Chicago Press
Chicago and London

Michael Largey is associate professor of music at Michigan State University. He is coauthor of *Caribbean Currents: Caribbean Music from Rumba to Reggae*.

The University of Chicago Press, Chicago 60637
The University of Chicago Press, Ltd., London
© 2006 by The University of Chicago
All rights reserved. Published 2006
Printed in the United States of America

15 14 13 12 11 10 09 08 07 06   5 4 3 2 1

ISBN (cloth): 0-226-46863-1
ISBN (paper): 0-226-46865-8

Library of Congress Cataloging-in-Publication Data
Largey, Michael D., 1959–
    Vodou nation : Haitian art music and cultural nationalism / Michael Largey.
        p.   cm.—(Chicago studies in ethnomusicology)
    Includes bibliographical references and index.
    ISBN 0-226-46863-1 (cloth : alk. paper)—ISBN 0-226-46865-8 (pbk. : alk. paper)
        1. Folk music—Haiti—History and criticism.   2. Voodoo music—Haiti—History and criticism.   3. African Americans—Haiti—Music.   4. Haiti—Social life and customs.   I. Title.   II. Series.
ML3565.L35   2006
780'.97294—dc22

2005023830

For Allison

CONTENTS

ILLUSTRATIONS

ACKNOWLEDGMENTS

I have benefited from the support and counsel of many people during the writing of this book. First, I thank the students and staff of the Section Musicale at Ecole Sainte Trinité where I worked as a music teacher in 1981. The founder of the music school at Sainte Trinité, the late Sister Anne-Marie Bickerstaff, gave me my first experience with Haiti and its people when she invited me, as a sixteen-year-old French horn player, to play with the Orchestre Philharmonique Sainte Trinité. Since then, I have had the good fortune to work with many musicians and artists from Haiti, including Julio and Nina Racine, John Jost, Maryse Bayard McNeeley, Yvrose Philippe-Auguste, Micheline Dalencour, James Smith, Alzire Rocourt, Nicole Saint Victor, Jean Brierre, Lina Mathon-Blanchet, Férère Laguerre, Hughes Leroy, Ciceron and Jean-Claude Desmangles, Claude Dauphin, Solon Verret, Lydia Jeanty, Pierre Blain, Colonel Iphares Blain, Marjorie Garnier, Luc Garnier, Sister Lesly-Anne, Ralph Hyppolite, Tony Belizaire, Père David César, Dickens Princivil, Judith Princivil, Jean-Luc Princivil, Jean Montes, Nadine Lucas, Serge Villedrouin, Micheline Laudun Denis, Raoul Denis, Fritz Benjamin, Simone Elie Stecher, Jean-Claude "Tiga" Garoute, Frantz-Gerard Verret, Carole Demesmin, Muller Louissaint, Wykinson Théodore, Stephenson Joseph, Dieubon Joseph, Estimon Estinril, and Jean Edouard Jovin. Anna-Maria Jaegerhuber and Tony Jaegerhuber gave me permission to reprint Werner A. Jaegerhuber's musical scores and his photograph. John Jost provided the photograph of the score of "1804."

In the United States, many friends and colleagues have read and commented on my work in progress: Allison Berg, Maurea Landies, Stephen Rohs, Mary Gebhart, Noel Allende-Goitía, Mary Procopio, Margaret Furioso, Stephanie Krehbiel, Isaac Kalumbu, Hanna Griff, Robbin Lee Zeff, Caroline LeGuin, Robert Dover, Katherine Borland, Felicia Roberts, Ronald R. Smith, Ruth Stone, Anthony Seeger, Austin B. Caswell, and Richard Bauman. Gage Averill's friendship and intellectual example have given me ample inspiration over the years. Lois Wilcken was a great help as I prepared the manuscript for publication.

I thank Suzanne Flandreau, librarian at the Center for Black Music Research, Columbia College Chicago, and Elizabeth H. Scobell, director of the Drain-Jordan Library at West Virginia State University, for their help in locating manuscripts by William Grant Still and John F. Matheus respectively. Noel Allende-Goitía produced the musical examples, while Mark Sullivan and Elizabeth Bollinger helped produce digital scans of all the photographs. The anonymous readers at the University of Chicago Press helped this to become a better book, and my editors, Elizabeth Branch Dyson, Richard Allen, and Claudia Rex, made the publication process enjoyable.

I have been supported financially by the following organizations through generous grants: a Watson Fellowship in 1981–82, a summer fellowship from the Indiana Federation of Clubs in 1985, a Foreign Language Area Studies fellowship at Indiana University in 1986, a Fulbright-Hays Doctoral Dissertation Fellowship in 1987–88, the 1987 Richard Dorson Prize from Indiana University, a sabbatical leave from Michigan State University in 2000, and an Intramural Research Grant at Michigan State University in 2001.

Finally, I thank my family, Arthur Largey Jr, Marjorie Largey, Meg Largey, CJ Jennings, Tad Largey, Marie Largey, Hugh Largey, Shannon Largey, Devon Borges, Tony Borges, Sandra Sampson, and Charles Sampson for their support. My daughter, Nina Mei-Ling Largey, has been an unending source of joy to me. My wife, Allison Berg, is my first and best reader. She has helped me immeasurably with this manuscript and has been a supportive and encouraging companion during this long process. This book is dedicated to her.

~ ~ ~

I am grateful for permission to reprint portions of chapters 2, 4, and 5, which appeared in the following publications:

"Recombinant Mythololgy and the Alchemy of Memory: Occide Jeanty, Ogou, and Jean-Jacques Dessalines in Haiti." *Journal of American Folklore* 118:327–53. © 2005 by the American Folklore Society (www .afsnet.org).

"Ouanga! An African American Opera about Haiti." *Lenox Avenue: A Journal of Interartistic Inquiry* 2:35–54. © 1996 Center for Black Music Research, Columbia College Chicago.

"Ethnographic Transcription and Music Ideology in Haiti: The Music

of Werner A. Jaegerhuber." *Latin American Music Review* 25, no. 1: 1–31.
© 2004 The University of Texas Press. All rights reserved.

The following publishers allowed me to use their copyrighted materials:

Justin Elie, "Queen of the Night," from *Babylon: a Suite of Four Orientalist Sketches* for full orchestra (piano reduction), measures 1–6 and 41–42. © 1928 by Carl Fischer Music, Inc., New York.

Justin Elie, "In the Temple of the Sun God," from *Kiskaya: An Aboriginal Suite for Orchestra* (1928) for full orchestra (piano reduction), measures 34–38. © 1928 by Carl Fischer Music, Inc., New York.

Justin Elie, "Dance to the Sun God," from *Kiskaya: An Aboriginal Suite for Orchestra* (1928) for full orchestra (piano reduction), measures 1–12 and 44–46. © 1928 by Carl Fischer Music, Inc., New York.

Vèvè (image) of Erzulie, from *Secrets of Voodoo,* by Milo Rigaud. San Francisco: City Lights Books, 1985. © 1985 by City Lights Books. Reprinted by permission of City Lights Books.

NOTE ON ORTHOGRAPHY

Haitian Kreyòl, or *kreyòl ayisyen,* is the language spoken in Haiti. The orthography for Kreyòl, called IPN for the Institut Pédagogique National d'Haïti, was standardized only in the late 1970s. I use the IPN orthography in this book, except for direct quotations using earlier ethnographic systems.

PERFORMING
THE NATION

Musical Constructions of Haitian
Cultural Identity

Booker T. Washington's 1895 Atlanta Exposition Address is justly recalled as a pivotal statement of African American racial uplift ideology. Speaking to a racially diverse audience, Washington intended, in his words, "to cement the friendship of the races and bring about hearty coöperation between them" (Washington 1901/1965, 146). Recognizing his position as a spokesperson for African Americans and as a supplicant to white Americans, Washington used his considerable rhetorical skill to convince both groups of their mutual dependency, articulating his most memorable argument in the form of a parable:

> A ship lost at sea for many days suddenly sighted a friendly vessel. From the mast of the unfortunate vessel was seen a signal, "Water, water; we die of thirst!" The answer from the friendly vessel at once came back, "Cast down your bucket where you are." A second time the signal, "Water, water; send us water!" ran up from the distressed vessel and was answered, "Cast down your bucket where you are!" And a third and a fourth signal for water was answered, "Cast down your bucket where you are!" The captain of the distressed vessel, at last heeding the injunction, cast down his bucket, and it came up full of fresh, sparkling water from the mouth of the Amazon River. To those of my race who depend on bettering their condition in a foreign land or who underestimate the importance of cultivating friendly relations with the Southern white man, who is their next-door neighbour, I would say: "Cast down your bucket where you are"—cast it down in making friends in every manly way of the people of all races by whom we are surrounded. . . . To those of the white race who look to the incoming of those of foreign birth and strange tongue and habits for the prosperity of the South, were I permitted I would repeat what I say to my own

race, "Cast down your bucket where you are." (Washington 1901/1965, 146–47)

Significantly, Washington first exhorts African Americans to remain loyal to the South in their search for stable, dignified employment; only then does he employ his "cast down your buckets" slogan to enjoin whites to hire African Americans instead of recently arrived immigrants to the United States. In a post-Reconstruction climate of political disenfranchisement, racial violence, and black unemployment, Washington's modest demands were applauded by both blacks and whites in the Atlanta Exposition audience. His message reached even larger audiences when he included it in his autobiography *Up From Slavery* (1901).

While central to the history of race relations in the United States, Washington's call to "cast down your bucket" also reached an international black audience that was inspired by Washington's message of racial uplift for the black masses through vocational training. Washington's parable of ships at sea had particular resonance for Haitian educator, physician, politician, and ethnographer Jean Price-Mars, who first met Washington in Paris in 1903 and who visited Washington in 1904 at Tuskegee Institute in order to bring Washington's message of educational reform to the dilapidated Haitian school system. Price-Mars was attracted to Washington's idea that "no race can prosper till it learns that there is as much dignity in tilling a field as in writing a poem" (Washington 1901/1965, 147). As director of Public Education in Haiti from 1912 to 1916, he sought both to extend educational opportunities to the Haitian masses and to reform a French educational model that stressed literature over vocational training.

Price-Mars's vision of educational reform was constrained, however, by the invasion of Haiti by U.S. forces in 1915. For nineteen years, U.S. Marines occupied Haiti with a paternalistic condescension that angered Haitian elites like Price-Mars.[1] While initially inspired by Washington's vocational messages, Price-Mars eventually used Washington's parable to make a statement against U.S. imperialism and to rally Haitian resistance toward the colonial presence of U.S. military forces. In the last years of the U.S. occupation, Price-Mars wrote an article titled "A propos of the 'Harlem Renaissance in the United States,'" in which he quoted Washington's story about "casting down your bucket," but in Price-Mars's version of the story, the point was to change the minds of elite Haitians who were antagonistic toward Haitian popular culture, especially the practice of Vodou. Price-Mars urged Haitian intellectuals to "Plongez vos basquets" (Cast your buckets) into the wealth of Haitian folklore (Price-Mars 1932, 14) because

Haitian traditional culture would serve as a potent antidote to cultural imperialism.

To begin with, the "fresh, sparkling water" pulled up in the buckets represented to Price-Mars the pure, authentic folk tradition of the Haitian peasantry, a heritage capable of satisfying Haitians' thirst for a cultural legacy that could defy the U.S. occupation. If we take this formulation as a metaphor for U.S.-Haitian relations, the vast ocean of salt water was like the rapacious imperialism of the United States, threatening to pollute the fresh water of Haitian folklore. U.S. culture—labeled "Anglo-Saxon" by most Haitian critics at the time—was seen as an unpalatable contaminant, potentially undermining the connections between the Haitian nation and its African-derived past. Price-Mars was one of the first Haitian intellectuals to call for Haitian elites to turn to Haitian lower-class culture as the basis of a new, anti-U.S. Haitian nationalism. Price-Mars specifically asked Haitian elites to reconsider their antagonistic position towards Vodou, the religion practiced by the majority of Haitian peasants.[2]

Blending several West and Central African spiritual traditions with Roman Catholicism, Vodou is a religious practice focused on the spiritual and emotional well-being of its practitioners. Healing is effected through group worship and individual consultations with *oungan* and *manbo* (male and female Vodou priests respectively). Practitioners believe that spirits, called *lwa,* travel from ancestral Africa, or *Ginen,* to help their followers in the material world. Through a series of prayers, songs, and dances, lwa are invited to possess the bodies of worshippers and to provide counsel— from friendly advice to stern admonition—through the mouths of their devotees.[3] Lwa are anthropomorphic and have individual personalities; worshippers are drawn to those lwa with whom they have a personal and spiritual affinity. Worshippers learn about lwa not only through Vodou ceremonies but also through the successive retelling of stories about lwa in which their personal attributes and extraordinary qualities are recounted. Such storytelling has both religious and political significance; worshippers use Vodou narratives to connect themselves with spiritual values and to make sense of political situations in the present. For Haitian elites, however, the spiritual aspects of Vodou were considered to be little more than superstition.

Until Price-Mars's 1928 call for a national music based on the songs of the Vodou ceremony, most elite Haitians traced their cultural roots to Europe. During the eighteenth century, colonial Saint-Domingue was an important center of European-derived musical activity. Between 1764 and 1791, there were over 3,000 musical and dramatic performances in the colony (Fouchard 1955/1988a). After Haitian independence in 1804,

European music remained popular among elite Haitian audiences. In 1860, the Haitian government founded the Ecole Nationale de Musique where students followed the curriculum from the Conservatoire Impérial de Musique de Paris (Dumervé 1968, 40–41). After the invasion of Haiti by the United States in 1915, Haitian composers reevaluated their attitudes toward Haitian peasant music. Composers used Haitian folk sources as the basis of an art music tradition that both claimed a unique, Haitian cultural identity, and established an artistic tradition of resistance by elite Haitians toward U.S. imperialism.

Vodou Nation examines Haitian art music, or *mizik savant ayisyen*, as it reflects the complex interplay of artistic production, cultural nationalism, and ethnography in the early twentieth century. I argue that Haitian composers turned to Vodou, a lower-class Haitian religious practice, to bolster their claims of an "authentic" national identity during the United States occupation of Haiti from 1915 to 1934. Composers treated Vodou ceremonial music as a cultural resource by selectively appropriating, decontextualizing, and, in some cases, repressing ideas in Vodou that were in conflict with elite values.[4]

Haitian composers also helped to create what I term the "Vodou Nation," an elite vision of the Haitian nation that, in times of political strife, selectively associated Haitian elites with Haitian lower classes or *pèp ayisyen*. Nationalist rhetoric employed by elites had to differentiate Haitians from an invading force from the United States while protecting their class interests. By evoking the pèp ayisyen as their symbol of an un-Americanized and hence unpolluted Haitian culture, Haitian elites embraced those aspects of lower-class culture that met their ideological goals while containing those features that challenged their control. Haitian composers such as Occide Jeanty, Ludovic Lamothe, Justin Elie, and Werner Jaegerhuber used the musical materials of the Haitian lower classes to write concert works that evoked the passion of the rural *fèt chanpèt* (country dance) and yet were sufficiently *cultivé et raffiné* (cultivated and refined) to number them with the "serious" composers of concert music in Europe and the United States.

The cultural construction of the Vodou Nation came at a time when foreign interest in Haiti as both a symbol of black distinctiveness in the Americas and as a site of African cultural retention was at its height. African American musicians William Grant Still and Clarence Cameron White each wrote operas about the Haitian revolution (1791–1804) in which Vodou figured prominently. Like elite Haitian composers, Still and White evoked the Vodou ceremony with musical clichés including hand drumming and frenzied dancing while setting their arias in European *bel canto* style. Their models for creating such "vodouesque" musi works were Haitian composers like Ludovic Lamothe and Justin Elie, who similarly sought to pique audience interest with references to Haitian cultural practices within the confines of recognizably "classical" forms.

This study focuses on Haitian cultural nationalism in the late-nineteenth to mid-twentieth century as expressed through musical composition. I follow Thomas Turino's definition of cultural nationalism as "the use of art and other cultural practices to develop or maintain national sentiment for political purposes" (Turino 2000, 14). As Turino points out, cultural nationalism is not simply a matter of stirring nationalist sentiment for patriotic display; it is a means for dealing with the contradictory nature of nationalist thought, what Turino calls the "twin paradoxes" of nationalism (15–16). The first paradox is that nation-states are simultaneously dependent on cosmopolitanism (which connects individual nations to a larger international community) and threatened by it (since an overactive cosmopolitan ethos challenges the nation from without). The second is that "nation-states celebrate and depend on local distinctiveness, but are simultaneously threatened by it," since too much local diversity undermines the unity of the nation-state from within.[5]

In Haiti, music has functioned as a particularly powerful medium for negotiating the tension between cosmopolitanism and local distinctiveness, a tension that reflects longstanding conflicts arising from race, color, class, and language differences.[6] Composers of mizik savant ayisyen combined aspects of the cosmopolitan and the local in order to satisfy multiple audiences' expectations. I argue that in order to foster both domestic and foreign respect for Haitian culture, Haitian composers attempted to write classical music that was both culturally unique and musically universal.[7]

Reconciling the expectations of domestic and foreign audiences was, however, difficult given the particular historical and political constraints on Haiti, beginning with its pariah status in the nineteenth century. Haiti was founded on a slave revolt at a time when most other countries in the Americas had thriving slave economies. As a result, Haiti was frequently reviled by other countries because it offered a model of freedom for black people. Between the declaration of Haitian independence on 1 January 1804 until the Vatican recognized Haiti in 1860, Haiti received diplomatic recognition from one nation—France—only after Haiti paid a multimillion dollar indemnity to offset French losses during the Haitian Revolution. Although the United States traded with Haiti throughout the nineteenth century, formal recognition for Haiti came only in the 1860s. During the latter part of the nineteenth century, foreign interventionism in Haitian affairs grew, culminating in the United States' occupation of the country in 1915. As Mary Renda points out in her study of paternalism during the U.S. occupation of Haiti, Haitians were often infantilized in the U.S. press and by armed forces personnel who saw Haitians as their legal wards (Renda 2001, 16). Frequent journalistic reports of cannibalism, human sacrifice, and orgiastic rituals reinforced Haiti's alleged inferiority by presenting Haiti as a dangerous locale that would benefit from intervention from its "civilized" neighbors.

Until the U.S. occupation of Haiti, most Haitian elites distanced themselves from negative foreign impressions of Haitian culture by identifying with European cultural models. Haitians' attitudes toward culture were influenced by the colonial experience in which French models of cultural refinement were held up as exemplary. During much of the nineteenth century, Haitian intellectuals made passionate arguments for "black capability" in artistic and political pursuits. Anténor Firmin and Hannibal Price both wrote lengthy treatises rebutting prevalent racialist theories while asserting that black people would, given enough time and resources, achieve the same degree of advancement as whites (Firmin 1885; Price 1900). It was only in the twentieth century that Haitian intellectuals, inspired by the African-oriented nationalist writings of Jean Price-Mars, would assert the quality of Haitian artistic production without resorting to the defensiveness assumed by most earlier writing on black capability.

While Haiti was isolated politically for much of its history, many of Haiti's intellectuals saw themselves as part of a larger black intelligentsia that included their African American neighbors. The cultural connections linking Haitian and African American intellectuals exemplifies the historical movement described by Paul Gilroy in *The Black Atlantic* (1993). According to Gilroy, "the history of the black Atlantic . . . continually crisscrossed by the movements of black people—not only as commodities but engaged in various struggles towards emancipation, autonomy, and citizenship—provides a means to reexamine the problems of nationality, location, identity, and historical memory" (Gilroy 1993, 16). Because Gilroy's work looks specifically at the black experience in English-speaking parts of the black Atlantic, Haiti is not included in his study. When his analysis is extended to the relationship between Haiti and the United States, however, it becomes apparent that black people in the Atlantic region crossed linguistic as well as political boundaries to forge intellectual connections with black people from other nation-states.

Indeed, Haitians and African Americans have had a long history of transnational contact. From the beginning of the nineteenth century, Haiti's successful slave revolt provided African Americans with an inspirational example of successful resistance and black sovereignty. In the mid-nineteenth century, Haiti was a destination for African Americans in the colonization movements formed to resettle black people from the United States. While the colonization movement, with its promise to deport masses of freed slaves, appealed to some white racists, it was embraced by some African Americans, most notably the Reverend James Theodore Holly, who took his Hartford, Connecticut congregation to Haiti in 1861 and founded the Episcopal Church of Haiti. In the early twentieth century, African American intellectuals such as W. E. B. Du Bois, Booker T. Washington, and James Weldon Johnson forged their own relationships with Haiti, with Johnson making a lengthy trip to the country in 1920.

In addition, during the U.S. occupation of Haiti, African Americans looked to Haiti as the embodiment of what J. Michael Dash has called a "racial Geist" (Dash 1988, 55) that emphasized the value of black culture in the face of both racist threat and cultural assimilation. As J. Martin Favor (1999, 4) has observed in his study of the "folk" in the New Negro Renaissance, African American rural, vernacular culture has tended to dominate notions of black identity. Drawing from Herderian notions of the rural folk as the root of an authentic, national culture, Du Bois used the "sorrow songs" in his *The Souls of Black Folk* (1903) to connect his readers with what Paul Anderson calls "a repository or archive of African American social memory" (Anderson 2001, 28). But, as the experience of African American slavery grew distant chronologically, African American intellectuals turned to Haiti as an alternative repository of African-based folk culture. Haiti appealed to African Americans not only as a storehouse for those cultural qualities that were believed to be an "authentic" foundation for an African-based national culture but also as a politically-independent black nation.

Indeed, the transnational relationships between Haitians and African Americans, especially in the twentieth century, constitute a form of black nationalism. As Wilson Moses points out:

> Black nationalism has sometimes, but not always, been concerned with the quest for a nation in the geographic sense. But often it has been "nationalism" only in the sense that it seeks to unite the entire black racial family, assuming that the entire race has a collective destiny and message for humanity comparable to that of a nation. (Moses 1987, 16)

This concept of nationalism resembles Stathis Gourgouris's notion of the "dream nation" in which a territory (usually thought of in terms of a state) goes beyond the commonly understood borders of a geographic locality (Gourgouris 1996, 42). For African American nationalists, Haiti was an imagined territory that fell outside the geographic and political purview of the United States. Yet, because Haiti, while sovereign, was nonetheless denied full participation in the Western capitalist system, Haiti was also a reminder of the price of resisting white hegemony. Cedric Robinson claims that:

> Like their European predecessors in the eighteenth and nineteenth centuries, and their contemporaries in the twentieth century all over the world, the Black middle classes—that is, the Black intelligentsias of the United States, the Caribbean, and Africa—were captives of a dialectic: on the one hand, their continued development was structurally implicated in the continued domination of their societies by the Atlantic metropoles; on the other, the historic destiny of their class was linked to nationalism. Put bluntly, the future of the Black middle class was embedded in the contradictions of imperialism. (Robinson 1994, 146)

This paradox is one African Americans and Haitians shared. They dealt with this conundrum by positing a black nationalism that transcended territorial boundaries and that was predicated on a dynamic, political collaboration between oppressed societies. Music was one form of cross-cultural imagination that brought Haitians and African Americans together. To understand how music functioned transnationally, we must first understand Haiti's class dynamics and the role of Vodou in the construction of Haitian cultural nationalism.

SOCIAL CLASS AND DOMINATION IN HAITI

One of the principal constraints on theorizing nationalism, especially in countries where elites have a tenuous grip on authority, is that the concept of nationalism itself emerges from an elite historiographic tradition (Guha 1988, 37). The tendency in early Haitian historiography has been to ignore the contributions of Haitian lower classes to the national struggle and to cast Haitian history as a series of events scripted by Haitian elites. Recent historiographic work on Haiti has demonstrated a more complex relationship between elite and subaltern classes and has raised questions about internal Haitian understandings of historical events (Trouillot 1995).[8]

This study of the elite historiography of Haitian art music interrogates claims of a "national music" in light of the competing and contradictory goals of Haitian subalterns. Gage Averill makes a strong case for the ineffectiveness of elite ideology on the practices of lower-class Haitians following James Scott's critique of "paper-thin hegemony" in which subordinate classes engage in "hidden transcripts" that challenge "public transcripts" of the powerful (Averill 1997, 241, n. 12; Scott 1990, 77–90). I agree with Averill that Haitian elites "never achieved anything like hegemony in rural Haiti" (1997, 7) and that Haitian art music had little effect on the musical practices of Haitian subalterns. However, Haitian elites do have power over Haitian subalterns and have used their authority to enforce their positions on political and social issues. Haitian elites practiced what Ranajit Guha (1997) has termed "dominance without hegemony" in which elite desire for political and social control is channeled into cultural programs in which "universal" (read elite) values are projected onto Haitian subalterns through the appropriation of their music and culture.

Class difference has been a factor in Haitian society since the days of the colony when wealthy French landowners and their light-skinned off-spring from unions with slave women—known as *afranchi* or "freed per-sons"—controlled much of the available capital in Saint-Domingue. After the revolution and the elimination of the white planter class, light-skinned persons of color—known as *lelit milat* (mulatto elites)—and dark-skinned people with access to power (most often through military service), who were known as *lelit nwa* (black elites), assumed positions of power in the newly founded republic. At the bottom of the social ladder were the pèp ayisyen (Haitian lower classes or masses). As Gage Averill has observed, Haitian lower classes include the *abitan* (peasants), who are either *moun mòn* (mountain people) or *moun laplenn* (plains people), with the moun-tain dwellers generally being poorer due to the harshness of the agricul-tural conditions (Averill 1997, 4). During the nineteenth century, a small middle class formed as wealthier peasants experienced upward social mo-bility. This middle class (*klas mwayen*)—with its mulatto and black mem-bers—played an important role in the emergence of a Haitian nationalist consciousness in the early twentieth century.

While skin color plays an important role in establishing and maintain-ing social difference in Haiti, skin color is only one of several characteris-tics that determine a person's social standing. Other factors include an in-dividual's phenotype, education, and something Michel-Rolph Trouillot calls a person's "social direction," or "the measure of the social distance between what is thought to be known of an individual's origin and what is thought to be known of his or her future" (Trouillot 1990, 121). Individ-uals may move up or down socially, depending on their achievements in government, business, and marriage. Trouillot tentatively asserts that while movement from the dark-skinned to the light-skinned side of the social lad-der generally indicates an upward movement (and movement in the dark-skinned direction means a downward movement), the social standing of a family moves slowly over time, making it difficult to measure changes in social direction in a single generation.

Another important factor in determining a person's social status is language, specifically the ability to speak French. The majority of the Haitian population speak Haitian Creole or Kreyòl, a language that grew out of the contact between French planter society and the enslaved African population in colonial Saint-Domingue. In the nearly two centuries since Haitian independence, French retained its associations with wealth, power, and prestige; official transactions were conducted exclusively in French during the nineteenth and early twentieth centuries. In 1959, sociolinguist Charles A. Ferguson identified the linguistic situation in Haiti as "diglossic," where a high-prestige language (French) was used for administrative and educational purposes and a low-prestige language (Kreyòl) was relegated to informal discourse. Today, most linguists refer to Haiti as having two separate linguistic communities: a small, bilingual elite who speak French and Kreyòl and the majority of the population who speak only Kreyòl (Schieffelin and Doucet 1998, 288; Valdman 1984, 80). While the bilingual elite use Kreyòl on a daily basis among themselves (and with their hired help), and in some cases may value the ability to speak colloquial Kreyòl or *kreyòl rèd* (hard Creole), many elite Haitians consider the Kreyòl language to be an inferior form of communication at best and a bastardized form of French at worst.[9]

Despite their superior position in the Haitian social ranks, Haitian elites have occupied a precarious position of power vis-à-vis their lower-class cohorts. Upper-class Haitians were reminded of their tenuous class position during the occupation of Haiti, when many white U.S. military personnel, ignorant of Haitian social codes, tended to categorize all Haitians as inferior to whites despite their social status. Haitian elites internalized this foreign threat and came to identify themselves symbolically with lower-class Haitians.

Haitian elites have never been in a position to assert hegemonic control over the pèp. For one thing, Haitian elites, most of whom live in Haiti's urban areas, had limited contact with the rural population. Prior to their twentieth century interest in indigenous culture, elites ignored the rural sectors of society. Despite the pèp's overwhelming numerical superiority over the elite classes (roughly 75 percent of the population lives in rural Haiti), the pèp are both physically and psychologically distanced from the elite. This social isolation is reproduced in elite ways of speaking about the pèp; rural dwellers are known as *moun andeyò* (literally, "the outside people"), indicating their status as outside the social mainstream as defined by elite society. When elites refer to pèp (people or masses) or abitan (rural farmers), frequently the words employed define the pèp for what they lack. For example, some common elite terms for non-elites include: *malpwòpte* (unwashed), *malelve* (ill-bred), *malere* (fem. *malerèz*) (without money, poor), *mizerab* (pitiful, poor). Conversely, as Trouillot (1990) notes, pèp often refer to elites as *leta* (the state) regardless of an individual's connection to the government.

Besides their isolation from pèp, elites, especially those associated with the federal government, were economically dependent on the abitan for food and tax revenues. After independence, the plantation system was broken up and the abitan population spread out to the Haitian countryside, where they formed small, family-centered agricultural units. Abitan provided the cities with food for local consumption as well as crops for export. In the nineteenth century, through a process of indirect taxation on export commodities, the government placed a disproportionate tax burden on single-crop peasant farmers (Trouillot 1990, 60–62). Thus, urban dwellers depended on abitan not only for food but also for the tax revenues that supported them. This pattern has persisted through the twentieth century, forcing peasants to squeeze more product out of decreasingly productive farmland.

Haitian elites were also in a precarious position as defenders of their country in the face of foreign invasion. During the nineteenth century, the effectiveness of the Haitian military eroded significantly. According to Trouillot, "since the days of Louverture, military rank had functioned as a mechanism for socioeconomic advancement, and after 1825, with the French threat receding, the army became a fustian network of political sinecures, utterly useless for the protection of the country when it was menaced by the very same individuals who furnished its uniforms" (Trouillot 1990, 66). After the U.S. occupation of Haiti, the ineffective Haitian army was transformed into the Garde d'Haiti, an internal police force focused on quelling disturbances within the country rather than repelling foreign invasions. In addition, the Haitian government established an unhealthy dependence on foreign commerce during the nineteenth century. Instead of using tax revenues to build capital that could be reinvested in public works and social programs, politicians spent large sums of money bolstering their regimes and enriching foreign merchants.

In short, Haitian elites were caught between a Western capitalist system that favored the exploitation of Haitian markets and a hostile lower class that bore the financial burdens for the country but threatened to rebel at any time. As Partha Chatterjee observed about a similar situation in India, upper classes in Haiti aspired to hegemonic control over lower classes but were constrained by their own subordination to the larger capitalist system.

In other words, Haitian elites were "simultaneously placed in a position of subordination in one relation and a position of dominance in another" (Chatterjee 1993, 36). Haitian elites experienced subalternity in the international realm even as they dominated their own country's national life.

In the late nineteenth and early twentieth centuries, African American elites were in a similar position vis-à-vis the black lower classes in the United States. In his study of the politics of "racial uplift" ideology, Kevin Gaines shows that African American elites espoused assimilationist ideas for the social "improvement" of black lower classes. According to Gaines:

> Uplift ideology's argument for black humanity was not an argument for equality. Indeed, the shift from race to culture, stressing self-help and seemingly progressive in its contention that blacks, like immigrants, were assimilatable into the American body politic, represented a limited, conditional claim to equality, citizenship, and human rights for African Americans. Black elites espoused a value system of bourgeois morality whose deeply embedded assumptions of racial difference were often invisible to them. It was precisely as an argument for black humanity through evolutionary class differentiation that the black intelligentsia replicated the dehumanizing logic of racism. (Gaines 1996, 4)

Similarly, Haitian composers used the rhetoric of racial uplift in their rationalizations for using the artistic materials of the Haitian underclass to produce an authentic, yet refined, version of Haitian music.

Yet, by including the music of the Vodou ceremony as a means toward racial uplift, Haitian elites also self-consciously invoked a cultural practice that eschewed bourgeois values and promoted black agency. Vodou's status as a black religious tradition challenged the assimilationist tendencies of the racial uplift movement, positing a black tradition as the basis of a national identity and embracing a cultural practice that did not curry favor with white audiences abroad.

VODOU AND CULTURAL INTIMACY

The title *Vodou Nation* draws attention to the apparent rhetorical contradiction in elites using a Haitian lower-class cultural practice to represent the nation. As a religion practiced by the majority of rural Haitians, Vodou has been viewed by elite Haitians as a threat to civil society and moral order since the establishment of the Haitian state. Many Haitian presidents took hard anti-Vodou stances, especially during times of peasant unrest. Vodou has also come to represent those characteristics of Haitian society that are feared and reviled by foreign observers. Since the Haitian Revolution in 1804, which established the first independent, black-ruled republic in the Americas, Vodou has been blamed for Haiti's problems and has been the target of racially motivated prejudice that depicts Haitians as pathological (Hurbon 1995). Although other African-derived religious practices such as Santería in Cuba, Shango in Trinidad, and Kumina in Jamaica share similarities with Vodou—including their use of music and dance to achieve spirit possession and their veneration of spirits from ancestral Africa through sacrificial offerings—Vodou has drawn a disproportionate amount of criticism from foreign observers.

In its capacity to instill revulsion in Haitian elites and fear in foreigners while providing a potential rallying point for Haitians wanting to distinguish themselves from outsiders, Vodou invokes what Michael Herzfeld calls "cultural intimacy," or "the recognition of those aspects of a cultural identity that are considered a source of external embarrassment but that nevertheless provide insiders with their assurance of common sociality" (Herzfeld 1997, 3). Cultural intimacy's capacity to bring elites and lower-classes together in order to feature the inherent conflicts within a given society makes it a useful tool for understanding Haitian cultural nationalism.

This study views nationalism not as a monolithic ideology but as a rhetorical flashpoint for internal debates about race and color, class, gender, and religion, among other issues.[10] As Prasenjit Duara has observed, "nationalism is rarely the nationalism of *the nation*, but rather marks the site where different representations of the nation contest and negotiate with each other" (Duara 1995, 8). Debates about the Haitian nation are not readily reconciled but are continually played out in cultural performances that underscore the dynamic tensions embedded in national life. Nationalism can thus be seen as a "form of mediation" in which inflammatory cultural ideas are used by different social groups for their own purposes (Chatterjee 1993, 72). Vodou is just such a volatile touchstone for debates about Haitian national identity. As a practice of lower-class Haitians that has been put to use by elite Haitians in a variety of contexts, Vodou provides a look into the workings of elite historiographic constructions.

During the colonial period, Vodou was seen by the predominantly white French planters as little more than superstition, a holdover from African ancestral rites. In his chronicle of pre-revolutionary Haiti (or, as it was called at the time, Saint-Domingue), Médéric-Louis-Elie Moreau de Saint-Méry (1798) described Vodou thus:

> In a word, nothing is more dangerous, according to all the accounts, than this cult of Voodoo [Vaudoux]. It can be made into a terrible weapon—this extravagant idea that the ministers of this alleged god know all and can do anything. (Moreau de St. Méry 1985, 6–7)

Moreau St. Méry's reference to Vodou's potential role as a weapon against slaveholding society was more than idle speculation. On 22 August 1791, a group of slaves led by runaway slave Boukman Dutty met at Bois-Caïman and held what historians believe was a Vodou ceremony in which they pledged their commitment to overthrowing the slave society of Saint-Domingue (Fick 1990, 102–104). While historians have debated the influence of Vodou on the Haitian Revolution, most agree that the slave revolt used Vodou imagery as part of its promotional arsenal and that Vodou ceremonies provided important opportunities for slave organization (Geggus 1983).

In the nineteenth century, after the success of the revolution and the establishment of the Haitian state, Vodou retained its dangerous associations, especially in the eyes of the newly established Haitian ruling class. During the first forty years after Haitian independence, Haitian presidents rigorously suppressed Vodou practice. Jean-Jacques Dessalines, Haiti's first president (later, emperor) and Henri Christophe (the leader of a Haitian northern kingdom between 1807 and 1820) "feared not only the latent potential of Vodou as a catalyst for revolution, but also the effects of magic done against them" (Desmangles 1992, 45). Elite fear of Vodou as a political and spiritual force motivated frequent anti-Vodou purges during the nineteenth and twentieth centuries. Political leaders also used Vodou to underwrite their own designs on power. Faustin Soulouque, who ruled Haiti as president from 1847 to 1849 and then as Emperor Faustin I from 1849 until 1859, curried favor with the masses by allowing the open practice of Vodou while officially claiming Haiti to be a Catholic nation (Nicholls 1979, 83).

Roman Catholicism in Haiti suffered a major setback after the Haitian Revolution. In the years between independence in 1804 and 1860, no foreign priests (save a few immigrants from South American countries) came to Haiti, forcing the Haitian government to appoint priests without the consent of the Vatican. By 1860, Haitian Catholicism was in shambles while Vodou grew with little interference from Haitian officials. Consequently, despite Catholicism's status as the religion of the ruling elite, Vodou gained significant strength during the first fifty years after Haitian independence. As the dominant religious practice of the Haitian masses, Vodou was considered by Haitian elites to embody those cultural characteristics that were drawn from African rather than French culture. With its focus on ancestor veneration and its use of nomenclature drawn from African sources, Vodou was seen by Haitian elites as proof that the Haitian pèp were culturally closer to African culture than were the upper classes.

As the nascent Pan-African movement gained some support in Haiti, Haitian intellectuals reconsidered Vodou's association with African culture as a potentially positive trait. When U.S. Marines invaded Haiti in 1915 and began a nineteen-year occupation of the country, elites turned to Vodou as a potential defense against foreign cultural encroachment. Dr. Jean Price-Mars's *La vocation de l'élite* (1919) and *Ainsi parla l'oncle* (1928/1983), exhorted Haitian elites to take their place as leaders of the country, to reconsider their relationship to Haitian lower classes, and to embrace the African side of their cultural legacy.

Price-Mars's call for a "Haitian national music" gave early twentieth-century composers the opportunity to write works that were not entirely derived from European cultural or linguistic idioms. Haitians routinely engage in what Gage Averill calls "discourses of authenticity" when discussing the relative "Haitianness" of a particular musical genre (Averill 1997). Averill also notes that for many Haitians, musical genres are considered to be more or less Haitian depending on their relationship to music of the Vodou ceremony (Averill 1989). *Mizik savant ayisyen,* with its reliance on Western musical notation and stylistic forms, is, according to Averill's typology, the Haitian musical genre farthest from the "center-post" of Haitian musical authenticity, Vodou music. By including Haitian rhythms, melodies, and language in their works, Haitian composers tried to deflect criticism of their music as overly European, or, as Haitians sometimes call it, *mizik blan* (white or foreign music). At the same time, Haitian elites were concerned that using the music of the Vodou ceremony in an unrefined form might bring the undesirable aspects of lower-class culture into the elite salons. By labeling Vodou-derived music as *fòklò* (folklore), elites distanced themselves from the religious aspects of Vodou music while maintaining a cultural connection to rural Haiti.

As Haitian elites promoted Vodou as a valuable cultural resource, foreign audiences developed a taste for cultural practices that reinforced their exoticized impressions of Haiti. Foreign journalism and literature about Haiti in the nineteenth century was based on exploiting Vodou's dangerous reputation in order to bolster foreign claims of Haitian backwardness and barbarism. During the U.S. occupation of Haiti, soldiers laid down their weapons long enough to pen "first-hand" accounts of Vodou attractions and atrocities (Craige 1933 and 1934; Renda 2001; Wirkus and Dudley 1931).

As Vodou was adopted and adapted by different audiences in the twentieth century, it soon took on aspects of a cultural commodity. By incorporating Vodou into Haitian art music, Haitian composers tried to retain the "use value" of Vodou music with its connection to Haitian lower-class culture while expanding the "exchange value" of Vodou in an international market, thus demonstrating their connection to a larger, cosmopolitan audience.[11]

However, Haitian elites underestimated the degree to which their subordinate position in the Western capitalist system would constrain their ability to control the "exchange value" of Vodou once it became an international commodity. In this context, Haitian composers were unable to overcome the exoticized reception their works received in the international market. For example, Haitian composer Justin Elie, who had a successful career as a composer and pianist in New York City in the 1920s, was forced to write music that misrepresented and exploited Vodou and Native American culture, two popular forms of exotica at that time.

VODOU AND CULTURAL MEMORY

While Haitian composers could not eliminate foreign control of Vodou as a market commodity, they were active in promoting their own Vodou-inspired art music as a site of Haitian cultural memory.[12] According to Marita Sturken, cultural memory is "memory that is shared outside the avenues of formal historical discourse yet is entangled with cultural products and imbued with cultural meaning" (Sturken 1997, 3). The musical works of Haitian composers are what Pierre Nora has called "lieux de memoire" or sites of memory that "are constantly evolving new configurations of meaning . . . their constant revision mak[ing] them part of the dynamism of the historical process" (O'Meally and Fabre 1994, 8–9). As a site of cultural memory, mizik savant ayisyen is chronicled in "unofficial" documents of personal narratives, poems, creative nonfiction, and correspondence.

Mizik savant ayisyen allows the ritual enactment of the potentially volatile cultural practices of Vodou in a controlled yet aesthetically transformative space. Vodou's relationship to Haitian elite culture is continually reshaped through performances of Haitian art music. While the religious functions of Vodou have been removed for the most part, the cultural significance of the Vodou trace—what Nestor García Canclini calls the "praised residue" of popular practice (García Canclini 1995, 148)—remains as a "bodily social memory" (Reily 2001, 5; Connerton 1989). Such a "bodily memory" is enacted through musical performance in ways that allow an individual to move beyond "imagining" the nation through print-capitalism (cf. Anderson 1991). As Sue Tuohy has observed about musical nationalism in China, "in musical performance, citizens do not merely 'read' the nation; they see, hear, and participate in it" (Tuohy 2001,

124). By using Vodou in Haitian art music, composers create opportunities for performers to embody Vodou ritual, taking the melodies, rhythms, and in some cases, the movements from Vodou ceremonial rituals as the basis of a new, culturally informed understanding of Haitian culture. Mizik savant ayisyen also allows Haitian audiences to "engage cultural elements to produce concepts of the nation" (Sturken 1997, 2–3). For example, Haitian composer Occide Jeanty wrote band music during the U.S. occupation that prompted civil unrest by encouraging Haitian crowds to imagine themselves as fighting a second Haitian Revolution.

The construction of cultural memory depends on remembering the past, but forgetting part of it as well. This forgetting may take the form of the large-scale "silences about the past" that Michel-Rolph Trouillot has analyzed in his historiography of the Haitian Revolution (Trouillot 1995). Or, it may involve the systematic elimination of disruptive elements of Vodou practice from the performance of Haitian art music. As one Haitian composer told me during an interview, he was uninterested in the religious aspects of Vodou ritual, calling it *vye bagay* (old or nasty stuff). In either case, forgetting brings the practice of Haitian art music into relationship with similar cultural processes.

Vodou Nation analyzes four modes of cultural memory through which new understandings of cultural identity are formed over time. The first mode is *recombinant mythology*, the practice of using mythologically oriented language to highlight praiseworthy characteristics of cultural heroes through a series of concatenated stories. Recombinant myths are, like the Vodou ancestral tradition, built on successive retellings of archetypal stories in new historical contexts. They are part of what Raymond Williams calls a "selective tradition" in which salient features of cultural narratives are chosen for their efficacy in linking the power of the past with the concerns of the present (Williams 1977, 116). As Joseph Roach points out, however, the selectiveness of tradition does not necessarily guarantee that ideas from the past fit comfortably into present-day contexts. Rather the process of "surrogation," what he calls the "three-sided relationship of surrogation memory, performance, and substitution" (Roach 1996, 2) shows that in new performances of ideas from the past, what is "substituted" in may precipitate new conflicts or "may congeal into full-blown myths of legitimacy and origin" (3). In the case of Haitian composer Occide Jeanty, narratives about his loyalty and bravery during the U.S. occupation of Haiti were infused with ideas from Vodou religious imagery to produce mythologically inflected rhetoric that reinforced his persona as a Haitian cultural hero.

Another mode of cultural memory is the use of class-specific practices to produce cross-class performances of important cultural ideas, which

I term *vulgarization* and *classicization.* Vulgarization—the use of lower-class performance genres in upper-class performance contexts—occurs when composers borrow popular musical forms to reinforce elite authority. Ludovic Lamothe's use of the Haitian dance genre the méringue, in both its elite parlor form and its popular politicized form as a Carnival song, brought Haitian elite audiences into a relationship with lower-class Haitians without the threat of cultural contamination. Classicization—the use of historically and geographically distant ideas to link current practice to an esteemed "classical" past—allows composers to ignore the political divisions of the present in favor of an idealized, ahistorical musical tradition. According to Partha Chatterjee, such a "classicization of tradition" is "a prior requirement for the vertical appropriation of sanitized popular traditions" (Chatterjee 1993, 73). For example, Justin Elie wrote works that commemorated idealized notions of a Haitian past by emphasizing Haitians' connections to ancient African and Native American civilizations while trying to sidestep what elites viewed as the more unsavory aspects of Vodou practice.

Haitian and African American composers developed a third mode of cultural memory that allowed them to merge their race and class interests in ways that circumvented dominant narratives of cultural influence through what I term *diasporic cosmopolitanism.* As Thomas Turino has claimed about popular music in Zimbabwe, producers of music engage less in an overtly "nationalistic" promotion of their cultural products and more in a "cosmopolitan" formation of culture. In Turino's model, "particular cosmopolitan lifeways, ideas, and technologies are not specific to a single or a few neighboring locales, but are situated in many sites which are not necessarily in geographical proximity; they are connected by different forms of media, contact, and interchanges" (Turino 2000, 7–8).

Diasporic cosmopolitanism describes the process by which Haitian and African American elites deliberately adopt values associated with intellectuals from African, African American, and Caribbean cultures (as opposed to white cultural models). In his critique of Eurocentric formulations of nationalism, Partha Chatterjee suggests that non-European nationalist movements may rely on very different criteria for the formation of their own nationalist ideologies (Chatterjee 1993). If, as Turino suggests, elites share a cross-cultural connection with members of similar class backgrounds in other nation-states, then it is possible to see Haitian and African American elites as participating in a shared vision of black nationalism (cf. Moses 1987). For example, African American composers Clarence Cameron White and William Grant Still wrote operas about the Haitian Revolution that linked African American cultural and political concerns with the most significant event in Haitian history. Haitian composer Werner Jaegerhuber also employed African and African American musical concepts to promote his work on the Haitian peasants to an Afrodiasporic audience. All three composers were interested in connecting their local art music traditions with a larger, African-influenced artistic world.

Finally, Haitian composers developed a fourth mode of cultural memory that linked the transcription of peasant music to the composition of art music through what I term *music ideology*. Following sociolinguists Bambi Schieffelin's and Rachelle Charlier Doucet's work on "language ideology," in which decisions about a language's orthography are based on competing ideologies of power and authority, I argue that Haitian composers applied their own "music ideology" to the transcription of Haitian peasant music and its incorporation into Haitian art music. Werner Jaegerhuber conducted ethnographic fieldwork and collected dozens of Haitian songs which he incorporated into his own compositions. Jaegerhuber's belief that irregular time signatures conveyed both the African origins of Haitian folksong and the sophistication of his own compositions reflected his own music ideology that tried to reconcile African and European musical aesthetics.

Each of these modes of cultural memory—recombinant mythology, vulgarization and classicization, diasporic cosmopolitanism, and music ideology—produces narratives that connect the present with an idealized past, a past in which Vodou religious practice is transformed from a threat to elite Haitian sovereignty into what Christine Yano has called an "internal exotic, a resource once removed from people's lives, yet central to their version of national-cultural identity" (Yano 2002, 15; cf. Ivy 1995). By basing a nationalist ideology on a potentially threatening cultural practice, Haitian elites invoked the revolutionary spirit of Vodou at a time when Haitian national sovereignty was threatened by the U.S. occupation. The Vodou Nation is, then, a project of cultural nationalism which manufactures national sentiment through emotional attachments to an imagined past (Anderson 1991; Yano 2002).

In the chapters that follow, I explore the relationship between ethnography, musical production, and cultural memory from the 1890s to the 1950s. By examining the historical period in which the United States occupied Haiti, including the years preceding and following the occupation, this study places the cultural practice of mizik savant ayisyen in its historical and political contexts. Composers used ethnography to explore the roots of Haitian culture at a time when the Haitian state (and Haitian culture) was under threat. Composers produced musical works that invoked modes of cultural memory to preserve Haitian culture under the threat of political intervention and cultural assimilation.

Chapter 1, "The Politics of Musical Ethnography: Jean Price-Mars and the Ethnological Movement," examines the work of Jean Price-Mars, one of the founders of the Haitian *négritude* movement and an advocate for a Haitian national music. Price-Mars's work as an ethnographer of Haitian Vodou and social critic of Haitian elite prejudice toward lower-class Haitian cultural expressions made it possible for composers to turn to the music of the Vodou ceremony as an inspirational resource. Specifically, Price-Mars's publications brought the activities of the Vodou ceremony to a hitherto hostile Haitian elite audience. I suggest that Price-Mars's political efforts to promote Haitian nationalism were realized through his championing for Haitian culture, specifically music.

Chapter 2, "Recombinant Mythology and the Alchemy of Memory: Occide Jeanty, Ogou, and Dessalines," examines early twentieth-century literature and oral accounts of Haitian composer Occide Jeanty's role in the resistance against the U.S. occupation of Haiti. I argue that Jeanty's historical image as a composer and nationalist have been combined with myths about Jean-Jacques Dessalines, the first leader of the Haitian state, and with Ogou, a Vodou spirit who is associated with warfare, fire, and military activity. While Dessalines and Ogou had already been linked through a process of traditionalization in which the attributes of the fierce Ogou were transposed onto Dessalines in the early twentieth century, Jeanty's image folded into the preexisting Dessalines/Ogou fusion through a process I call "recombinant mythology." By composing works during the U.S. occupation of Haiti in the early twentieth century that invoked the Haitian Revolution of the eighteenth century, Jeanty used Haitian history and folklore as powerful tools of resistance to foreign occupation.

In Chapter 3, "Africans and Arawaks: The Music of Ludovic Lamothe and Justin Elie," I compare the work of two Haitian composers who had very different ideas about the cultural provenance of Haitian music. Elie, who conducted ethnographic fieldwork among different Native American groups during his tours of the Caribbean and South America, posited a Native American, specifically Taíno Arawak, origin for the "national" music style of Haiti. Lamothe, who wrote several articles about "national" Haitian music, turned to the African side of the Haitian cultural patrimony for his inspiration. I demonstrate that both composers were interested in fusing their respective non-Western cultural inspirations with a European-derived concert music style in order to make their music palatable to foreign and domestic audiences.

Chapter 4, "Visions of Vodou in Operas about Haiti: *Ouanga* and *Troubled Island*," examines the work of African American composers Clarence Cameron White and William Grant Still, who wrote the operas

Ouanga and *Troubled Island* respectively. White and his librettist John Matheus both traveled to Haiti to conduct "research" for their work, while Langston Hughes, the librettist for *Troubled Island,* also visited Haiti. Their operas, which exposed U.S. audiences to the Haitian Revolution and to the Vodou religious tradition, were part of a larger process of Afrodiasporic artistic production. Their work demonstrated the ways in which people in the black Atlantic forged ties with each other across political and linguistic boundaries.

In Chapter 5, "Ethnography and Music Ideology: The Music of Werner A. Jaegerhuber," I examine Jaegerhuber's contributions to the study of Haitian music and folklore, which include his ethnographic research in the Haitian countryside and his incorporation of folksong transcriptions into his compositions. Born in Haiti and trained in Germany as a musician, Jaegerhuber was forced to leave Germany when the Nazi Party rose to power in the mid 1930s. Jaegerhuber was an important contributor to the post-occupation ethnographic movement directed by Jacques Roumain, the first director of the Haitian Bureau d'Ethnologie. I argue that Jaegerhuber's efforts to use Haitian Vodou music in his classical music compositions were part of his own music ideology that sought to reconcile the African and European elements of Haitian music.

Vodou Nation traces the processes by which Haitians and African Americans addressed each other through politically inflected artistic practice. The modes of cultural memory described here extend not just to Africa but also to African Americans as part of a larger African diaspora. Haiti never had a "back to Africa" movement linked to Garveyite political activities. However, Haiti was already connected to Africa in the eyes of many Haitian elites because of Vodou's strong ties to African cultural practices. Haitians did not need to return to the land of Africa if, in their minds, the idea of Africa already existed within the confines of their nation-state. As the self-proclaimed representatives of African culture in the Americas, Haitians were well situated to encourage a vision of an authentic, black, African-based culture among other black constituencies in the Americas.

~ 1 ~
THE POLITICS OF MUSICAL ETHNOGRAPHY

Jean Price-Mars and the Ethnological Movement

Early twentieth-century composers of Haitian *mizik savant* were part of a larger process of Haitian cultural change. Stimulated by abrupt changes in Haiti's political and economic relations with foreign powers, Haitian elites constructed a nationalist discourse that became a touchstone for most aspects of Haitian cultural production, especially music. A full understanding of Haitian mizik savant produced during the early twentieth century requires knowledge of the prevailing ideological currents in late nineteenth-century Haiti. Several Haitian nationalist schools of thought emerged in Haiti during the first two decades of the twentieth century, due in large part to the disruptive influence of the United States occupation that began in 1915.

This chapter discusses how Haitian elites' concerns shifted from a preoccupation with internal class and color conflicts to a determination to establish a Haitian national identity in the face of foreign intervention. The United States occupation of Haiti from 1915 to 1934 sparked a "nativistic movement" (Linton 1943) that resulted in several indigenous Haitian responses. The indigenous responses I am concerned with center around the development of the ethnological movement (sometimes called the *mouvement indigène* or *mouvement folklorique*) that advocated a reevaluation of Haiti's African ancestry and the establishment of criteria for evaluating the authenticity of Haitian cultural productions. Haitian composers of mizik savant, influenced by the ethnological movement, created new forms of Haitian musical expression that fused indigenous instruments, lyrics, and rhythms with European-influenced musical forms and textures.

While Haitian elites were turning to the Haitian rural underclass as the root of an "authentic" national culture, they were simultaneously considering how Pan-African ideologies affected their relationships with other black populations in the Americas. African American intellectuals such as W. E. B. Du Bois, Booker T. Washington, and James Weldon Johnson included Haiti as part of a larger, Pan-African diaspora by stressing the common concerns of black people around the world. At the same time, Haitian writers like Jean Price-Mars looked to African American intellectuals for ideas about how to posit an African diasporic culture that embraced similarities with Africans in the United States while maintaining a unique, Haitian culture that resisted absorption into the growing imperial presence of the United States.

The emergence of a Haitian nationalist consciousness in the early twentieth century was tied not only to political and social changes but also to the articulation of scholarly discourses about the nature and origins of national identity. Scholarly interest in constructing a culture to study—epitomized by the work of Jean Price-Mars and members of the ethnological movement—inspired nationalists to adopt Pan-African anthropological rhetoric in service of the nation.

RESEARCH ON MUSIC AND ETHNOGRAPHY

Although Price-Mars is often attributed with first calling attention to the folkloric heritage of the Haitian working class, musical composers, including those he enjoined to use folk sources, had already been borrowing ideas and inspiration from non-elite sources since the late nineteenth century. For example, Haitian military band composer Occide Jeanty, especially in his concert méringues, sought a characteristic Haitian sound for his popular compositions and achieved a high degree of notoriety for his efforts.

Haitian composers of the early twentieth century were similarly interested in incorporating Haitian characteristics before Price-Mars published his *Ainsi parla l'oncle*. These composers practiced a form of musical ethnography that had specific goals and processes, some of which anticipated the ethnographic approaches Price-Mars promoted in the 1930s.

The most important technique of the composer was *rechèch* (research). The research techniques of Haitian composers included a form of fieldwork in which composers collected material for their compositions during sojourns either in the countryside or on the streets of Port-au-Prince. For these composers, all members of the Haitian elite, music was a raw material to be molded by the skilled hands of the composer.

Rechèch trips were rarely planned; elites circulated in the countryside, pursuing a vigorous constitutional or some other amusement, like hunting or fishing. On one such trip to a rural area in Haiti in 1920, Jean Price-Mars had an impromptu encounter with a group of Haitians performing a

Vodou ceremony. While out on horseback hunting for wild game, Price-Mars stumbled upon a ceremony in progress, much to the dismay of the participants. Both he and his surprised hosts had reason to be apprehensive about his discovery:

> I interrupted a legally forbidden ceremony and my clothes were a principal reason for my mistake that caused the participants of the ceremony to scatter. In effect, clothed in a horseback-riding outfit, wearing a khaki helmet, legs encased in a yellow flannel, a gun in a bandolier, I resembled an officer in the rural police force. Thus my initial attempt to dissuade the runaways, my engaging pleas, failed to inspire their confidence and I was unable to ascertain the principal elements of the celebration and what it was celebrating. (Price-Mars 1938, 21)

While Price-Mars eventually gained access to Vodou ceremonies, which were the focus of his ethnographic interests, most Haitian elites' experience with Vodou as practiced in the countryside was more akin to Price-Mars's first exposure: an unsettling, frightening, and vaguely dangerous encounter with people who feared reprisals.

Most Haitian elites, however, did not have to go on expeditions to hear music of the Vodou ceremony. In many cases, the folk songs that composers heard in Haiti were already familiar to them from their own experiences. Despite the fact that over 70 percent of the Haitian population lived in countryside in the early twentieth century, abitan (rural workers) had a ubiquitous presence in urban life. The U.S. occupation of Haiti from 1915 to 1934, with its *corvée*, or work gangs, and its repression of rural resistance, forced large numbers of abitan to the urban areas, especially Port-au-Prince and Cap Haïtien. Abitan worked in the homes of the urban elite as maids, gardeners, house servants, and cooks. Children growing up in these elite households were exposed to the stories, legends, and folksongs mentioned in Price-Mars's *Ainsi parla l'oncle* without having to leave the house (Victor 1943).

Another locus of folkloric exposure among elites was the summer home. For those elites who could afford more than one dwelling, the hot Haitian summers were often spent in the mountains east of Port-au-Prince. The towns of Kenscoff and Furcy, both around 1,000 meters above sea level, provided relief from the dirt and heat of the city and gave elites opportunities to mingle with each other. Lyonel Paquin claims that Kenscoff was an important social center for Haitian elites: "Kenscoff had many purposes: to restore health, and maintain the homogeneity of the class. Every Mulatto of importance and status had a summer home there" (Paquin 1983, 224). As an important component of elite social life, a vacation in Kenscoff provided an investment in the social future of the elite family. Sunday promenades in the countryside provided exposure to rural workers in their natural setting, giving elites an image of life as they imagined it was lived in the Haitian countryside.

Kenscoff also provided elite society with an extreme example of the class inequalities in Haiti. Writers and musicians came to Kenscoff not so much to collect songs and stories but to absorb the ambiance of lower-class life and to experience what it was like for less fortunate members of Haitian society, albeit in a controlled and comfortable way. Haitian poet Andre Liautaud's 1928 poem, "O Beaux Soirs de Kenscoff" (O Beautiful Evenings of Kenscoff), evoked the surreal atmosphere of the mountain town. The poem's speaker, lying upon his *natte*, or woven sleeping mat, hears the voice of an abitan calling his dogs through the fog that is "thick enough to be parted with a cutlass":

> His voice has the strange rhythm of Vaudou,
> And to hear his songs trailing along in his rasping throat
> We quiver at the deep feeling we share
> Like a faint tremor of our mutual ancestry.
> (Liautaud 1928/1971, 23)

According to this poem, the speaker and the abitan are joined by their shared Haitian ancestry. However, it takes the rattling in the abitan's throat to set off the "quiver of deep feeling" in the writer. The two men, while socially distant from one another and physically separated, commune with each other through the "strange rhythm of Vaudou." Also, notice that the abitan is not necessarily singing a Vodou song; the writer's "deep feeling" is triggered by the sound of the abitan's voice alone, for that voice, the writer imagines, has been formed by the abitan's long experience with Vodou.

Other writers penned more indulgent prose that conflated exoticized depictions of Vodou with the sensual pleasures most elites associated with lower-class people, especially women: drinking, dancing, and sex. Jules Blanchet, in his "Cadences Créoles," reminisces about languorous days spent consuming *klerin* (cane alcohol) and *pates* (Haitian meat pies), kissing women's "juicy and drooping lips," and singing to the Vodou spirit "Erzulie" (Kreyòl: Ezili), whose association with sensuousness and beauty attract the upper-class Haitian male against his will.

> I spent my pocket change drinking klerin
> Klerin pure and thirst-quenching
> Eating meat pies, fish and sugar cane
> Cane fresh and sugary

I wasted my time dancing with women
   Women supple and lascivious
Embracing their bodies and kissing their lips
   Their lips drooping and juicy

I wasted my time tasting pleasures
   Pleasures sumptuous and delicate
Singing to Erzulie under the red arbor
   Red with the blood of sacrifices
Dancing Congo in a conical rhythm . . .
(Blanchet 1932, 15)

Blanchet's narrator is a flâneur, someone who strolls about town without plan or aim; in Haitian Kreyòl, a flâneur is said to "pa gen pwogram" (have no program or schedule). Significantly, while the crowd enlivens the flâneur, he (the flâneur is gendered male) is not a *moun lari* (street person); he is a member of the bourgeoisie.

In the context of Blanchet's verse, the flâneur "wastes his time" by ignoring his class duties and indulging in the carnal pleasures of the street. Klerin, or cane alcohol, is the "poor man's rum" that is often sold by the *fresco* (shaved ice) push-cart vendor for a few centimes a shot. Pates or meat pies are street food; they are sold by itinerant vendors who call out "pate" as they wander from house to house. The women described in the poem are also of the street; Haitian prostitutes commonly work the bars in search of patrons and use dancing as a means of solicitation. Finally, Blanchet's flâneur "sings to Erzuile" under the red arbor, turning the Vodou ceremonial song into a drunken anthem to debauchery and decadence and the Vodou religion into an exciting diversion from the flâneur's usual bourgeois existence.

In both of the previous poems, the narrator assumes a bourgeois subjectivity. While there is a tradition of bourgeois ventriloquism in Haitian literature in which upper-class subjects impersonate lower-class protagonists (most notably in the example of Oswald Durand's poem "Choucoune," examined in chapter 2), many of the poems and stories about Haitian lower-class life are told by upper-class people *about* lower-class subjects. This tradition of speaking *for* lower-class subjects—as opposed to impersonating them or transcribing their words—characterizes most Haitian composers' attempts to use Haitian peasant culture as artistic inspiration before the U.S. occupation of Haiti. As Gayatri Chakravorty Spivak has observed, there is an inherent difficulty with the interpretation of subaltern subjectivity through discourse produced by and for elites (Spivak 1988). However, as the example of Haitian composer Franck Lassègue shows, some composers used Haitian peasant music as a site of appropriation without paying attention to Price-Mars's call to "uplift" peasants through education. For Lassègue, the Haitian peasant was oblivious to his or her status as artistic inspiration for elites.

Franck Lassègue (1890–1940), a Haitian amateur musicologist and composer who lived most of his adult life in Paris, wrote several works on Haitian culture that cultivated the image of the Haitian composer who suffered for his art. In 1919, before Lassègue's departure for Paris, he wrote *Etudes critiques sur la musique haïtienne*. The *Etudes critiques* were brief vignettes describing the personal characteristics of some contemporary Haitian composers. Lassègue's descriptions of these composers gave them the power to speak for the Haitian people, even those with whom the composer had no social intercourse. Lassègue likened Haitian composer Ludovic Lamothe's music to the strains of a young woman singing of love or sadness:

> To be truly intimate and to open a field of dreams to our imagination, it is best that [music] be, like the waltzes of Mr. Lamothe, a melancholy music, without noise, something tender and sweet that speaks of love or of sadness, a music that addresses itself rather to the heart than the mind, the only music that is able to raise up profound emotions, and to allow the critic to recount the adventures of his soul through a masterpiece. (Lassègue 1919, 16)

At the end of his article about Lamothe, Lassègue begged the readers' indulgence for his free interpretation of the sources of Lamothe's inspiration. His apologies for any misinterpretation of Lamothe's intentions did not diminish Lassègue's presumptions about the importance of the native music critic, especially in cases involving Haitian music.

Lassègue, as a Haitian, felt he had an advantage as music critic by virtue of his knowledge of Haitian culture and music. For Lassègue, music criticism was an exercise based on the fusion of the feelings expressed in a piece of music with incidents from the life of the artist. Lassègue likened musical criticism to poetic analysis; the motifs and phrases themselves were subject to scrutiny and the important elements of the composition would yield themselves to the trained observer (Lassègue 1919, 17). It took a critic who was sufficiently versed in the musical and cultural background of the composer to interpret the composer's message properly.

Another important aspect of the critic's job was to judge music according to external criteria of quality. A song might be a piece of music, but was it beautiful? And, more importantly perhaps, was it art? Beauty in art, according to Lassègue, resided in its ability to make objects capable of inspiring an individual, of "speaking to the heart." The heart that is spoken to, however, was one that was sufficiently "cultivé [et] raffiné" (cultivated and refined):

> The sensations of art in a musical page of value are always non-existent for the vulgar crowd. . . , I believe that is as difficult for the thrill of the artist to penetrate the crowd as it is for the crowd to feel it. (Lassègue 1919, 22)

According to Lassègue, the crowd, or *foule,* was incapable of sensing artistic emotions. Only those possessing sufficiently "cultivated and refined" hearts were able to apprehend the technical criteria of beauty (such as musical form and style) and appreciate the artistry of the performance. Without referring directly to the social class of the crowd to which he was referring, Lassègue implied that those persons who did not possess sufficient education to discern the technical proficiency of music were condemned never to understand it. He also saw the crowd as an impenetrable mass that no amount of effort on the part of willing artists could overcome. This belief in the inability of the crowd or masses to feel even those tragedies that befall them gave the musician and critic power over the interpretation of the abitan's suffering as well as exclusive rights to express and appreciate that suffering. Lassègue's essay epitomizes the ambivalent relationship between urban elites and rural workers. Abitan were effectively eliminated from any discussion of the evaluation of musical art through Lassègue's categorization of them as "impenetrable" and "insensitive."

In one of Lassègue's own compositions for piano, *Les Chansons du Rivage* (The Songs of the Shore; ex. 1.1), the composer claimed that the piece evoked in him a painful nostalgia for Gonaïves, the seaside city in northern Haiti that inspired the piece. Looking over the bay of Gonaïves, Lassègue likens the rhythmic motion of the ocean waves and fluttering sails to the undulations of his own tormented soul. Claiming that no one else on the wharf could understand his interior suffering, Lassègue sighs:

> I see myself alone, alone, completely alone on the wharf—[in an] inflexible folding chair—sinking in the bank of the brown sand, the songs of the sailor and those of the ocean which, in their monotonous refrains, have the effect of a tragic chorus. They are mingled in the same sadness and the same mystery, calling up an atavistic sadness, because nature, that unequalled artist, created between herself and us, to tune our feelings with her proper martyrdom, indissoluble liaisons. (Lassègue 1929, 42)

Seated on the shoreline, Lassègue is not only physically but psychically alone as he listens to the sounds of the ocean. The dock workers, food

Example I.I. Franck Lassègue, *Les Chansons du Rivage*, mm. 1–25

merchants, and mobile vendors are too busy and uninterested to heed the lessons that nature shares with Lassègue.

Evoking Haiti's physical environment was a consistent theme in Lassègue's music. As a expatriate living in Paris, Lassègue often consciously linked his musical themes to places or activities characteristic of Haitian life in order to evoke nostalgic memories of his homeland. In his "Le Marchand de Pâtés" (Meat Pie Vendor), Lassègue referred to the singing meat pie vendors common in Haitian towns. Early in the morning, the *marchands de pâté* would circulate through the neighborhoods of the middle-class and wealthy Haitians singing short tunes like the one in example 1.2 to advertise wares for sale: Haitian composers used invocations of Haitian locales or the folk music that might have been part of that environment. Usually, the singer of the folk song, the Haitian abitan, was

Example 1.2. "Le Marchand de Pâtés" (in Victor 1943, 65)

Pa - té,   pa - té,   pa - té, pa - té   chaud.

absent from this idyllic vision of the Haitian countryside. It was the composer, not the peasant, who felt the passion and the pain of the tune's
heartfelt lyrics.

Lassègue's attitude toward the Haitian lower classes was common
among Haitian intellectuals and was indicative of a larger conflict going
on in Haitian society at the end of the nineteenth century. As elites became increasingly dependent on tax revenues from peasant farmers to
support their lifestyles, Haitians concentrated their energies on maintaining control over rural populations as they attempted to assert control over
Haitian political life. The conflicts between *milat* (light-skinned, upper-
class Haitians) and *nwa* (dark-skinned, middle- and upper-class Haitians)
were expressed through a complex rhetoric of black authenticity and class
privilege.

COLOR AND CLASS IN
NINETEENTH-CENTURY POLITICS

Although Haitian economic markets had been thoroughly penetrated by
German, French, and U.S. business interests by the end of the nineteenth
century, Haitian intellectuals were more concerned with power relations
within Haitian politics than with foreign intervention. Milat and nwa elites
had long been engaged in a power struggle for political and economic
control. With the fall of the Fabre Geffrard government in 1867, light-
and dark-skinned factions struggled for control of the Haitian government for the rest of the century. Two political parties with strong affilia-
tions with milat and nwa interests formed in the 1870s and by the 1880s
had established considerable influence in Haitian politics. The Parti Liberal, or Liberal Party, which supported a milat ideological outlook, advocated a ruling policy of "power to the most competent." The Liberals emphasized the common African ancestry of all Haitians, denying the
existence of racial prejudice, especially in governmental matters. Yet, the
only political leaders who were deemed "competent" by the Liberals usually belonged to the milat elite, whose position of privilege, especially with
regard to educational opportunities, made them "natural" leaders for the
Haitian people (Nicholls 1979).

The Parti National, or National Party, was associated with the interests of the black elite. Its slogan was "power to the greatest number," identifying the party with the black majority, including the disenfranchised rural masses. The Parti National challenged the milat elite vision of Haitian society that denied racial prejudice, denouncing milat control of political and economic interests in Haiti.

Despite each party's ideological identification with a different sector of Haitian society, they shared a common vision of social relations within Haiti. Both the National and Liberal parties were firm in their insistence that Haiti be run by an elite cadre consisting of educationally "well-formed" individuals. Members of the Parti Liberal avoided direct references to issues involving color in an effort to present themselves as "enlightened and progressive" on matters concerning race. Milat politicians, including Léon Laroche, J. N. Léger, Justin Dévot and Léon Audin insisted that there was "no such thing as color prejudice in Haiti" (Nicholls 1979, 120–21).

The Parti National, while criticizing milat influence in the political and educational spheres, saw Haiti as a country torn by racial prejudice since the early days of the republic. According to the "nationals," the black elite was uniquely suited to rule the country; on one hand, they could represent the black masses on the basis of their "racial affinity" with the dark-skinned portion of the population, and, on the other hand, their superior social status gave them the responsibility to look after their less fortunate compatriots.

According to David Nicholls, both milat and nwa historians upheld what he calls "legendary accounts" of Haitian history to support their visions of how Haiti should be governed. These legends were manifestations of conflicting elite ideologies that demanded interpretation and debate in and of themselves (Nicholls 1974a, 25–26). Thomas Madiou, a light-skinned historian who challenged the milat legend, published his three-volume history of Haiti in 1847. His lenient evaluations of Haitian leaders hostile to the milat cause prompted several revisionist versions of Haitian history by other milat writers who resented Madiou's tolerance of the milat's rivals. Most notable among these histories were Beaubrun Ardouin's *Etudes sur l'histoire d'Haïti suives de la vie du Général J.-M Borgella* in eleven volumes (1853–60) and Joseph St. Rémy's *Pétion et Haïti* in five volumes (1853–57) (Nicholls 1974b, 23–24).

In Ardouin's and St. Rémy's accounts of Haitian history, racial differences within Haitian society were downplayed. Rather than refer directly to the milat and nwa conflict, the focus of national contempt was trained on the ever-present threat of white invasion and reenslavement. In this version, milat generals were cast as defenders of Haitian soil in the face of white imperialism, and the contributions of nwa leaders, such as Toussaint Louverture and Jean-Jacques Dessalines, were deemphasized or ignored.

Milat historians like Ardouin and St. Rémy saw their task as arbiters of Haitian history, preserving the legacy of the revolutionary past (whose defendants were rapidly disappearing) for the sake of the national patrimony. History was, for Ardouin and St. Rémy, a patriotic preservation of national culture and an assertion of the national character, albeit a milat vision of that character.

In contrast, in the nwa "legend" of Haitian history, milat politicians of the past were excoriated for their insensitivity to the needs of the black masses (and, by association, the black elites). Black generals who participated in *la politique de doublure* (or "government by understudy" in which pliable nwa candidates were supported by milat political interests) were criticized for their part in the support of regimes that did not hold the best interests of dark-skinned Haitians in mind (Nicholls 1979, 114). The nwa interpretation of history favored those rulers who embodied the image of the benevolent protector: the *bon Papa*, or good father, who had nothing but fatherly concern for his *timoun yo*, or children. However, the nwa legend of the Haitian past did not simply laud the rulers that the milat legend criticized. Nwa historians, like Louis Joseph Janvier, praised only those rulers who had advocated the distribution of former plantation property into the hands of the Haitian rural masses. Thus, while Haitian ruler Henri Christophe was held as a good example of a *bon Papa* whose skin was black and who adopted a liberal land distribution policy, Toussaint Louverture,[1] another black general who struggled against the milat power structure, was criticized for trying to nationalize the plantation system.

The nwa vision of the past was, like the milat historical version, an elitist view, one based on the belief that black people were capable of enlightened self-government, but that only those from privileged social classes were fit to rule. Nwa ideologues, like Janvier, identified the struggle of the nwa elites with their milat counterparts as a class struggle, likening the nwa elite to the rural agricultural worker.

Despite their rhetorical differences, Liberal and National factions espoused similar political positions. As sociologist Alex Dupuy has argued, the Liberal and National parties of nineteenth-century Haiti should probably not be considered as political parties at all:

> Neither embodied the visionary program of a well-defined faction of the dominant class seeking to establish its hegemony over the society through its universalist principles and objectives. Rather, each "party"

reflected the particularistic ambitions of their leaders cast in appeals to biologically based bounds of solidarity. Both "parties" remained trapped in their own racism, in other words, and reduced all human achievements and possibilities to a matter of the epidermis. (Dupuy 1989, 124)

The Liberal and National parties both relied on rhetoric about race to consolidate their political strengths. They turned to the African heritage of Haitian culture for their inspiration while vying for control of the Haitian state as a means to further their economic interests (Dupuy 1989, 121).

RACE AND THE IMPORTANCE OF AFRICA

Haitian elites, both milat and nwa, constructed their own interpretations of the Haitian past. While their visions of the early days of the Haitian republic differed in content and tone, their beliefs about the importance and influence of their African ancestry were often congruent. Liberals and Nationals both accepted the importance of the African origins of Haitian peoples, but stopped short of looking to Africa as an example for Haitian cultural and political expression.

Africa, in the eyes of Haitian elites in the late nineteenth century, had declined in its influence and importance as a civilizing force. Though they acknowledged that the ancient African kingdoms of Egypt and North Africa were once as powerful as the Greek and Roman Empires and just as culturally influential as their European counterparts, they interpreted the decline in African political power to its nineteenth-century level of colonial dependence as an indication of the inherent weaknesses of modern African peoples. Haitians, who claimed their descent from the ancient, powerful kingdoms that ruled the continent before and during the epoch of massive slave exportation, thus disassociated themselves from the problems of nineteenth-century Africa.

Although all Haitians were biologically descended from Africans at some point in their family histories, elites traced their social and cultural backgrounds to France. The French concept of "culture" was identified with ideas of refinement and civilization, and Haitian elites largely accepted this European view. African artistic expression had never been seriously examined by Europeans prior to modernism. J. A. Gobineau's *Essai sur l'inégalité des races humaines* (1853–55) articulated the view that African peoples were incapable of emulating or appreciating the culture of Europe. His racialist theories were often cited to justify the belief in the racial inferiority of black peoples and the fear that "degeneration would result from racial mingling" (Dash 1988, 9).

Several Haitian writers criticized Gobineau, yet they were deeply ambivalent about their historical connections with African cultures. Rather than challenge the Eurocentric evaluations of African civilizations and culture, Haitian writers became apologists for the so-called "backwardness of modern Africa" (Nicholls 1979, 130). Anténor Firmin's *De l'égalité des races humaines* (1885) was an obvious response to Gobineau's racial theories and a refutation of the cultural stereotyping European writers foisted upon African descendants. Other Haitian authors, including Hannibal Price in his *De la réhabilitation de la race noire* (1900), and Louis Janvier in his *L'Egalite des races* (1884), asserted Haitians' capability to appreciate and augment European culture. Yet, Firmin and Price did not dispute Africa's "backwardness," nor did they consider the African influence on their culture as equal to European ideas. Instead, they complied with the European assessment of African culture as less advanced than Europe but *capable* of improvement and advancement according to European criteria. Haiti was, for these writers, a "symbol of black regeneration" (Nicholls 1979, 128), a modern hope for all black people. Elite Haitians felt that although they were descendants of Africans, they had culturally evolved from their so-called "primitive" pasts.

Thus, while Africa figured prominently in Haitian literature in the nineteenth century, there was never a "return to Africa" movement in Haiti (Nicholls 1979, 114; Dash 1981). Instead, Haitian intellectuals kept Africa at a distance, stressing that Africa's geographic isolation explained the region's political difficulties. This consideration of Africa as a distant geographic entity was consonant with nineteenth-century Haitian elite views of Haitian abitan. For Haitian elites, the rural masses were literally "Africans in the New World," emulating their ancestors' behavior and beliefs in customs and practices that reflected their technological and cultural deprivation. Abitan were considered *moun andeyò* (literally, "people outside," i.e. marginal) by the urban elite. The identification of abitan culture as an extension of the African past placed the rural masses both at a geographic distance (rural vs. urban) from the Haitian elites and at a temporal distance, since urbanites believed that abitan lived as their African ancestors did.

Before the ethnological movement in the twentieth century, Vodou, the religion of the rural masses, was treated by milat and nwa elites alike as evidence of the regressive, "African" tendencies of the abitan population. In the Catholic church, whose power in Haitian affairs had grown rapidly since the 1860 Concordat, Vodou was viewed as a pagan ritual that undermined Catholic dogma and threatened the hard-won stability of the Roman church. As a result, Catholic bishops mounted periodic "anti-superstition campaigns" throughout the nineteenth century.

Elites regarded peasant music-making in the countryside with a mixture of wonder and fear, apprehensive that such unrestrained activity would lead to disorder and violence. Vodou religious celebrations were considered especially pernicious since they eschewed not only elite, French-based musical aesthetics but also belief in the Catholic faith as practiced by Haitian elites. One member of the Haitian elite, General Guy-Joseph Bonnet, undertook a personal crusade in the early nineteenth century to replace indigenous musical practices with more European musical forms:

> [Bonnet] proudly recorded in his memoirs how he had tried to introduce the calinda dance, performed to the accompaniment of the violin, alongside the traditional African dances of the peasants performed to the beat of the tambour. Bonnet and a group of elite Haitians together with some French residents, founded in 1820 a society for "decent entertainment" in Port-au-Prince. The purpose of the society was to organize dances in the European style. (Nicholls 1979, 71)

While most Haitian elites looked to European culture, with its "socially acceptable" music, to be an inspiration for elite audiences throughout the nineteenth century, others looked toward African-oriented Haitian culture as an example of black resistance to white imperialism.

Haiti's status as a black nation that identified with its African roots attracted the attention of African Americans in the early nineteenth century as an alternative "homeland" ruled by black instead of white politicians. As Elizabeth Bethel notes about African Americans at mid-century, "Toussaint L'Ouverture and Crispus Attucks were claimed equally as Afro-American heroes; and the Haytian and American Revolutions were declared equally crucial political events in the shaping of Afro-American political and cultural identity" (Bethel 1992, 827). As it became apparent that large-scale resettlement in Africa was not feasible, Haiti looked like a promising site for the massive resettlement of free black populations. Unlike Liberia, which had been founded by white Americans as a resettlement colony for former slaves, Haiti was a sovereign black nation and was, especially after the passage of the Fugitive Slave Law in 1850, considered by many black people in the United States as a logical destination for escaping an economy based on slavery.

Haitian leaders also saw a potential benefit in bringing free black people from the United States to settle in Haiti. The settlers would, they hoped, bring stability to a volatile political situation. Haitian president Jean-Pierre Boyer, a light-skinned elite who ruled Haiti from 1818 to 1843, enforced domestic policies that brought back a form of plantation labor, thus replicating, at least in the eyes of the dark-skinned majority, conditions under slavery. In order to shore up his regime, Boyer used the money from sales of Haitian coffee to entice free black people from the United States to settle in Haiti (Lewis 1993, 43). One such person who traveled to Haiti as a potential settler was Alexander Du Bois, the paternal grandfather of W. E. B. Du Bois. Moving to Haiti around 1829, Alexander Du Bois remained in Haiti until 1833 or 1834 when, seeing that his fortune would not be made easily in the poverty-stricken country, he returned to the United States (Lewis 1993, 44). W. E. B. Du Bois's father, Alfred, was likely born in Haiti, the child of a sexual liaison Alexander had with a Haitian woman during his first trip to the country (44). While kindled by his personal connection to the place via his grandfather, W. E. B. Du Bois's interest in Haiti eventually developed into a more profound appreciation of Haiti's anti-colonialist, pro-black legacy.

In the 1860s, another small group of about two thousand African Americans eventually settled in Haiti (Dixon 2000, 178) at the behest of the Reverend James Theodore Holly, an African American clergyman from Hartford, Connecticut. Born in 1829, Holly became interested in black emigration from the United States in his early twenties when he worked for the American Colonization Society, a group that encouraged black people in the United States to move to Liberia. In 1854, Holly was appointed a commissioner for the National Emigration Convention to evaluate Haiti's suitability as a site for African American emigration (Pamphile 2001, 48). In 1855, Holly visited Haiti not only to evaluate the country's potential as a destination for African Americans but also to determine the willingness of the Haitian government to support such a large emigration project. As a result of Holly's visit to Haiti, in 1857 he published *A Vindication of the Capacity of the Negro Race for Self-Government and Civilized Progress*, a revision of a series of lectures he gave during his tours of the United States to encourage African Americans to consider Haiti as their new home. His concern in *Vindication* was to dispel notions of black inferiority:

> I wish, by the undoubted facts of history, to cast back the vile aspersions and foul calumnies that have been heaped upon my race for the last four centuries, by our unprincipled oppressors; whose base interest, at the expense of our blood and our bones, have made them reiterate, from generation to generation, during the long march of ages, every thing

that would prop up the impious dogma of our natural and inherent in-feriority. (Holly 1857/1970, 22)

Holly saw Haiti as an example upon which could be built a counterhistory that gave black people the agency denied them in most historical ac-counts. Holly understood that, in order to resist the tendencies in white historical writing that assumed black inferiority, an undisputable narrative of black heroism and valor was essential:

> I wish to remind my oppressed brethren, that dark and dismal as their horrid night has been, and sorrowful as the general reflections are, in regard to our race; yet, notwithstanding these discouraging consider-ations, there are still some proud historic recollections, linked indissol-ubly with the most important events of the past and present century, which break the general monotony, and remove some of the gloom that hang[s] over the dark historic period of African slavery, and the ac-cursed traffic in which it was cradled. (Holly 1857/1970, 23).

Holly's tract focused on the history of the Haitian Revolution, stressing that Haiti's overthrow of Napoleon's forces and its continuous defense against European reinvasion made Haitians profoundly dedicated to the defense of black people.

One problem with Holly's depiction of Haiti, however, was the fact that when *Vindication* was published, Haiti was a monarchy ruled by Faustin Soulouque, a general who, in 1849, proclaimed himself Emperor Faustin I. Holly tried to address the seeming contradiction of advocating emigra-tion to a place ruled, according to most accounts, by a despot. "There is far more security," he wrote, "for personal liberty and the general welfare of the governed, among the monarchical negroes of Hayti where the rulers are held individually responsible for their public acts, than exists in this bastard democracy" (Holly 1857/1970, 63). By casting the United States as a country that squandered its birthright as the "land of the free," Holly could avoid issues of Haitian political instability and focus his at-tention on providing a suitable destination for African Americans.

Despite Holly's apologies for the excesses of Faustin I's reign, he chose to emigrate to Haiti in 1861 only after General Fabre Nicolas Geffrard overthrew Soulouque in a coup d'état. While Holly promoted a vision of Haiti as a haven for black people from different political and linguistic backgrounds, his status as an Episcopal deacon and eventually as Bishop of the Episcopal Church of Haiti put him at odds with Soulouque's open support for Vodou. The African-associated practice of Vodou was not in-cluded in most late nineteenth-century elite visions of a Pan-African world.

By the beginning of the twentieth century, however, the deep ambivalence of the Haitian elite toward their African ancestry turned to a cautious interest in things African, especially as the nascent Pan-African movement gathered momentum. Among the Haitian intellectuals who were part of the early Pan-African movement was Benito Sylvain (1868–1915), who attended the first Pan-African congress in 1900 (Nicholls 1979, 134). Sylvain was a political activist who founded the journal *La Fraternité* in 1889 while living in Paris. He traveled extensively during his lifetime, visiting the newly crowned Emperor Menelik of Abyssinia (modern Ethiopia) three times between 1897 and 1904 (Bervin 1969, 156). Sylvain was outspoken in his criticism of Europe's colonies in Africa but was still convinced that European culture was a beneficial influence, even if it was responsible for most of the world's suffering for the previous nine hundred years (Sylvain 1901, 523).

As Haitians cautiously reconciled with their African ancestry, however, foreign merchants and governments sought ways to penetrate Haitian markets and ensure their economic interests. German merchants had made significant inroads into the Haitian economy, investing large sums of money in coffee plantations. They also intermarried with members of the milat elite and obtained Haitian citizenship, thereby eluding Haitian laws forbidding land ownership by foreigners. According to Brenda Plummer, the French government focused on "collecting [their foreign] debt, protecting the interests of French residents, preserving their part of the foreign trade that catered to the bourgeoisie, and cultivating Haitian Francophones for ideological purposes" (Plummer 1988, 80). British merchants enjoyed an active trade relationship with Haiti since the early nineteenth century, but their importance in Haitian markets waned by the beginning of the twentieth century.

U.S. business interests were thus the most influential in Haitian affairs in the late nineteenth and early twentieth centuries. The U.S. government tried to bring Haiti into its economic sphere, not only to secure favorable conditions for their own businesses in Haiti but also to stem the increasing influence of the German merchants and bankers on the Haitian economy. The German government, eager to establish a secure foothold in the Caribbean, engineered several small military campaigns against Haiti, ostensibly to protect their citizens. German ships invaded Port-au-Prince harbor in 1872 for property reparations and again in 1887 to demand the release of German citizens arrested for assaulting the police. In 1902, the German warship *Panther* sunk the Haitian ship *La Crête-à-Pierrot*, and returned in 1911 to oust President Antoine Simon (Bellegarde 1938, 142; Léger 1907/1970, 250). The threat of German naval power and immanent loss of economic influence over Haitian markets made military intervention in the Caribbean an increasingly attractive proposition to President Woodrow Wilson, especially after the outbreak of the First World War in 1914.

As Alex Dupuy has argued, Haitian governments throughout the nineteenth and early twentieth centuries were loath to grant foreign governments territorial concessions (Dupuy 1989). However, several Haitian administrations brokered financial deals with foreign governments in order to maintain their economic advantage. Perhaps the most damaging economic incident for Haitian governments was the decision to allow the establishment of the French-controlled Banque Nationale d'Haïti in 1880 as the principal financial institution of Haiti. The precedent of having a foreign bank oversee the financial health of the country prompted the United States to step up its participation in Haitian financial affairs. In 1910, the United States, with the cooperation of the French government, established the Banque Nationale de la République d'Haïti (BNRH). Through the BNRH, the United States was able to control German economic expansion in Haiti. Then, in 1915, one year after the outbreak of World War I, American forces landed in Haiti to quell the anarchy that followed the downfall of President Vilbrun Sam. The U.S. quickly seized the assets of the BNRH, thus securing the occupation's jurisdiction over Haitian economic affairs.

THE UNITED STATES OCCUPATION OF HAITI

The invasion of Port-au-Prince by American forces on 28 July 1915 was one of the most traumatic moments in modern Haitian history. Not since the era of French colonial domination had Haitian citizens been under the control of a foreign power. The invasion and subsequent occupation of Haiti engendered resistive responses, not only in Haitian political and economic life, but also in the arts, most notably in literature and music.

In Haiti, elites who had previously disclaimed any cultural affinities with their African past reevaluated the importance of Africa in Haitian culture. The resulting intellectual curiosity about African culture prompted what has been called "the ethnological movement" (Nicholls 1979, 152), also known as the *mouvement indigène* or *mouvement folklorique* (Averill 1997, 80). The indigène movement had neither a unified cadre of followers nor an explicit program for cultural change. It was, like the Haitian elite movements of the nineteenth century, a confluence of intellectual currents that combined different ideological approaches to a series of cultural questions. Indigènisme, in its widest sense, had racial, social, and political currents that were often at odds with each other.

Indigènisme was fundamentally concerned with issues of race. Specifically, indigènistes refuted the racialist theories of black inferiority that had been in vogue on the European continent since J. A. Gobineau's *Essai sur l'inégalité des races humaines* (1853–55). With the invasion of U.S. Marines in 1915, Haitians had to deal with different but equally damaging foreign prejudices concerning race. As the U.S. occupation wore on, milat and nwa elites alike felt the sting of American racism. The Americans ignored the Haitians' own distinctions and lumped milat and nwa into a single category of "black," which connoted social, cultural, and biological inferiority in the minds of the U.S. occupation force. Patrick Bellegarde-Smith cited two examples of the American attitude:

> When U.S. Secretary of State William Jennings Bryan was briefed on the Haitian situation by an officer of the National City Bank, he exclaimed "Dear me, think of it! Niggers speaking French!" Admiral H. S. Knapp wrote the following to the secretary of the Navy: "The people of Haiti had no immediate contact with the superior cultivation and intelligence such as the negroes of the United States have had. . . . I consider that the bad traits are more in evidence in Haiti than in the United States, where they [blacks] are under better control." (Bellegarde-Smith 1990, 77)

Although Americans tended to favor lighter-skinned Haitians in their business and social dealings, milat elites still experienced overt racism within their own country during the occupation. While "American officers [initially] attended social functions at elite clubs, danced with Haitian women, and were received in elite homes" (Schmidt 1995, 136), their social intercourse with Haitians was curtailed with the arrival of the soldiers' wives and families. "Jim Crow" laws implemented by the Americans further alienated an already uneasy milat elite. Nwa elites, who were more familiar with overt racial discrimination, continued to be discriminated against as they had been under milat control.

As Hans Schmidt observed in his history of the U.S. occupation, "the cultural clash between Americans and the Haitian elite was all the more exacerbated because the Americans, who subscribed to the political ideologies of democracy and egalitarianism, were repulsed by the very concept of elitism that was fundamental to the social and economic positions of the elite in Haiti" (Schmidt 1995, 146). As a result, U.S. officials could excoriate Haitian elites for maintaining an attitude of superiority vis-à-vis the Haitian peasant even as they themselves felt a cool condescension that placed the Haitian poor in a position of inferiority. John Craige, a U.S. Marine who wrote a book about his "adventures" during the U.S. occupation of Haiti, characterized Haitian peasants this way: "A man who is born with a semi-ape's brain cannot rise in life's competition. That was the kind of brain ninety percent of the Haitian peasants seemed to have" (Craige 1933, 133).

Before the U.S. occupation, Haitian intellectuals had not been overly concerned with how their culture appeared to foreigners:

> They sometimes sought French publishers for their texts, but the vast majority of Haitian books were published in Port-au-Prince for domestic consumption. . . . Unlike much contemporary Third World literature, the Haitian *oeuvre* was traditionally directed inward, and polemics and apologetics also focused on a home constituency. (Plummer 1988, 73)

Only after the U.S. invasion did Haitian intellectuals posit a new theory of Haitian culture, one founded on the supposition that Haitian cultural authenticity was tied to non-European models. With the publication of *La Revue Indigène* in 1927 and the "political literary" journal *La Relève* in 1932, Haitian writers used poetry, essays, and reviews to critique Haitian intellectual complacency and to exhort readers to "understand the literature and soul of Latin America" (Sylvain 1927, 5). The indigèniste rejection of Europe as the sole model of civilization worthy of aspiration reflected not only Haitians' reevaluation of their African cultural roots but also their resistance to the political encroachment of foreign powers in Haiti.

Although both European and U.S. economic interests had controlled the Haitian economy throughout the nineteenth century, the invasion of Haiti by U.S. Marines made Americans—and by association, their culture—a primary focus for Haitian animosity. Haitian writers espoused an anti-American nationalism by claiming an "Afro-Latin" cultural descent, thus distancing themselves from what they termed the United States' "Anglo-Saxon" culture. J. Michael Dash quotes from a Haitian historical work written in the 1920s as an articulation of the Anglo-Saxon/Latin cultural tensions:

> The Occupation has one advantage—in that it forces us to understand . . . how much our black French backgrounds, our afro-latin feelings, our French culture was opposed to the crude materialism, rough anglo-saxon mentality of North-Americans, scornful of subtlety, ignorant of refinement and convinced that all civilization is purely materialistic. (quoted in Dash 1981, 50)

These sentiments reflect the fluidity of indigèniste discourse at its best. Conflating their conceptions of French sensibility with African sensuality, elite writers combined their use of French forms with more indigenous themes, all of which resisted the materialism and violence of the American invasion.

However, Haitian elite claims of an "Afro-Latin" patrimony were interpreted by white U.S. writers as a sign of Haitian decadence and anti-democratic tendencies. U.S. diplomat Stuart Grummon characterized the difference between U.S. "Anglo-Saxon" and Haitian "Latin" cultures this way:

> In general, while the Anglo-Saxon has a deep sense of the value of social organization and of the obligation of democratic government to assume a large share of responsibility for the social welfare of the masses, and has in addition a profound conviction of the value of democratic government, the Latin mind, on the contrary, is apt to scorn democracy and neglect activities looking to the health and educational welfare of the masses. . . . The Anglo-Saxon, who excels in collective action, is apt to be impatient with the Haitian characteristic of intense individualism inherited from the French regime. . . . The action of the Haitian, in common with the Latin in general, is in the main directed by emotion rather than by reason, which in the main dictates the action of the Anglo-Saxon. (quoted in Schmidt 1995, 145–46)

Haitian intellectuals and white critics from the United States were in a rhetorical standoff during much of the U.S. occupation, each accusing the other of democratic abuses while extolling the virtues of their cultural patrimonies.

JEAN PRICE-MARS AND THE ETHNOLOGICAL MOVEMENT

Dr. Jean Price-Mars, a Haitian physician, ethnographer, and sometime political candidate, first articulated a new vision of the Haitian peasant in the late 1920s as Haitian resistance to the U.S. occupation gained momentum. Price-Mars outlined a new relationship between Haitian elites and peasants, one that would bring Haitian social classes together to fight the cultural and political occupation of their country by U.S. forces. For Price-Mars, education and ethnographic research were the principal tools for forging this new alliance between social classes that were accustomed to fighting each other for control of the Haitian state. In his vision for Haiti, elites would provide uplift to the poverty-stricken masses through educational reform. The masses, in turn, would provide their single most valuable resource: the African-derived folklore that distinguished Haitian culture from other nations in the Americas. While Price-Mars believed that Haitian peasants were keepers of Haitian culture, he also saw folklore as a cultural product that elites and peasants shared in Haiti. By providing education to the masses in exchange for Haitian folklore, Price-Mars thought the Haitian elite could demonstrate the appropriateness of upper-class Haitian control of the state. Eventually, Price-Mars would identify the cultural practices of Haiti as a link not only to an African past but also to a black transnational future.

Jean Price-Mars was born in 1876 in Grande Rivière du Nord, near Cap Haïtien. Son of Jean Eléomont Mars, member of the National Assembly and a practicing Baptist, and Fortuna Delcour Michel, a Catholic, Price-Mars was educated at local schools. Magdaline Shannon has speculated that it was perhaps through his exposure to his father's Baptist beliefs and the practices of his maternal grandmother's Catholicism that Price-Mars learned respect for different forms of religious practice (Shannon 1996, 16).

Price-Mars's political connections enabled him to move to Port-au-Prince where, beginning in 1892, he lived in the home of his cousin, Tirésias Simon Sam, President Hyppolite's minister of war (Shannon 1996, 17). He matriculated at the prestigious Lycée Pétion in 1892 and in 1895 enrolled in the National School of Medicine. During his days in medical school, Price-Mars developed an interest in politics which remained with him throughout his career. He helped found the politically critical *Journal des Etudiants* (1898) while in medical school. In 1896, his cousin Tirésias Simon Sam assumed the presidency of Haiti. In 1899, Price-Mars was awarded a scholarship by the Haitian government to finish his medical degree in Paris.

The heady intellectual atmosphere of the French capital gave Price-Mars ample stimulation. When he was not busy with his medical studies, the young Price-Mars attended social science lectures at the Sorbonne and the Collège de France and engaged in private study at the Musée Trocadero and the Museum of Natural History (Antoine 1981, 35). He read widely in the current sociological literature and encountered Gustave Le Bon's *Lois psychologiques d'évolution des peuples* (1894). Le Bon's racialist theories stood in direct opposition to ideas that Price-Mars valued. Specifically, Le Bon advocated a view that culture could only be absorbed by those racial groups disposed toward advancement. In Le Bon's view, the culture of Europeans could be learned by non-Europeans, but it could not be absorbed by members of Asian or African cultures. Further, according to Le Bon, European culture was a "varnish" that, with little effort, could be worn off to reveal the so-called true nature of non-Europeans: unlettered, uncultured, and uncouth. Price-Mars was incensed at this condescending and unsympathetic characterization of non-Europeans and later made the counter claim that Haitians, despite the scorn of most nations of the world, had managed to keep their independence in the face of repeated violations of their sovereignty (Price-Mars 1928/1983).

Price-Mars continued his study of anthropology and sociology in Paris until political problems in Haiti forced him to return home. Price-Mars served several Haitian administrations as official representative of the Haitian government, first as part of the Haitian legation to Berlin in 1900 and then as Haitian representative to the Louisiana Purchase Centennial Exposition in 1904. While he was used to the racialist discourse of intellectuals in Paris and the color conflicts in his home country, it was during his visit to the Centennial Exposition that Price-Mars had a formative racial experience. Later, in his *Vocation de l'élite* (1919, 200), Price-Mars wrote of his encounter with a group of people from the Philippines who had been brought to the exposition as an example of people who conformed to the contemporary cultural evolutionary constructions of the "primitive." Price-Mars described how these "poor ones" mocked him and laughed at his suit and tie. Price-Mars noted:

> What went through the minds of these primitives? Perhaps they considered me as one of their own who denied the faith of the ancestors because I was dressed like a white person. . . . Perhaps they found me supremely ridiculous in my clothing. . . . In any case, what is undeniable, is that between me and them, they sensed incalculable differences of taste and manners and probably they ought to have judged that it was I who was wrong for having changed. (Price-Mars 1919, 200)

While he was in St. Louis for the exposition, Price-Mars contacted Booker T. Washington, whom he had met the previous year on one of Washington's speaking tours of Europe. Price-Mars was eager to visit Tuskegee Institute to see if Washington's ideas of technical education could be adapted for Haitian schools. Upon his return to Haiti in 1904, he made a successful bid for the Haitian legislature representing his home district near Cap Haitian. By 1909, Price-Mars was sent to Washington, D.C., to work for the Haitian legation to the United States.

From this position of political influence, Price-Mars wrote a blistering critique of public education in Haiti; he had made several trips to the Haitian countryside, especially in the northern provinces where he spent much of 1910 and 1911. In his article "La reforme de l'enseignement primaire" (The reform of primary education, 1912), Price-Mars asserted that one of the essential functions of a state was to provide, "at a *minimum,*" an education for all its citizens so that its people could, "with dignity, exercise their rights as citizens" (Price-Mars 1912, 313). Blasting the

Haitian school system as having illiterate instructors, bankrupt facilities, and insufficient supplies, Price-Mars asserted that "the [Haitian] state ought to make sacrifices in order to raise the miserable conditions of Haitian schoolteachers" (315).

Going against the prevalent practice of teaching in French, Price-Mars promoted the use of the Haitian Kreyòl language in the elementary grades and suggested that texts be produced that focused on the achievements and history of Haiti. When textbooks were available to Haitian schoolchildren, they were usually from France and stressed French history, literature, and culture. Price-Mars was appalled that Haitian children knew more about the geography of France than of their native Haiti:

> In our primary schools—the same in the countryside—we use texts that are specially edited for French schoolchildren, that is to say, children who are placed in other physical and social conditions. You can see the absurdity of the system. (Price-Mars 1912, 316).

Price-Mars thought that the Haitian elite should have a stake in the improvement of Haitian education and that they should work diligently to raise the level of education for the entire Haitian population. Without the participation of the elite, Price-Mars speculated, the failure of the educational system could be used against all Haitians as an example of how the Haitian people were incapable of improving their social conditions:

> One often hears how our race is inferior. Following our illustrious predecessors, I have rebelled against the pseudo-scientific arguments advanced to support that erroneous doctrine. But no defense seems to me more preemptive and more decisive than that of the removal of ignorance and superstition from the masses of our people. For if the proof is made of the perfectibility of the black mind, it seems clear to us that for the elite, so much of our apathy and our bad faith have left our lower-classes with the double servitude of stupidity and poverty. (Price-Mars 1912, 317)

Due in part to his critical articles about the Haitian educational system, Price-Mars was appointed the General Inspector of Haitian Schools; he served from 1912 to 1915 (Shannon 1996, 23–24). In 1915, Price-Mars was appointed Haitian minister to Paris, but he returned to Haiti abruptly at the beginning of the U.S. occupation of Haiti.

Upon his return to Haiti, Price-Mars organized academic conferences and introduced his socio-political ideas to the Haitian elite. In his speeches, he called upon the members of Haiti's elite to put aside their prejudices against the vestiges of their African heritage. Published in 1919 as *La Vocation de l'élite*, these academic papers introduced Price-Mars to the Haitian intellectual community and established him as an opponent of the U.S. occupation. In *La Vocation de l'élite,* Price-Mars exhorted the Haitian elite to assume their positions as leaders of the Haitian people, charging that those who had the benefit of an education had a moral duty to lead and serve their country. In Price-Mars's estimation, the elite had failed to resist the U.S. occupation forces and had turned their backs on their responsibilities as stewards of the Haitian economy. By clinging to a sharecropping system that effectively drained agricultural surpluses from the rural population through burdensome taxation, the elite contributed to the economic decline of rural workers:

> [Elites] preferred, all the while maintaining nominal control over the land they acquired, to live elsewhere, in the cities, where they enjoyed easier and more immediate profits from politics, and to leave the administration of their plantations to the ignorance and routine of the "lower half" [sharecroppers]. This was the first great mistake of the elite: the desertion of the land. (Price-Mars 1919, 62)

Price-Mars understood that education was a contributing factor to the alienation of the elite from the sharecropping majority. Haitians with the financial means sent their children to the best schools in Haiti (like the Lycée Pétion) or in France where they would be tutored in literature, philosophy, history, and other subjects in the arts and humanities. Elites did not, for the most part, send their children to study agricultural subjects to prepare them to run large-scale plantations.

The ideological divide between rural workers and elites was exacerbated by the two-tiered educational system. Price-Mars's suggestion that Haitian elites involve themselves in the vocational training of the rural underclass borrowed from Booker T. Washington's model of technical education, whereby rural workers would continue to provide manual labor in exchange for a stake in a growing national economy fueled by elite and working-class cooperation. Citing the successes of African Americans in the United States in raising money to help less fortunate members of their communities, Price-Mars urged the Haitian elite to activate their dormant sense of civic responsibility: "It is necessary for all social forces—religion, school, corporate groups—to have one doctrine, one vision: to save the moral patrimony from the disaster that has struck the political patrimony. This cannot be done except by private initiative for a better education" (Price-Mars 1919, 89–90).

Price-Mars's call for educational reform anticipated one of the most important conflicts between the Haitian students and the U.S. occupation forces. During the U.S. occupation, the Haitian educational system was operated by two different bureaucratic agencies: the Haitian-controlled Ministry of Public Instruction and the U.S.-controlled Service Technique. The ministry oversaw the primary and secondary school systems in Haiti as well as the private schools operated by the Catholic church. The Service Technique controlled the agricultural and vocational programs in Haiti and was run by U.S. bureaucrats who were paid extravagant sums financed by the Haitian treasury (Pamphile 1980, 169–73). When the Service Technique was looking for ways to cut expenses at the agricultural campus at Damien, they tried to withdraw "incentive scholarships" that had been offered to students who were willing to perform manual labor to help with new building construction at the school (Pamphile 1980, 191; Schmidt 1995, 197). Students who were fearful about losing their scholarships met with Dr. George F. Freeman, the director of the Service Technique, to discuss their concerns. Freeman told the students that they could leave the school if they didn't like the situation and that they would be summarily replaced (Savaille 1979, 12). Agricultural students quickly organized a strike at the Service Technique; students in the Haitian law and medical colleges joined the agricultural students in a sympathy strike. After a protracted struggle, the Service Technique gave in to the strikers' demands. The student strike—La grève de '29 as it became known (Savaille 1979)—was the first in a series of civil disobedience actions that forced the U.S. government to reassess its goals for the occupation.

The educational reforms advocated by Price-Mars were principally directed toward Haitian elite men; women were not included in the student body at the Damien agricultural school. However, Price-Mars thought that Haitian elite women had an equally important role in maintaining Haiti's civic "health" through their capacity to bear children. As Lora Romero points out in her study of domesticity in the antebellum United States, "nationalism organizes itself around a gendered division of labor between the task of founding the nation and the task of guaranteeing its posterity—even if these activities are never wholly distinct or necessarily diachronic in their performance" (Romero 1997, 66). In Price-Mars's view, Haitian elite women had a national responsibility to produce civic-minded Haitian citizens. Working-class women were, according to Price-Mars, ill-suited to produce tomorrow's leaders: they were too physically disfigured by their incessant work at home and in the fields (Price-Mars 1919, 103). As the keepers of Haiti's national future, Haitian elite women were supposed to instill the values of patriotism and black pride while resisting potentially debasing activities. Price-Mars criticized Haitian women who were content to be "objects of luxury and pleasure" (103).

By focusing their attention on pleasure and ignoring their charge to "raise up the race," Haitian women were, according to Price-Mars, contributing to Haiti's descent into the imperial orbit of the United States.

While *La Vocation de l'élite* articulated Price-Mars's views on the importance of education and eugenics for the maintenance of Haitian political sovereignty, it was his *Ainsi parla l'oncle* that first brought Haitian culture into theoretical focus. Published in 1928 as another series of lectures about Haitian folklore and Haiti's African heritage, each of the speeches given in the collection was addressed not specifically to an academic audience but to a broader audience of elites for whom Price-Mars's exhortations were intended. In *Ainsi parla l'oncle,* Price-Mars turned his attention to the folklore of the Haitian people as the source of a new Haitian nation. Elaborating a theory of Haitian culture that included the Haitian elite and working classes, and claiming that both rural and urban sectors of Haitian society were important in understanding the cultural heritage of Haiti, Price-Mars could justify his interest in the customs of the Haitian working class as a member of the elite.

Despite his rejection of the black inferiority thesis of Le Bon, Price-Mars was influenced by anthropological writings that correlated race and culture. Following the work of Ellen Churchill Semple (1911), Price-Mars suggested there was an important relationship between the geography of a particular nation and the culture that lived there. Mountains, valleys, forests, and coastal areas each had their own effect on the people who inhabited them. For Price-Mars, no place better exemplified the cultural impact of geographic factors than Africa. According to Price-Mars, African people had been trapped in the African subcontinent and had been unable to mingle with races from other continents. This geographic isolation resulted in a cultural stagnation that explained the discrepancies between European and African technological advancement. Like his nineteenth-century predecessors, Price-Mars believed that Africans were at a cultural disadvantage vis-à-vis their European counterparts. These cultural differences were, however, due to the degree of geographic isolation, not to an inherent difference in African and European intellectual capabilities.

The rural worker or abitan was, for Price-Mars, an unreflective individual who, with a sigh of *si Dye vle* (God willing), was resigned to his or her future. Price-Mars described the so-called typical Haitian worker this way:

[A] people who sing and who suffer, who grieve and who laugh, who dance and are resigned. From birth to death, song is associated with his whole life. He sings when he has joy in his heart or tears in his eyes. He sings in the furor of combat, under the hail of machine-gun fire, or in the fray of bayonets. He sings of the apotheosis of victories and the horror of defeats. He sings of the muscular effort and the rest after the task, of the ineradicable optimism and humble intuition that neither injustice nor suffering are eternal and that, moreover, nothing is hopeless since "bon Dieu bon" (God is good). (Price-Mars 1928/1983, 26)

An important part of the abitan's image was his or her musical ability. Moreover, the song of the abitan represented the most typical expression of the peasant and was in the greatest danger of being lost:

Of all our popular traditions, the song is the one which persistently disappears with unaccommodating frequency since it is essentially oral tradition. I do not believe that a single one of the songs which appeased the cruelty of the hours of colonial servitude has come down to us. (Price-Mars 1928/1983, 27)

Price-Mars's belief that the folk songs of the Haitian peasant were part of a dying tradition allowed him to ask the rhetorical question: who will save this Haitian heritage?

Price-Mars thought that the Haitian elite had a responsibility to preserve, protect, and elevate the folkloric materials of the abitan. Elites had, however, allowed the culture of the Haitian abitan to deteriorate to its endangered condition. He blamed the elite for having the same class prejudices as the French colonials and for ignoring their duty as leaders of the country:

[T]he Haitian society of the present time closely resembles the one from which it issued. We know that the arrogant vanity of our elite forces them into an obstinate and fierce denial of this. The elite closes his eyes to the evidence. He has only to note, however, the demographic development of our people in order to realize how vain is his stupid claim that he alone typifies the whole Haitian society. For the bourgeoisie, as they exist now, are no more than a symbol. Having fallen from their historic role as leaders of the nation because of inertia, cowardice, or failure to adapt, although they still illustrate through their thinkers, artists, and industrial chiefs the height of intellectual development to which a part of the society has risen, yet by shirking their duty to mix with the rest of the nation they exercise only a sort of mandarinate which weakens and atrophies more each day. (Price-Mars 1928/1983, 105–106)

Not only were the elite unable to "mix with the rest of the nation" and acknowledge their cultural links with the abitan heritage, but they were guilty of "cultural bovaryism, meaning the faculty of a society of seeing itself other than it is" (Price-Mars 1928/1983, 8). According to Price-

Mars, the Haitian elite saw themselves as "colored Frenchmen" whose biological link to the Haitian abitan had long ago been overshadowed by the cultural influences of Europe. Price-Mars called elites to reconsider not only their cultural affinities with Africa, but also their social responsibilities to the Haitian abitan.

It was through folklore that Price-Mars envisioned a cultural rapprochement between the elite and working classes in Haiti. In a country with wide economic disparities between the urban elites and rural abitan, virtually no political power available to the rural population, and few educational opportunities for monolingual Haitian speakers, folklore was one of the few things that elite and abitan shared:

> [If] miraculous thinking [folklore] which is at the base of Haitian life and confers upon it its own identity—the mystical tonality—if all of that is drawn from the common reservoir of ideas, sentiments, acts, gestures which constitute the moral patrimony of Haitian society, then it will be in vain for the arrogant among the elite and plebeian to jibe at the joint responsibility for faults and transgressions, for dilettantist bovaryism to dictate to both acts of cowardice and falsehood, for imbecilic class egotisms to trigger attitudes and measures of ostracism. . . . [Folklore] constitutes in an unexpected and breathtaking fashion the materials of our spiritual unity. (Price-Mars 1928/1983, 174)

In short, Price-Mars thought that folklore could be put to use to bridge the class antagonisms in Haiti. The "cultural bovaryism" of the Haitian elites was, in part, a product of their lack of knowledge about the working class. Price-Mars thought that a careful exploration of abitan life would demonstrate the cultural similarities of rural and urban dwellers, rich and poor alike.

To this end, Price-Mars stressed the importance of considering Vodou as a religious system rather than a collection of superstitions. Questioning the assumption that African religions constituted a crude "fetishism" in which irrational attachments were placed on inanimate objects in the environment, Price-Mars suggested that Africans were "animists" (or "dynamists") who believed in distinctions between a corporeal existence and a spiritual plane. He went on to cite the presence of such animistic practices in the early history of Judaism and Christianity, and to assert a similarity between the spirit possession of the Vodou ceremony and the practice of Christian mystics who achieve trance-like states. After all, he reasoned, "if more than one Christian mystic presents for observation some phenomena of obsession, of catalepsy, of possession, of sensori-motor difficulties, how could we deny to elementary forms of religious life the possibility of producing some cases of mysticism?" (Price-Mars 1928/

1983, 126). Vodou and Christianity, in Price-Mars's presentation, had far more in common than the "colored Frenchmen" of the Haitian elite cared to admit.

Price-Mars's program did not stop, however, with a bid for elites to accept Haitian Vodou. Once elites acknowledged their connection to their African-derived past, their next step would be to appropriate that past and use it in ways that reflected their own cultural perspectives. Unfortunately, folklore was, in Price-Mars's view, unusable for elite consumption in its unrefined form.

According to Price-Mars, the Haitian intelligentsia was responsible for transforming the raw materials of Haitian folklore, its tales, legends, beliefs, superstitions, riddles, proverbs, and folksongs, into a national literature and music. Price-Mars claimed that Haitians were capable of structuring a national literature that would combine the cultural values of the Haitian abitan with the formal criteria of European art:

> It is necessary to draw the substance of our works sometimes from this immense reservoir of folk-lore in which the motives for our decisions are compressed after centuries, in which the elements of our sensibility are elaborated, in which the fabric of our popular character, our national mind, is structured. (Price-Mars 1928/1983, 178)

While a new Haitian literature would draw inspiration from folklore's "immense reservoir," Haitian national music would be based on songs and chants specific to the Vodou ceremony (182). He complained, however, that despite the presence of Vodou rhythms in popular dances of the period, there was no similar tendency in Haitian art music to incorporate Vodou elements: "Although we may not be qualified to speak in a technical sense, we have not found a single decisive work in all this mass of production that in recent times may be designated: 'Voodoo music'" (182).

Price-Mars's final words in *Ainsi parla l'oncle* thus enjoined Haitian composers of his day to draw upon Haitian folklore and allow their music to be inspired by Vodou themes. A national music, like a national literature, was a political construction forged to assert the capabilities of the Haitian people and, by extension, the black race. What Haiti needed, according to Price-Mars, was a cadre of nationalist composers to carry on the musical message of the Haitian people:

> An Occide Jeanty already in his prime but with a head still brushed by the wings of the Muse, a [Ludovic] Lamothe whose perceptivity is an inexhaustible reserve of dreams and hopes, a Justin Elie with a talent ripened by so many auspicious essays that promises a great work, a

Franck Lassègue who, from the banks of the Seine, gives vent to the nostalgia of his vagabond soul in plaintive notes, and all the others who are obsessed with the problem of creating an original Haitian music, sensual and melancholic, all are guarantors who in the matrix of Time are preparing the work which will mark the capacity of the race for an individual art generating ideas and emotions. (Price-Mars 1928/1983, 183)

Price-Mars's concern with "marking the capacity of the race for an individual art" turned his call for nationalist musical composition into a larger idea to defend the race in the face of foreign criticism. By advocating the conscious construction of a national art out of elements from the historical past, Price-Mars conflated the needs of the Haitian artistic community with the political needs of the Haitian people during the U.S. occupation.

Although Price-Mars envisioned a folklore-inspired music and literature as a defense against U.S. imperialism, his interest in a larger black transnational culture led him to connect his ideas about Haitian culture with the ideas of like-minded blacks in the United States. In a 1932 article about the "Negro Renaissance," Price-Mars identified the center of black artistic activity not in Africa or Haiti, but in Harlem:

> One has reason to consider HARLEM as the greatest black city in the world. Nowhere on the planet does there exist a city that brings together so many black people. But HARLEM is not only the black capital due to its numbers, but also for its preponderance of intellectuals. (Price-Mars 1932, 8)

Citing many of the prominent black intellectuals of the day, including W. E. B. Du Bois, J. Rosamond Johnson and James Weldon Johnson, Jessie Fauset, Langston Hughes, and Countee Cullen, Price-Mars identified African American culture as another potential cultural resource; he laid claim to the folk genius of all black people. Price-Mars reached out to African Americans who themselves were searching for their cultural roots. Together, Price-Mars imagined, Haitians and African Americans could forge a black culture that would challenge both white criticism and black skepticism about the value of African-derived culture and religion.

BLACK ATLANTIC CONSCIOUSNESS
IN HAITI AND THE UNITED STATES

In his study of literature written about Haiti in the United States and in Haiti, J. Michael Dash characterizes white U.S. writers' commentary on Haiti as doing nothing more than "justifying America's 'civilizing mission' in Haiti at the time" (Dash 1988, 22). Dash points out, however, that U.S. black writers were "more generous" (46) to Haiti, perhaps because of their own marginalized status within the United States and their identification with Haitians under occupation.

Indeed, while Haitian intellectuals chafed at the presence of a foreign military force on their soil, African American intellectuals wrote passionately about the implications of the Haitian situation for the fate of Africans in the diaspora. At first, however, African Americans were likely to give the U.S. government the benefit of the doubt, citing the political instability in Haiti as the prime factor in the decision to invade. On 3 August 1915, just a few days after the invasion of Haiti by U.S. forces, W. E. B. Du Bois wrote President Woodrow Wilson saying that he was "deeply disturbed over the situation in Haiti and the action of the United States" (Du Bois 1973, 209). In his letter, however, Du Bois also expressed his hope that the occupation could help Haiti regain its political composure and take the lead as a nation ruled by black people. Du Bois asserted:

> Hayti is not all bad. She has contributed something to human uplift and if she has a chance she can do more. She is almost the sole modern representative of a great race of men among the nations. It is not only our privilege as a nation to rescue her from her worst self, but this would be in a sense a solemn act of reparation on our part for the great wrongs inflicted by this land on the Negro race. (Du Bois 1973, 212)

Haiti provided, for Du Bois, a site of racial redemption for the United States, since the U.S. government could, through helping the Haitian government establish a democratic government, right the "great wrongs" done to Haiti and, by extension, to black people everywhere.

Du Bois saw the problem of black sovereignty in Haiti as one component of a much larger issue of black political rights around the world. In an effort to build an argument that countered widely held beliefs about black people being unable to govern themselves, Du Bois wrote one of the first internationally comparative black history texts, *The Negro* (1915/1974). The book dealt with African history and the slave trade and included descriptions of places in which African-descended people were distributed around the world; it was favorably received by the contemporary press (Aptheker 1974, 20–23). *The Negro* identified the history of Haiti as "the struggle of a small divided country to maintain political independence" (Du Bois 1915/1974, 177). Du Bois's work not only introduced English-speaking audiences to the history of Haiti, it presaged the problems that the U.S. occupation would bring. In his concluding remarks about Haitian history, Du Bois remarked, "If modern capitalistic greed can be restrained from interference until the best elements of Hayti secure permanent political leadership the triumph of the revolution will be complete" (178).

While Du Bois's subsequent assessment of the occupation identified an opportunity for Haitians to assert themselves politically (Du Bois 1973), other prominent African American leaders interpreted the occupation as confirmation of Haiti's status as a degenerate failure. Booker T. Washington, in an article in the magazine *Outlook* (1915, 681), expressed his belief that Haitians were "a backward people in need of discipline and enlightenment" (in Plummer 1992, 121). Even James Weldon Johnson, who would eventually become one of Haiti's staunchest supporters, said in 1914 that "Haiti is again in the throes of a revolution, and we are once more compelled to feelings of regret at the thought that the only real independent Negro state in the world has not yet achieved stable government" (Johnson 1914/1995a, 230).

Soon, however, African American responses to the U.S. occupation of Haiti went from cautiously optimistic to profoundly outraged. The occupation government usurped the authority of the Haitian legislature, making it clear to African American observers that the U.S. government was not invested in promoting democracy in Haiti. In 1917, the Haitian National Assembly tried to pass a revised constitution that retained the longstanding stipulation that foreigners were forbidden to own Haitian property. Major Smedley Butler, the commandant of the newly formed and U.S.-sponsored Gendarmerie d'Haïti, forced Haitian president Sudre Dartiguenave to sign a decree dissolving the assembly. U.S. occupation forces supervised a constitutional referendum in 1918 that gave foreigners the right to own property and granted the military occupation forces more power to intervene in Haitian affairs.

To add insult to injury, the occupation government, desperate to repair the decrepit road system in the country, enforced a decades-old law allowing the government to conscript laborers for road work if those workers lacked the funds to pay an exorbitant road tax (Schmidt 1995, 10). This practice, known as *corvée*, was particularly odious to Haitian laborers since it involved tying the workers to each other with ropes, a practice that viscerally evoked chain-gang labor practices under colonial slavery.

African Americans were quick to condemn the abuses of the *corvée* system and expressed their anger and frustration with an occupation that not only replicated practices from slavery but also consistently denied Haitians redress for indignities suffered at the hands of U.S. Marines. The National Association for the Advancement of Colored People (NAACP) contacted Republican Party leaders, including Theodore Roosevelt, with the idea of sending an investigative team to Haiti to document reports of abuses (Plummer 1982, 132). In 1920, the NAACP sent their field secretary, James Weldon Johnson, to write a first-hand account of the situation in Haiti. In a series of critical reports published in *The Nation* and the NAACP's *Crisis* magazine, Johnson outlined the abuses of the military occupation, including the killing of innocent civilians, the U.S.'s interest in controlling the Haitian economy through the National City Bank of New York, and the draining of the Haitian treasury by cronies of the U.S. Democratic Party (Johnson 1920/1995b).

Johnson's essays on Haiti not only advocated a more enlightened attitude toward the occupation and respect for Haitian culture, they also emphasized a cultural and economic connection with African Americans, especially those living in poverty. Racist stereotypes about Haitians as shiftless, lazy, ignorant, and dirty paralleled similar attitudes of whites toward African Americans in the United States. In an article titled "The Truth About Haiti" (1920), for example, Johnson countered such claims that Haitians did not practice proper personal hygiene by reporting that Haiti imported "more soap per capita than any country in the world" (Johnson 1920/1995c, 249). He argued that despite reports to the contrary, Haitians were an industrious and innately intelligent people. Johnson also insisted that the economic problems in Haiti during the occupation stemmed not from Haitian misdeeds but from the mismanagement of the U.S. occupation government. Johnson concluded:

> The United States has failed in Haiti. It should get out as well and as quickly as it can and restore to the Haitian people their independence and sovereignty. The colored people of the United States should be interested in seeing that this is done, for Haiti is the best chance the Negro has in the world to prove that he is capable of the highest self-government. If Haiti should ultimately lose her independence, that one best chance will be lost. (Johnson 1920/1995c, 252)

Upon his return to the United States, Johnson called for an investigation into reports of abuses against Haitian citizens by U.S. military personnel. The Mayo Commission, headed by U.S. Admiral Henry T. Mayo, exonerated the U.S. military in Haiti, saying that reports of killing innocent Haitian civilians were unfounded (Antoine 1981, 120).

During his trip to Haiti, Johnson not only collected evidence for his publications, he pursued professional relationships with Haitian intellectuals and activists, encouraging them to organize themselves into a group resembling the NAACP in the United States. The Haitian "Union Patriotique," which presented witnesses before the Mayo Commission, was formed by Georges Sylvain, Pauléus Sannon, Sténio Vincent, and Jean

Price-Mars with the idea of ending the U.S. occupation of Haiti and form-ing a new, elected Haitian assembly (Nicholls 1979, 149).

After Johnson published his findings about the U.S. occupation, he made several attempts to lobby for Haitian causes in the United States. Since 1920 was an election year and the Democratic Party was under crit-icism for its policies abroad, Johnson met with Republican presidential candidate Warren G. Harding to make his case for ending the occupation of Haiti. Sensing an opportunity to win African American votes, Harding promised to investigate allegations of abuses in Haiti. After the election, however, Harding proved to be less interested in righting wrongs against the Haitian citizenry and more inclined to ignore his pre-election prom-ises to Johnson.

Johnson's efforts to humanize Haitians for U.S. audiences also led him to emphasize that not only did Haitians have much in common with their African American compatriots, but they were also part of a larger, Pan-African diaspora whose several nations deserved a chance at political sovereignty. In 1927, Johnson echoed Du Bois's ideas from *The Negro* in a pamphlet titled *Native African Races and Cultures*. Johnson described African political institutions in detail, emphasizing that African societies were more similar to European ones than his readers might have ex-pected: "It will be seen that in the case of African Negroes as indeed with all other races, political institutions beginning in such apparently simple needs as the desire to exchange commodities in markets have permeated every phase of life, leading to the development of cities, of kingdoms and empires and ceremonial life on a large scale" (Johnson 1927/1995d, 259–60).

As intellectuals like Du Bois and Johnson sought to educate readers in the United States about the economic and political situation in Haiti, other African American writers saw Haiti as an inspirational example for their artistic efforts. In the 1920s, Haiti emerged as a popular focus for writers eager to explore the creative possibilities of Pan-African culture. As a country founded on a successful slave revolt, Haiti was considered by African Americans to be a New World connection to West and Cen-tral Africa. As J. Michael Dash points out:

> This view of Haiti as a sensory experience, the source of natural luxu-riance, unbridled passion and the power of the supernatural, was meant not to establish Haiti's otherness but, on the contrary, its natural, or-ganic relationship to black American folk culture. Haiti would provide for black writers not a shudder of fear but a "frisson" of recognition. (Dash 1988, 56)

In order to produce such a cultural "recognition" between black writers from Harlem and Haiti, several writers turned to ethnography to unearth similarities between the poor, uneducated black populations in the rural southern United States and the farmers of Haiti. In Alain Locke's collection of essays *The New Negro* (1925), Arthur Huff Fauset encouraged black writers to leave the research into black culture in the hands of those trained to collect, organize, and annotate such material: the professional ethnographer. In his essay, "American Negro Folk Literature," Fauset asserted:

> The antiquity and authentic folk lore ancestry of the Negro tale make it the proper subject for the scientific folk-lorist rather than the literary amateur. It is the ethnologist, the philologist and the student of primitive psychology that are most needed for its present investigation. Of course no one will deny or begrudge the delightful literary by products of this material. . . . But a literary treatment based on a scientific recording will have much fresh material to its hand, and cannot transgress so far from the true ways of the folk spirit and the true lines of our folk art. (Fauset 1992, 243–44)

Several African American artists turned to the folk cultures of African Americans and Haitians in search of artistic subjects that could express a "racial Geist" (Dash 1988, 55) through literature and music. Langston Hughes (1902–67), whose travels to Haiti and creative writing about Haitian culture are discussed at greater length in chapter 4, not only traveled to Haiti but made the country the focus of his play *Emperor of Haiti* (1936/2002), his libretto for the opera *Troubled Island* (1949), and his children's book, *Popo and Fifina,* that he wrote with friend Arna Bontemps (Bontemps and Hughes 1932/1993).

Zora Neale Hurston (1891–1960), a novelist and ethnographer trained by Franz Boas at Columbia University, also traveled to Haiti to conduct research on Haitian culture. Hurston's *Mules and Men* (1935) was an ethnographic account of her work among African Americans in her home state of Florida and in Louisiana. In *Mules and Men,* Hurston examined "hoodoo," a spiritual practice derived in part from Vodou that was brought to Louisiana from Haiti by refugees from the Haitian Revolution. Hurston's *Tell My Horse* (1938) was a first-person account of her travels to Haiti and Jamaica. In the sections on Haiti, Hurston included detailed descriptions of Vodou ceremonies, secret societies, and Haitian folklore. Hurston's classic novel, *Their Eyes Were Watching God* (1937), while not about Haitian culture, was written while Hurston was conducting ethnographic research in Haiti.

Other writers made more explicit connections between Haiti and the United States. Claude McKay's *Home to Harlem* (1928) featured both African American and Haitian protagonists whose struggles against racism and xenophobia showed readers that Haiti and Harlem were inextricably tied together. John Lowney observes about McKay's *Home to Harlem:* "While Haitians comprised a small minority of Caribbean immigrants to Harlem, McKay's exposure of the devastating impact of the American invasion of Haiti underscored the necessity for a renewed counterhegemonic pan-Africanist solidarity" (Lowney 2000, 414). As Haitian and African American artists and intellectuals searched for ways to connect their experiences against white oppression in their different locales during the 1920s and 1930s, they simultaneously forged a model for a transnational identity that transcended political or linguistic boundaries. According to Michelle Stephens, "one could argue that the moment of transnationalism is less the transcendence of the national than the very moment of its construction: the real distinction lies in whether the 'nation' under construction is understood and represented in domestic or international terms" (Stephens 1998, 606).

Visions of the "nation," however, are constructed in specific historical contexts and often draw upon cultural resources that are articulated first in scholarly treatments of national art and music. In his work on the politics of culture in modern Québec, Richard Handler has noted that scholars and nationalists have often shared methods and conclusions: "Most scholarly writing on nationalism is to some extent a rationalization of native ideology, while the nationalists, in turn, borrow these scientific elaborations of their own more commonsense notions" (Handler 1988, 8). Certainly, nationalist rhetoric is essential to what Ralph Linton has called a "nativistic movement":

> What really happens in all nativistic movements is that certain current or remembered elements of culture are selected for emphasis and given symbolic value. The more distinctive such elements are with respect to other cultures with which that society is in contact, the greater their potential value as symbols of the society's unique character. (Linton 1943, 231)

By isolating such "elements of culture" in service of nationalism, nationalists turn culture into an object and imbue it with the qualities of "[historical] continuity, [territorial] boundedness, and [ethnic] homogeneity" (Handler 1988, 6). Once objectified, culture is more susceptible to what David Whisnant calls "systematic cultural intervention"—the process by which "someone (or some institution) consciously and programmatically takes action within a culture with the intent of affecting it in some specific way that the intervenor thinks desirable" (Whisnant 1983, 13).

Nationalist theorizing about the existence of a unique culture most often occurs at moments when national sovereignty and identity are challenged. The U.S. occupation precipitated a cultural identity crisis in which Haitian intellectuals supported a vision of the Haitian past based on a romantic and authentic vision of Haitian culture. That vision was shared by African American intellectuals who also saw evidence of an authentic African cultural past in the Haitian peasant. Isolated geographically from the elites of the urban areas, possessing a religious tradition that was believed to be a direct survival of an African past, and carrying on a way of life that was thought to be unchanged over many generations, Haitian peasants were seen by Haitian and African American intellectuals as the keepers of traditional African culture in the Americas. Moreover, the abitan were thought to be unaware of the materials they possessed. It was up to the trained scholar to locate and identify the folkloric treasures of the country and transform them into form that elites could appreciate. Price-Mars's efforts to bring the treasures of Haitian folklore to a wider audience underscored not only his commitment to improving the lives of the Haitian peasant, it also confirmed his and other Haitian elites' role as the advocate for preserving and disseminating Haitian rural culture.

~2~
RECOMBINANT MYTHOLOGY AND THE ALCHEMY OF MEMORY

Occide Jeanty, Ogou, and Jean-Jacques Dessalines

As a composer "brushed by the wing of the Muse," Haitian military band director Occide Jeanty (1860–1936) played a pivotal role in the musical and cultural changes called for by Haitian ethnographer Jean Price-Mars in *Ainsi parla l'oncle* (Price-Mars 1928/1983, 183). Although Jeanty's oeuvre did not directly conform to Price-Mars's idea of a nationalist music based on the rhythms and melodies of the rural Haitian underclass, his efforts to commemorate the Haitian Revolution through musical composition earned him a reputation as an important composer within Haiti and one of its most beloved nationalist figures during the period of the U.S. occupation of Haiti from 1915 to 1934.

Jeanty's image as a defender of the Haitian nation is significant because of the ways his loyalty and patriotism are imagined by Haitian audiences. By examining the legendary accounts of Jeanty's life—especially those infused with Haitian myths—both Jeanty's importance as an artistic and political figure and the cultural value placed on his musical compositions can be better understood. Rather than looking at myths and historical events as autonomous subjects that capture the attention of folklorists and historians respectively, it is possible to examine both as linked to larger notions of historical meaning. Including myth as a tool of history, however, forces scholars to examine assumptions about how historical meaning is constructed.

Myth and history are elements of larger discursive processes that forge relationships with the past. As Michel-Rolph Trouillot points out, "Theories of history rarely examine in detail the concrete production of specific narratives" (Trouillot 1995, 22). But specific narratives matter, particularly in the case of Jeanty, whose career began during a time when Haitian politicians were actively cultivating connections with the deceased heroes of the 1791–1804 war for Haitian independence, especially Jean-Jacques Dessalines, the first ruler of independent Haiti. While late nineteenth-century Haitian intellectuals strove to connect themselves rhetorically with Dessalines's qualities of bravery, courage, and industry, lower-class Haitians had already begun the process of incorporating the legend of Dessalines into the practice of Haitian traditional religion. Unlike the heroic image of Dessalines favored by Haitian politicians, the lower-class religious image of Dessalines focused on his death and dismemberment in 1806 by members of the light-skinned elite who feared that Dessalines's land redistribution plans would put their plantations in the hands of the newly liberated, dark-skinned majority. As "Ogou Desalin," a mythological fusion of the historical Dessalines and the West African-derived spirit Ogou, Dessalines's incarnation as a Vodou spirit or *lwa* fused two compelling and contradictory images: the powerful general who protected the Haitian state from invasion and the dismembered corpse torn asunder by his enemies. According to Joan Dayan, "The history told by these traditions defies our notions of *identity* and *contradiction*. A person or thing can be two or more things simultaneously" (Dayan 1995, 33).

Despite their differences, both elite and lower-class visions of Dessalines's legacy were concerned with connecting contemporary Haitians with the rhetorical power of politics and myth. As politicians like late nineteenth-century Haitian president Florvil Hyppolite (1889–96) discovered, formulating mythologically inflected rhetoric about Dessalines enabled politicians to be incorporated into the very myths they sought to exploit. Hyppolite's death, which had strong parallels with the death of Dessalines, has eclipsed his historical image and been passed on in a series of widely known songs. Each successive retelling of his story, especially in a politically charged situation, reinscribes Hyppolite's experience as a moral tale that warns audiences of the dangers of unbridled power.

I call this process, whereby people in the present use mythologically oriented language to highlight praiseworthy characteristics of cultural heroes, "recombinant mythology." Recombinant mythology, I argue, creates a chain of meaning linking Haiti's past with the present through a series of concatenated stories. In the case of Occide Jeanty, narratives about his bravery, loyalty, and courage draw upon the recombinant myths of Ogou, Dessalines, and Hyppolite, infusing the heroic rhetoric associated with the defense of the Haitian nation with ideas from Haitian traditional religion. Jeanty, who served as the director for President Hyppolite's band, was himself affected by the recombinant myths of Dessalines, Ogou, and Hyppolite.

President Hyppolite was absorbed into an ongoing fusion of Ogou and Dessalines through his deliberately inflammatory rhetoric and liberal use of Dessalines-inspired metaphors. His absorption into the Dessalines myth was not, however, performed exclusively in the sanctuaries of Vodou temples in the poor sections of Port-au-Prince. Writers, politicians, and intellectuals contributed to Hyppolite's cultural inscription as a subject of recombinant mythology. Alcius Charmant, a journalist from Jacmel, claimed that Hyppolite was subject to fits of insanity that were described as resembling the possession trance of a violent Vodou spirit. When Hyppolite was in the grips of such a fit, he "assumed the name and identity of 'Mabial,' a fact that strongly suggests that these seizures may have been *crises de possession* of Voodoo origin" (cited in Heinl and Heinl 1978, 319).

Although Vodou ceremonies are most often the focus of Haitian mythological analysis, writers and intellectuals from the upper echelons of Haitian society also participate in the creation of a Haitian historical consciousness through their mythologically inflected recountings of Haitian historical events. Such intellectuals may be termed "alchemists of memory," as Michel-Rolph Trouillot has called them, "proud guardians of a past that they neither lived nor wished to have shared" (Trouillot 1995, 32). Though Trouillot was referring specifically to his own family's involvement in a cultural society focused on the achievements of Haitian general Henri Christophe, I suggest that his sobriquet can be applied aptly to those members of Haitian society who use Vodou mythology as part of their cultural vocabulary despite their personal repudiation of Haitian traditional religion. As alchemists of memory, Haitian intellectuals use Vodou as a cultural resource to enliven their own writing and saturate their prose with culturally resonant ideas. Writings such as Charmant's may be seen as a type of cultural performance in which the culturally disruptive practice of Vodou is recast in a format more suitable for Haitian intellectual audiences.

For elite audiences, the competitive and contradictory characteristics embodied by a complex Vodou spirit are too volatile for immediate use. They need to be diluted into forms that both stir the patriotic passions of Haitian audiences and connect them to salient cultural images. John Roberts's (1989) idea of the "African American folk hero" describes one of the more easily assimilated forms of recombinant mythology because it draws upon cultural notions of what it means to belong to, and defend, a particular cultural group. Although the "hero" may share some general characteristics cross-culturally, its importance to a particular culture is specific to that culture's history.

Though Jeanty was not absorbed directly into the recombinant myths of Dessalines and Ogou, his musical works that invoked the spirit of Dessalines and his association with Hyppolite were interpreted by elite

Haitians as a sign of his importance to Haitian history and his status as a Haitian hero. As the following section will show, President Hyppolite revived Dessalines's memory for his own political purposes at the end of the nineteenth century and was absorbed into the Dessalines legend through a series of popular songs. Similarly, Occide Jeanty, the director of President Hyppolite's band, was himself enmeshed in the legend of Dessalines through his own musical compositions that commemorated the Haitian Revolution. Haitian elite writers worked as alchemists of memory to forge a heroic persona for Jeanty, drawing upon the rich tradition of Vodou mythology and Haitian military figures at a time when Haitian sovereignty was under siege. Jeanty's most important musical work, "1804," commemorated Dessalines's successful campaign for Haitian independence at a time when Haitians were occupied by the United States.

HYPPOLITE'S HAT AND OGOU PANAMA

On 24 March 1896, Haitian president Florvil Hyppolite mounted an excursionary force to put down a rebellion in the provincial city of Jacmel, a busy trading port and home to Mérisier Jeannis, Hyppolite's insurrectionary adversary. Jeannis was known as a "chat-marron" (runaway cat) for his guerilla tactics and renegade politics (Turnier 1982, 256). Hyppolite understood the importance of controlling outbreaks of unrest; in 1889, he himself had wrested the presidency from General François Légitime in a successful coup d'état (Nicholls 1979, 111). Hyppolite dealt with subsequent conflicts in a similarly expedient fashion. In 1891, Hyppolite's administration was threatened by a band of rebels from northern Haiti who overran the national prison in Port-au-Prince in an effort to liberate some of their incarcerated comrades. Hyppolite's forces successfully repelled the invasion and executed dozens of conspirators, thereby ensuring that rebels would think twice before attempting an overthrow of Hyppolite's regime.

General Jeannis knew that President Hyppolite was unassailable in Port-au-Prince. Hyppolite's administration, though rife with corruption, was popular with most Haitians because it established social programs such as the department of public works (Bellegarde 1938, 140; Léger 1907/1970, 248). The Haitian army was also firmly under Hyppolite's control. Regional military leaders—Nord Alexis in the north, Jean-Jumeau in the Artibonite valley, and Antoine Simon in the south—maintained authority over their respective militias. Jacmel was the only region in Haiti that was not under the direct supervision of Hyppolite. The president thus savored the opportunity to confront his nemesis in battle.

Hyppolite never had the chance to face Jeannis in combat. On the way to Jacmel to capture Jeannis, the president suddenly suffered a heart attack and died after he fell from his horse's saddle. Tirésias Simon Sam, Hyppolite's minister of war, became president and continued the fallen president's tendencies toward public works as well as graft and corruption. Jeannis consolidated his dominion in the Jacmel area, only to be ousted in 1908 as yet another Haitian president, Nord Alexis, was poised to turn over his office to a rival.

Although some Haitians may know the details of Hyppolite's final hours, most Haitians today are more familiar with the folklore surrounding Hyppolite's fateful trip. According to one popular song, Hyppolite was seen off on his trip by his wife and son:

Le lévé Mardi bon matin,	He arose early on Tuesday morning,
Le fai sélé cheval à li.	He saddled his horse.
En montant sa cheval li,	As he climbed on his horse,
Panama li sorti tombé.	His hat came off and fell.
L'Hérison rélé "Papa!"	L'Hérison called out, "Papa!"
Li dit'l, "Papa à moin,	He said to him, "Father,
Panama ou sorti tombé,	Your hat has come off and fallen,
Cé déjà youn mauvais signal."	That is already a bad omen."
Li répond ni, "Pitit à moin,	He replied to him, "My child,
Moin déjà met' l'armée déhors,	I have already sent the army ahead,
L'armeé moin déjà nan portaille.	My army is already at the city gate.
Y faudra que moin parti."	I have to go."
Ariveé sou Pont Gentil,	Arrived at Pont Gentil [Gentil Bridge],
Le tombé sans connaisance,	He fell unconscious,
Yo voyé rélé Doctor Jules,	They sent for Dr. Jules,
"Vin sauver Florvil Gélin!"	"Come to save Florvil Gélin!"
Ste. Anne dit, "'i faut mouri."	St. Anne said, "He has to die."
St. Augustin dit, "'i faut mouri."	St. Augustine said, "He has to die."
Li rélé St. Jacques Majeur,	He called to St. James the Great,
"Vine sauver Florvil Gélin!"	"Come to save Florvil Gélin!"
Mérisier rété Jacmel,	Mérisier waited at Jacmel,
Li souqué baksor à li.	He shook his sacred rattle.
Li conné ça qui gainyain.	He knew what was going on.
Tout ti trou déjà bouché.	All the small holes are filled.
Victoire dit con ça,	Victory said,
Quand Florvil ta va mourit	When Florvil dies

Li tap fai youn belle soirée	She will hold a beautiful party
Avec tout ti gens la yo.	With all the young people.
CHORUS	CHORUS
En allé Dodo!	We are going to dance!
En allé Dodo!	We are going to dance!
En allé ce soir	We are going this evening
Caille la belle Victoire!	To the house of beautiful Victory!
	[Hyppolite's young wife]

(Courlander 1960/1985, 151–52, his translation)

In this version of the story, Hyppolite's hat falls off as he mounts his horse. Referred to in the second verse as a "Panama," the hat has a wide brim designed to shield the wearer from the harsh sun. Hyppolite's son, L'Hérison, warns the president that a falling hat is a bad omen; after all, in Haitian folklore, the land of the dead is also called *peyi san chapo,* or "the country without hats." Later, Hyppolite falls from his horse; Dr. Jules is called, but cannot revive the president. Dr. Jules calls upon three saints— St. Anne, St. Augustine and St. James the Great—to grant a boon and spare the president's life. Anne and Augustine flatly deny the doctor's request while James the Great remains silent on the issue. In the next verse, Mérisier [Jeannis], Hyppolite's rival, shakes a *baksor* or *ason,* a sacred rattle that is a ritual object associated with an initiated male Vodou priest or *ougan.* The verse seems to say that Jeannis plotted Hyppolite's death and that the spirits overseeing Hyppolite's trip—Saints Anne, Augustine and James the Great—did nothing to stop the inevitable.

Although some Haitians know the words to the version of the song above, most are likely to know the popular song about Hyppolite's last campaign, "Panama m Tonbe" (My Hat Fell Down). In "Panama m tonbe," the action is focused on the falling hat itself:

Panama'm tombé	My hat fell down
Panama'm tombé	My hat fell down
Panama'm tombé; ça qui dèyè	My hat fell down; whoever is behind
Ranmassé'l pou ba moin.	Pick it up for me.
Moin soti la ville Jacmel	I left the city of Jacmel
Moin pralé la Valée	I'm going to the Valley
En arrivant carrefour Bainet	Arriving at the Bainet crossroads
Panama'm tombe.	My hat fell down.

(Michel 1970, 30, her translation)

"Panama m tonbe" places the historical event of Hyppolite's falling hat into a timeless context. The song seems to warn those who disregard ill omens as sealing their fate. It also distills the historical narrative to the omen itself, leaving the singers and audience of the song to fill in the rest of the story.

Yet another Panama song replaces Hyppolite with a figure taken from Vodou. In this song, Ogou, a spirit associated with the Nago *nanchon* or denomination of Vodou, is praised as a "nèg Panama" (Panama-wearing man):

M-di Panama ye,	I say Panama,
Papa Ogou se neg Panama ye.	Papa Ogou is a Panama man.
O Panama ye,	Oh Panama,
Neg Nago se neg Panama ye.	The Nago man is a Panama man.

(Brown 1989, 78, her translation)

Ogou is a warrior spirit, derived, in part from Yoruba and Dahomean mythological antecedents (Barnes 1989). As a patron spirit of iron, fire, and soldiers, Ogou asserts his military prowess when under attack. The symbol of the panama hat links Ogou and Hyppolite.

Ogou's response to the threat, however, takes an idiosyncratic form that is demonstrated during Vodou ceremonies when an *ousi,* or Vodou initiate, is spiritually possessed by Ogou. In her study of Ogou in Haiti, Karen McCarthy Brown observed that the ritual enactment of an Ogou possession often follows the same pattern:

> First, he attacks the imaginary enemy: he rushes wildly about the temple clanging the sword on doorframes and brandishing it in the air. Then he threatens the immediate community: with smaller gestures, he brings the sword's point threateningly close to the bodies of those standing nearby. Finally he turns the sword on himself: lodging the point in his solar plexus, he poses. This performance is to body language what proverbs are to spoken language. In one elegant series of motions, it conveys the message that the same power which liberates also corrupts and inevitably turns on itself. (Brown 1989, 70)

Few Haitians would confuse the historical events of Hyppolite's demise with an Ogou possession trance. The legend of Hyppolite's death, however, takes on a larger significance when compared with the regular pattern of Ogou's behavior. In the case of the fallen president, the power that he wielded eventually came back to kill him; ignoring the ill omen was a sign of Hyppolite's careless use of authority. As with most Ogou possessions, a lack of attention to the consequences of power eventually results in that same power coming back to topple the leader deluded by notions of invincibility. Hyppolite's story is transformed by Vodou through Ogou Panama; the falling hat is both historical event and religious parable.

On the surface, the first lyric, in which Hyppolite's family implores him to heed the omen of the falling hat, seems to be distantly related to the song for Ogou Panama. Yet, in the fifth verse of the song, Saints Anne, Augustine, and James the Great are called upon by the attending doctor to intervene and save the dying president. Anne and Augustine flatly refuse to intercede, while James the Great says nothing. In Haiti, Saint James the Great (Sen Jak Majè) is also known as the "senior Ogou," who is saluted in Vodou ceremonies before all other Ogou spirits (Brown 1989, 71). Saint James the Great might have been expected to save Hyppolite since they are both military men, known for their loyalty and bravery under fire. In addition, Hyppolite's fate is foretold by Merisier Jeannis's shaking of his *ason*, or sacred rattle. Jeannis was known to have presided over two Vodou *oufò* or temples, one in his hometown of Jacmel, the other on the outskirts of Port-au-Prince in the Bizoton neighborhood (Turnier 1982, 390).

Hyppolite's compatibility with Ogou spirits may have been due to his activities as a devotee of Vodou. According to Michel Laguerre, "Hyppolite was a devotee of Nan Kanpèch [a Vodou temple] to which he gave lavish gifts" (Laguerre 1993, 56). Hyppolite's association with Vodou was not unique among Haitian presidents. Several presidents were known for their associations with Vodou temples, including Nord Alexis (1902–8), who was denounced by Alcius Charmant as the "grand pontife du vaudouisme ("the grand pontiff of Vodouism," cited in Nicholls 1979, 111); Faustin Soulouque (1847–59), who crowned himself Emperor Faustin I in 1849 and who openly permitted the practice of Vodou (Nicholls 1979, 278, n. 99); and, most recently, Dr. François Duvalier (1957–71), who promoted himself as Bawon Samdi (Baron Saturday), a Vodou spirit closely related to death and the cemetery (Largey 2000, 240).

Hyppolite's alleged involvement in Vodou is not, however, the only issue that makes his story compelling. The legend of his courting disaster while marching on his enemies resembles a story about another important Haitian soldier-statesman: Jean-Jacques Dessalines. In 1804, General Dessalines led the Haitian army to victory and served as Haiti's first president. Dessalines took a bold step by giving newly emancipated slaves an opportunity to own land, the same land to which they had previously been bonded. Consequently, Dessalines's land reform plan was resisted by wealthy, freeborn persons of color who had inherited slave plantations from their white, French-planter fathers. In 1806, as Dessalines marched on his adversaries, he was ambushed and killed at the Pont Rouge, or "Red Bridge." According to most accounts, the embattled president was stabbed and shot repeatedly, then hacked to pieces by his enemies.

Dessalines's story does not end with his violent death. As Joan Dayan points out, the historical figure of Jean-Jacques Dessalines was absorbed into Vodou religious practice as a figure of defeat as well as of resurrection: "Born in Haiti, Dessalines is called a *lwa krèyol* (Creole god). As *Ogou Desalin* he walks with the African Ogou, the gods of war and politics that remain in Haiti in their multiple aspects" (Dayan 1995, 30). Emperor Dessalines may have perished on the Red Bridge, but his spirit is called upon to inhabit the bodies of contemporary Vodou initiates to show Haitians both the desirability and the risks of maintaining their national sovereignty.

Dessalines, Hyppolite, and Ogou are linked to each other through their respective overlapping myths. Taken as a group, these three figures limn a cultural space where myth, religion, and history work together to create social meanings that transcend a single historical moment. Their individual narratives derive their authority from Haitian traditional religion as well as from their importance to Haitian political history.

MYTH, MEANING, AND MEMORY: RECOMBINATION AND HISTORICAL CONSCIOUSNESS

In Haiti, myths provide important contextual information that enriches current understandings of Haitian history. But myth is not simply a spicy condiment for bland historical narratives. Myth can provide opportunities for individuals to experience historical ideas through metaphors that allow for multiple interpretations in the present. In a predominantly oral culture such as Haiti's, the enactment of mythic ideas is perhaps the preeminent way in which individuals create a usable past.

Oral narratives of Haitian myths do not place spirits in a distant, ancestral past. Rather, they are enacted in Vodou ceremonies through what Karen McCarthy Brown has called "possession-performances" in which spiritual energy is channeled in constructive ways, bringing the power of the spirits into contact with the human world (Brown 1987, 155). The term "possession-performance" does not imply that the possession experience of the Vodou devotee is false or staged for an audience. Rather, the performative aspects of Vodou possession contribute to the quality of the ceremony. Vodou ceremonies are cultural performances that create relationships between spirit and devotee in the present, providing opportunities for negotiating issues through performative display. When Vodou devotees are possessed by spirits during a ceremony, they often invoke complex and sometimes contradictory personality traits that provide opportunities for participants to interpret their behaviors. As the legend of

Ogou Desalin demonstrates, the spirit of the revolutionary general provides an example of a brave and selfless warrior pitted against the forces of slavery as well as a gruesome reminder of the peril of attempting to bring about social change in the face of determined resistance.

The analysis of myth is important in understanding the formation of a historical consciousness, especially in places like the Caribbean where written history has privileged colonialist perspectives. According to Edouard Glissant, "Myth anticipates history as much as it inevitably repeats the accidents that it has glorified; that means that it is in turn a producer of history" (Glissant 1989, 71). In Haiti, the persistence and persuasiveness of myth has complicated the colonialist vision of history, making it difficult for students of Haitian culture, most notably folklorists, anthropologists, ethnomusicologists, and literary scholars, to ignore Vodou mythology entirely (Courlander 1939 and 1960/1985; Brown 1987, 1989, 2001; Dayan 1995; Desmangles 1992; Herskovits 1937). Joan Dayan has suggested the term "vodou history" as a corollary for the combination of mythical and historical narratives in Haiti. Calling such accounts "sinkholes of excess," Dayan asserts that "these crystallizations of unwritten history force us to acknowledge inventions of mind and memory that destroy the illusions of mastery, that circumvent and confound *any* master narrative" (Dayan 1995, 54; emphasis in original).

Other scholars have proposed new, hybrid terminology to emphasize the interconnectedness of history and myth. Liisa Malkki, in her study of Hutu refugees in Tanzania, suggests that historical narratives, when combined with myths, represent "not only a description of the past, nor even merely an evaluation of the past, but a subversive recasting and reinterpretation of it in fundamentally moral terms" (Malkki 1995, 54). For Malkki, the term "mythico-history" embraces events of the past with their cultural and moral interpretation by local agents.

Myths that have salience in the present may be used by contemporary subjects in traditions that "establish connections with a meaningful past and endow particular cultural forms with value and authority" (Bauman 1992, 128). Elsewhere, I have argued that Haitians are adept at taking cultural expressions from Haitian history and religion to forge new, symbolically constructed ideas through traditionalizing processes that connect them with their past and, hence, their power (Largey 2000, 240). Traditionalizing processes bring the past into a relationship with the present, giving contemporary subjects discursive power to negotiate authority over their history.

One type of traditionalizing process in which historical narratives are infused with mythological ideas is what I term "recombinant mythology," making historical events more culturally saturated, and hence more resonant, to culturally competent audiences. As the stories of Hyppolite, Dessalines, and Ogou show, certain historical narratives may be legitimated over others when they have affinity with mythological ideas. Because it has been combined with the cultural story of Ogou Panama, Hyppolite's story has become part of a larger narrative about the use and abuse of power.

Recombinant myths do not spring whole from the fertile ground of Haitian cultural imaginations. If they are to have meaningful applications, they must be connected to historical, political, or cultural institutions. The first stage of recombinant mythology is connection; people in the present make a demonstrable link to some idea, practice, person, or event in the past that carries contemporary significance. Recombinant myths rely upon "selective tradition"—that is, they exploit similarities between the present and the past, leaving behind traits that do not serve an explicit purpose in the present (Williams 1977, 116–17). Ogou is a particularly effective point of connection for recombinant mythology in Haiti. Known primarily as a soldier, Ogou brandishes his machete as part of his possession-performance and often wears the sash of a Haitian army officer. In addition, since every Haitian president between 1804 and 1913 was drawn from the ranks of the Haitian army, the military has been closely associated with the control and abuse of political power. Dessalines's and Ogou's mutual affinity comes from their shared associations with the military. Both the Haitian president and the Vodou spirit are identified as brave and selfless soldiers, willing to put themselves in physical danger despite the risk. They are prototypical Haitian folk heroes who sacrifice themselves for the good of the nation.

Selective traditions bring the present and the past together in specific discursive forms, but they do not replace alternative explanations of the past. They exist in what Homi Bhabha calls the "Third Space," where they are available for use in a myriad of ways, some of which may be in direct contradiction with each other. According to Bhabha, "it is that Third Space, though unrepresentable in itself, which constitutes the discursive conditions of enunciation that ensure that the meaning and symbols of culture have no primordial unity or fixity; that even the same signs can be appropriated, translated, and rehistoricized and read anew" (Bhabha 1994, 37). In the "Third Space," ideas coexist in contrary and competitive forms, available for use depending on the specific context. In Haiti, Vodou spirits are often used as sources of recombinant myths and can be, as Karen McCarthy Brown shows, "moral exemplars" whose possession-performances demonstrate particular points. Vodou spirits are not "moral" in the sense that they are "perfect." Rather, their exemplary status is derived from their moral complexity, their ability to show worshippers that human interactions are always imbricated with power relations. In the case of Ogou, the power he wields is neither good nor bad; it is his relationship with power that makes him a focal point for his followers. Thus, "Haitians call Ogou a 'saint' not because he is good, but because he is whole, complete" (Brown 1987, 151).

Recombinant myths made in the present with the ideas of the past, however, are not arbitrary. They cannot be formed with just *any* ideas selected from the past. Recombinant myths involve combination, or the alignment of salient traits between appropriate subjects. Combination, the second stage of recombinant mythology, connects ideas that are, to paraphrase Claude Lévi-Strauss, good to think *together* (Lévi-Strauss 1962, 128). Ogou, the patron of the Haitian soldier-statesman, combines well with Haitian generals and presidents like Hyppolite whose power eventually overcame them. Other legendary Haitian generals, such as Toussaint Louverture and Henri Christophe, are rarely depicted as having Ogou characteristics. Although they are both regarded as Haitian heros, their stories do not lend themselves well to combination with Ogou.

Toussaint Louverture, the first military leader of the Haitian Revolution, had the requisite courage, resolve, and willingness to risk his safety to make him a focal point for recombinant mythology. His image as a brave defender of the Haitian nation, however, was complicated by his attitudes toward the soon-to-be freed slaves in Haiti. As Alfred Hunt points out, Louverture was admired by slaveholders in the southern United States for his insistence that Haitian workers continue to work plantations under conditions similar to those they suffered under slavery. For many U.S. slaveholders, and by extension, for many Haitians, "Toussaint thought like a white man" (Hunt 1988, 89). In addition, before Louverture came fully into his own power, he was captured by French forces and imprisoned in the Joux prison in France, dying less than a year before Haiti declared its independence.

Henri Christophe, on the other hand, emerged victorious from the Haitian Revolution and consolidated his power in the northern part of Haiti. Originally from Grenada, Christophe participated as a French mercenary in the Battle of Savannah, helping the emergent United States win its independence from Britain. After the success of the Haitian Revolution, Christophe built an elaborate mansion that he named Palais Sans Souci and a mountaintop fortress called La Citadelle Laferrière that was designed to repel invasions of European forces bent on reestablishing slavery in Haiti. Crowning himself emperor of northern Haiti in 1811,

Christophe waged war against the regimes of Presidents Alexandre Pétion and Jean Pierre Boyer, who controlled the southern and western
portions of the country. According to Michel-Rolph Trouillot, in 1820,
"having engaged unsuccessfully in various rituals to restore his failing
health and knowing that he had lost the personal magnetism that made his
contemporaries tremble at his sight, a paralyzed Christophe shot himself,
reportedly with a silver bullet, before a growing crowd of insurgents at
Sans Souci" (Trouillot 1995, 60). Like Ogou, Christophe is ultimately
overtaken by his own power, but his final act is one of cowardice. Ogou
does not usually kill himself as part of a possession-performance; he
merely demonstrates that power can easily slip from a warrior's control.

Compare the ignominious deaths of Louverture and Christophe with
that of Dessalines. Dessalines was violently dismembered by his enemies
as he rode into battle. The forces that conspired against Dessalines were
interested in reestablishing involuntary plantation labor, a form of de
facto slavery. Dessalines's attitudes toward slavery and colonialism—his
demand for freedom for black people and his rejection of white domination—made him a target for those Haitian elites who pursued their own
continued prosperity at the expense of the Haitian poor.

The final stage of recombinant mythology is transformation, or the
emergence of a recombinant myth in a specific place and time. When a
recombinant myth is transformed, it takes its place in a concatenated
chain of narratives each of which is simultaneously linked to specific historical and mythological antecedents. It is, like the "minstrel lore cycle"
described by W. T. Lhamon (1998) in his work on blackface minstrelsy in
the United States, built upon previous performances of similar material.
As the songs about Hyppolite demonstrate, singing about the "falling hat"
evokes the historical Dessalines and the mythological Ogou in the *current
historical moment* through performance. Dessalines's rise as a cultural hero
came as Hyppolite and his contemporaries traced the emperor's footsteps
and laid claim to the first Haitian president's heroic lineage.

It was the centennial of Haitian independence in 1904 that gave a sense
of urgency to the efforts to reclaim Dessalines's patriotic legacy. Dessalines
was, along with Christophe and Pétion, recommended for a commemorative statue at a location to be called "place de l'Indépendance" (Dévot
1901, 19). The association in charge of the centennial organized a competition for a Haitian national anthem and chose Nicolas Fénélon Geffrard's (1871–1930) "La Dessalinienne," set to lyrics written by Alexis
Justin Lhérisson (1873–1907).

During the first part of the nineteenth century, however, Dessalines's
image as a Haitian patriot waned, due in part, to a succession of upper-class

rulers, predominantly light-skinned Haitians who shared the attitudes of Dessalines's enemies on the status of the lower-class, mostly dark-skinned population of the country. As a result, especially before the 1870s, Dessalines was often cited as one of the sources of Haitian political turmoil; his warlike demeanor and his antipathy toward Haitian light-skinned elites made him a suitable scapegoat for the many problems facing the country, especially in the eyes of the light-skinned elite. As elite control of the Haitian government was challenged by rural revolts in southern Haiti in the 1840s, however, government officials gingerly invoked the name of Dessalines as an ideological defense against the charge of elitism and color discrimination against dark-skinned Haitians. It was Haitian President Charles Rivère Hérard, a light-skinned elite who, in 1844, first praised Dessalines as a hero of all Haitians (Dayan 1995, 27). Hérard's public praising of Dessalines was mere showmanship; as Dayan points out, although the president was lauding Dessalines in public, Dessalines's body lay in an unadorned grave (28).

Dessalines's transformation into a national, mythic hero was tied to the emergence of what some have called a "cult of Dessalines" in the late nineteenth century (Heinl and Heinl 1978, 336). Both light- and dark-skinned politicians used the memory of Dessalines to promote their particular political regimes. Haitian President Lysius Salomon, who ruled from 1879 to 1888, was perhaps the first Haitian president to rehabilitate the image of Dessalines. According to David Nicholls, "Salomon was instrumental in establishing a revised view of the Haitian past and of Dessalines in particular—a black legend" (1985, 37). This "black legend" was an ideological construct promoted by nwa elites who were marginalized by the milat elite. It directly countered the mulatto legend promulgated by the milat elite, in which the contributions of nwa leaders Toussaint Louverture, Jean-Jacques Dessalines, and Henri Christophe were denigrated while those of milat leaders such as Aléxandre Pétion and Jean-Pierre Boyer were praised (Nicholls 1974b, 1979, 1985).

Salomon's choice of Dessalines as a political ancestor allowed the president to identify his regime with the protection of Haitian sovereignty and the defense of Haitian economic interests. It also provided political cover for Salomon's dealings with foreign powers, notably the United States and France. As Salomon decried his political adversaries' failure to protect Haiti's sovereignty, Salomon himself was negotiating to make Haiti a protectorate of the United States, and later, of France as a way to keep British political intervention at bay (Nicholls 1985, 43).

Whereas Salomon's use of Dessalines for political promotion was a transparent case of self-interested grandstanding, Florvil Hyppolite's treatment of Dessalines verged on a state-sponsored religious movement. With the overthrow of François Légitime by Hyppolite in 1889, Dessalines found his most ardent devotee. Hyppolite established the first public monuments to Dessalines and began construction on a mausoleum for Dessalines's remains (Brutus 1947, 246–65).

In addition to his personal interest in promoting Dessalines's legend, Hyppolite, like Salomon before him, courted foreign governments to help him maintain his grip on power. According to Brenda Gayle Plummer, "A U.S. steamship company with intimate ties to ranking American navalists had bankrolled Hyppolite's campaign" (1988, 27). In exchange for their support, the U.S. government expected the Hyppolite administration to turn over the deepwater port of Môle St. Nicolas for the construction of a U.S.-run naval base. David Nicholls notes:

> In a speech made after his election to the presidency, Hyppolite denied that he had promised to cede the Môle, and explicitly linked his defence of territorial integrity with his racial identity. "I am not white," he declared, "I belong to the same race as you do; the day when there should be a question of such an act, I should prefer to see this country disappear like Gomorrah." (Nicholls 1979, 140)

Like Dessalines before him, Hyppolite defied his enemies when they sought political concessions. In his speech, Hyppolite upheld Dessalines's vow to prevent foreign (or white) ownership of property within Haiti and promised to defend his vow to the death. Significantly, his identity as a black person superseded his loyalty to the Haitian state. In this rhetorical situation, Hyppolite preferred to lose Haiti in a biblically inspired conflagration than deny his identity as a *nèg natif natal* (native-born black). Like Dessalines, Hyppolite identified himself as the defender of the Haitian people, despite the danger that position entailed.

As an outspoken supporter of the Dessalines legend who also self-consciously identified himself with the martyred hero, Hyppolite was himself subject to the same traditionalizing processes that merged the first Haitian president with the warrior spirit, Ogou. When Hyppolite tried to manipulate the Dessalines legend toward his own ends, the legend eventually overtook him. For Haitians today, Hyppolite's defense of Môle St. Nicolas is less well known than the story of the president's falling hat.

As a focus for recombinant mythology, Hyppolite has grown beyond his importance as a political figure. He is, like the African ancestral spirits associated with Vodou, subject to renovation and renewal. In their transfer from Africa to Haiti, Vodou spirits have themselves been "recombined" in new forms as attributes of one spirit are grafted on to another spirit or group of spirits (Cosentino 1987, 267). For example, the West African Fon spirit Legba, like his Haitian counterpart of the same name, is the guardian spirit of the crossroads and the first spirit ritually saluted in a ceremony; however, the Fon Legba is also associated with a voracious sexual appetite, something that the geriatric and slightly lame Haitian Legba is not. According to Cosentino, the sexual side of the Fon Legba's personality was passed on in Haiti not to Legba but to the Gede spirits of the dead (1987, 268–72). As tricksters, the Gede spirits use sexually charged behavior, often including liberal doses of profanity, to make their presence known in a ceremony. The risqué aspects of the Fon Legba are thus conserved in Haitian religious practice through a form of religious syncretism.

In his landmark ethnography of Haitian life, Melville Herskovits first described the transformative aspects of Haitian spiritual figures through the concept of syncretism, in which African spiritual personalities were combined with Roman Catholic saints into a new spiritual form that reflected the social world of the slaves (Herskovits 1937). Building on Herskovits's idea of syncretism, Karen McCarthy Brown has observed that the physical shift of African populations to the Americas has resulted in a similar shift of the cosmological structure of Haitian spiritual life:

> The African slaves brought their religions with them, religions whose wisdom and insight operated on many levels in both the social and natural worlds. Slaves were drawn from specific population subgroups, and they therefore had selective memory. But, once on the other side of the ocean, they also had selective needs. Slaves in the New World reground the lens of their religion to allow it to focus in exquisite detail on the social arena, the most problematic one in their lives. The spirits they brought with them from Africa shifted and realigned in response to their needs. (Brown 1991, 100)

According to Brown, "The cosmos became thoroughly socialized" (100) as a result of the large-scale movement of African slaves to the Americas.

Recombinant mythology resembles the concept of syncretism, especially in its endless transformations of mythological ideas to suit contemporary situations. Recombinant mythology, however, assumes not only a socialization of the cosmos but also a politicization of it, as it uses cosmological stories to underscore historical and contemporary issues of power, control, and domination. As Joan Dayan observes, Vodou practitioners have long used narratives that invoked issues of power in their religious observances:

> Gods were born in the memories of those who served and rebelled, and they not only took on the traits or dispositions of their servitors but also

those of the former masters, tough revenants housed in the memories of the descendants of slaves. While de-idealizing, by reenacting to the extreme, a conceit of power, the figure of Dessalines became a proof of memory: something gained by those who were thought to have no story worth the telling. (Dayan 1995, 30)

Although the practice of Vodou is more often associated with the disenfranchised, or those "who have no story worth the telling," its *lwa* are also used by those in power, like Hyppolite, to highlight those character traits that have cultural resonance with Haitian history and folklore.

Just as Hyppolite's importance to Haitian history cannot be measured solely by his political and diplomatic contributions, Haitian band director Occide Jeanty's contributions to Haitian music similarly can best be evaluated by his cultural salience to Haitian audiences. Jeanty's importance to Haitian audiences is documented in what VèVè Clark, following Pierre Nora, has called, "*milieux de memoire*—discrete, regional remembrances beyond the pale of official history—so insignificant as to be known only to practitioners, a living chronology revealed to members only" (Clark 1994, 190). These *milieux de memoire* include such disparate genres as myths and legends about Jeanty's prowess as a musician and patriot; personal experience narratives by Jeanty's contemporaries in which his positive traits are selected and magnified through heroic rhetoric; poems written about Jeanty that blur the distinction between his actual role in historical events and his inspirational value; and a genre I term "experiential programs," personal interpretive statements—in the form of newspaper articles, poems, or incidental writings—made by audience members upon listening to a piece of music, in this instance by Jeanty.

Poems, personal experience narratives, and experiential programs were written down so that Haitians as well as foreigners could read about the exploits of important Haitians. Each genre was a type of "autoethnographic text" (Pratt 1992, 7; Reed-Danahay 1997, 7) in which Haitians expressed their version of events in terms acceptable to both Haitian and foreign audiences.

MUSIC AND THE MILITARY:
OCCIDE JEANTY'S PROFESSIONAL CAREER

Occilius Jeanty fils (junior), better known to Haitian audiences as Occide, was born in Port-au-Prince in 1860 during a period of relative political stability under President Fabre Geffrard. The young Jeanty was an elementary school student at the L'Ecole Polymathique de Coupeaud and attended high school at the prestigious Lycée Pétion. According to Dumervé

(1968, 124), Jeanty was an indifferent student, preferring to sing children's songs to himself while beating time with his ruler or pencil.

Occide Jeanty was part of a musical family. His mother was Mulerine Obin and his father was Occilius Jeanty père (1830–82). Occilius père was the director of the Ecole Centrale de Musique and a professor of mathematics at Lycée Pétion, as well as the director of the Corps de Musique, a military band attached to the National Palace in Port-au-Prince. He began his studies at the Ecole Wesleyenne and finished his high school studies at the Lycée Pétion. In contrast with his son, Occilius père was a talented student, excelling in mathematics and music. According to Dumervé (1968, 57), the flutist Franklin Carpentier gave Occilius père his first flute. Soon afterward, Occilius père was conscripted to play in the Grenadiers de la Garde, the official band of Emperor Faustin I. He later served Haitian presidents Fabre Geffrard, Nissage Saget (who disbanded the presidential band), Michel Domingue (who reestablished the band), Boisrond Canal, and finally Lysius Salomon.

Like most individuals who are accorded folk hero status, Occide Jeanty inspired several legendary narratives about his childhood. Jeanty was, according to his informal biographer, Marat Chenet, a naturally talented musician. Chenet recounted several examples of how the young Jeanty displayed a precociousness that "rivalled Mozart," including his first composition, "Les Pleurs d'Estelle," written at age twelve (Herissé n.d.).

Occilius père encouraged his son, Occide, to study music from a young age. The younger Jeanty proved adept at music, eventually opening his own course of solfège at the Ecole Centrale de Musique under the Boisrond Canal regime (Dumervé 1968, 60). In 1881, Jeanty was awarded a scholarship to study trumpet in Paris with Jean Baptiste Arban. Despite the backing of the legendary Arban, Jeanty failed to win the first prize for the annual instrumental competition at the Paris Conservatory. To make matters worse, political problems in Haiti caused Jeanty's scholarship payments to stop shortly after he arrived in Paris. A frustrated Jeanty played in the streets of Paris for money to support himself. According to Herissé, rumors were flying that Jeanty was spending more time chasing after women (referred to as "les blondes des boulevards" in Herissé's narrative) than studying music. Whether or not the rumors about Jeanty's behavior were true, his reputation was already damaged in the eyes of the Haitian government. Jeanty was recalled to Haiti and dressed down personally by President Salomon.

Jeanty's supporters, however, resolved to quell President Salomon's wrath. Père R. P. Saint Clair, a priest of the Saint Esprit order who had served on the jury that awarded Jeanty his scholarship to study in Paris, arranged an audience with President Salomon and other well-respected Haitian musicians, including Edmond Roumain, Toureau Lechaud, and Louis Astrée père (Dumervé 1968, 125; Herissé n.d.).[1] Jeanty's brilliant playing prompted Salomon immediately to appoint the young cornetist to the ranks of the Musique du Palais National, the Haitian president's official military band (Herissé n.d.).

Jeanty wrote at least eight processional marches, six funeral marches for Haitian dignitaries and their families, and four patriotic marches, as well as various polkas, gavottes, and méringues. Most of his works were originally written for the Musique du Palais National. His dance pieces were often scored for wind band so that the Musique du Palais National could play them in their weekly concerts on the Champs de Mars in Port-au-Prince.

It was during his tenure with the Musique du Palais National from 1882 to 1916—first as a cornet soloist and then as director of the group—that Jeanty turned his creative talents fully toward musical composition. Most of his early works were intended for the official functions of the Haitian government, including marches for military processions and funerals. In 1892, Jeanty wrote his first funeral march, "Imprécations de Dessalines" (Dessalines's curses). Originally titled "Jacques Ier" (Jacques the first), the work was commissioned by President Hyppolite to commemorate the building of an official mausoleum for Dessalines. According to Herissé (n.d.), the work was divided into five sections: Introduction, the Prayer, the Curse, the Agony, and the Last Breath. Herissé claimed that, in the Prayer section, Dessalines invoked divine powers to curse his attackers; the abrupt "sforzando" in the Prayer conveyed the emperor's desperation. In the Curse section, again the basses "in a powerful sonority, reproduced these words: Vous serez, à jamais, l'assassin de vos chefs" (You will forever be the assassin of your leaders). According to Herissé, not only did "Imprécations de Dessalines" have a program outlining the death of Haiti's first president, but the musical structure itself paralleled the agony and suffering of the dying leader.

Jeanty provided other official funeral marches, including two for President Florvil Hyppolite ("Chery Hyppolite" [Dear Hyppolite], and "Nos L'Armes"), one for Tirésias Augustin Simon Sam ("Ti Sam" [Little Sam]), and one for Nord Alexis ("Sur la Tombe" [On the Tomb]). Jeanty also wrote patriotic pieces, including the "Chant National" (with lyrics by Haitian poet, Oswald Durand) in 1897 and the commemorative march "1804" in celebration of the centennial of Haitian independence.

While Jeanty's official job was to create ceremonial music for a series of Haitian governments, he was also active composing musical works that engaged issues of political sovereignty and national security. During the 1870s, 1880s, and 1890s, Haiti experienced an increasing degree of interference from foreign powers, especially in the areas of trade and politics. French, British, and American interests in Haiti grew steadily during this period, while other, smaller foreign groups such as Levantine Christians moved into commercial activity (Plummer 1981).

The German government was especially interventionist in its dealings with Haiti. During what came to be called the "Batsch Affair," several German merchants lost their businesses during a bombardment of Cap Haïtien by British ships in 1865. When the Haitian government refused to compensate the German businessmen for their losses, the German government intervened diplomatically on behalf of its citizens. After its demands went unanswered, Germany sent two frigates to Port-au-Prince in 1872 to claim reparations forcibly for its citizens. In the process, German ships seized two Haitian ships and demanded monetary compensation (Nicholls 1985, 109). After the Haitian government paid the ransom, the German navy returned the ships, but not before German sailors smeared the ship's Haitian flag with their feces (Heinl and Heinl 1978, 256).

During Jeanty's tenure with the Musique du Palais National, Haiti witnessed yet another notorious example of German interventionism: the Emile Lüders affair. Lüders, the son of a Haitian mother and a German father, retained his German citizenship while living and working in Haiti. In 1894, he assaulted a Haitian soldier and was sentenced to six days in jail (Léger 1907/1970, 250). In 1897, Lüders tried to stop a Haitian police officer from arresting one of his employees. In the ensuing melée, he assaulted the officer and resisted arrest. In light of his earlier offense, Lüders was fined and sentenced to a year in prison. Upon receiving the news of Lüders's sentence, Count von Schwerin, the German chargé d'affairs, bypassed the usual diplomatic channels and demanded a personal audience with President Simon Sam. Under pressure from the American legation, Simon Sam released Lüders on 22 October; Lüders left Haiti immediately. In order to further humiliate President Simon Sam, Schwerin called for German naval intervention. On 6 December 1897, the German ships *Charlotte* and *Stein* sailed into the bay of Port-au-Prince and the German navy demanded a $20,000 indemnity from the Haitian government, a salute to the German flag, as well as a four-hour reception for the German chargé d'affairs (Bellegarde 1938, 142).

Simon Sam complied with the German demands, due largely to the encouragement of the United States embassy. He was later decorated with the Legion of Honor by the French government as a consolation for his capitulation. While Simon Sam weathered the political situation, other Haitians were outraged at the disrespectful treatment their country received from the Germans. Pierre Frédérique, director of the Haitian newspaper *L'Impartial,* published the following announcement after the incident:

> You are invited to attend the funeral of young Haiti, cruelly assassinated by President Tirésias Augustin Simon Sam. The funeral procession will leave the mortuary, located at the National Palace, to give itself to the court of Berlin. Port-au-Prince, 6 December 1897. (Herissé n.d.)

Frédérique was sentenced to death for his impudence, but was spared thanks to a last minute intervention by William F. Powell, the U.S. ambassador to Haiti.

Haitian artists responded to German interventionism with similar vitriol, but directed their anger at Germans rather than the Haitian government. Occide Jeanty composed "Les Vautours de 6 Décembre" (The vultures of 6 December) shortly after the incident to protest the treatment Haiti suffered at the hands of the German navy. While Jeanty was experienced in writing patriotic music for the needs of the Haitian government—marches for Fête Dieu parades, two funeral marches for Florvil Hyppolite—"Les Vautours" was Jeanty's first explicitly political work that was not geared toward presidential praise or military procession.

POLITICS, POETRY, AND CROSS-CLASS MUSICAL PERFORMANCE

Jeanty's turn toward more explicitly political and controversial subjects was part of a larger Haitian cultural movement during the late-nineteenth century to consider Haitian subjects as worthy of artistic attention. Perhaps the most well-known exponent of Haitian subjects for his artistic work was the poet Oswald Durand (1840–1906). Like Jeanty, Durand had a patriotic response toward colonialist powers' efforts at political interventionism. On 14 June 1872, just four days after the German navy seized the Haitian warships during the "Batsch Affair," Durand composed "Ces Allemands" (These Germans) in protest of the indignity (Durand n.d./1896, 103). Durand was one of the earliest Haitian poets to inject a politicized sensibility into his poetry. According to J. Michael Dash, "in what can be considered the poetic equivalent to the polemic works defending Haiti and the black race, a note of earnest declamation enters Durand's verse as he attempted to re-establish the old ideals of patriotism and national consciousness" (Dash 1981, 20). One of Durand's best known patriotic poems was his "Chant National" (National Song), a work written in 1887 and set to music by Occide Jeanty in 1897.

Durand's poems ranged from the patriotism of "Ces Allemands" and "Chant National" to works more grounded in Haitian culture. Durand was one of the first writers to treat the Vodou religious tradition as something other than an illegal activity or devil worship. According to Dash, "his evocation of voodoo rituals may appear stylized today but is unprecedented in its treatment of this sensitive area of Haitian culture" (1981, 19). Durand wrote several poems that draw upon Vodou culture, including "Sur le Morne Lointain" (cited in Dash 1981, 19) and "Le Vaudoux" (Durand n.d./1896, 52–53). In "Le Vaudoux," Durand describes a bourgeois Haitian man taking a walk in the Haitian countryside. As the man encounters the natural beauties of the environment, he hears drumming in the distance. Approaching the source of the music, he is entranced by a young woman dancing in what appears to be a Vodou ceremony. Noting her "zoune rond" (round buttocks) and "dents blanches" (white teeth), the man is entranced by both the hypnotic rhythms of the music and the woman's physical appearance, especially her "fluttering shoulders." Not only is Durand's scene a good example of a masculine gaze upon an exoticized feminine subject, it also captures the class dynamic of bourgeois observers and Haitian laborers. His privileged class position is erased in the poem, allowing Durand's subject to project his eroticized interpretation onto workers without speaking to them. Durand's male protagonist is all eyes, able to walk into what would have been, at the time, a surreptitious and possibly illegal activity without having to explain his presence.

Durand's description of a Vodou religious ceremony in the Haitian countryside brought the hitherto reviled practice of Vodou to bourgeois Haitian audiences. As a demonstration of a working-class Haitian sensibility toward ecstatic dancing and eroticized behavior, Durand's depiction of the Vodou ceremony set the tone for subsequent considerations of Haitian religion. As later poets and creative writers turned toward lower-class Haitian culture as the source of their creative inspiration, Durand's image of the poor, earthy, and exuberant peasant became a staple of Haitian verbal and musical art.

Durand's most enduring example of a feminized romanticization of peasant life, "Choucoune," was also "the first really successful effort to write poetry in Haitian creole" (Dash 1981, 20). In "Choucoune," the narrator admires a woman nicknamed Choucoune who is a "marabout," a woman with black skin and silky hair. Each verse describes Choucoune's beauty, from her "p'tits dents blanch' com' laitt'" (little teeth, white like milk) to her "tété doubout" (upright breasts). Originally, the poem was titled "Frè P'titt Pierr" or "Little Brother Pierre" for its male narrator, a slave who is doomed to admire the beautiful woman from a social and physical distance. While Brother Pierre catalogues Choucoune's physical attributes, he laments that "dé pieds moins lan chaine" (my feet are in chains).

Durand's poem, set to music by Michel Mauléart Monton (1855–98), became an anthem for bourgeois Haitians interested in connecting themselves with their local culture. At the first performance of the song at the Palais National for President Salomon, Durand himself dressed as Little Brother Pierre. Emulating a bourgeois ideal of the "country bumpkin," Brother Pierre carried a "halefor" (*alfò* or straw bag) and smoked a "cachimbo" (*kachimbo* or clay pipe) (Dumervé 1968, 93). Mugging for the assembled dignitaries, Durand visually fused the image of the unlettered but culturally authentic peasant with that of the educated, elite poet.

Durand not only engaged in some of the "transgressive glee" that such cross-class performances produce (Lott 1993), but also demonstrated for lettered Haitian audiences that the job of the poet was to act as a conduit between the rarified experiences of his bourgeois audience and the harsh reality of the common people in Haiti. In his poem "Le Chanteur des Rues" (The Street Singer), Durand made an explicit link between the lower-class entertainer and the bourgeois poet:

> Our destinies, alas! are quite comparable:
> People laugh at the two of us when they pass us;
> For that is our fate, we miserable ones,
> To amuse the crowd with our songs!
> (Durand in Saint-Louis and Lubin 1950, 43)

Occide Jeanty engaged in his own version of cross-class performance with pieces written to evoke the folkways and mores of lower-class Haitians. His programmatic piece, "Coq, Poules, et Poussins" (Roosters, Hens, and Chicks), imitates the sounds of the barnyard, complete with crowing rooster courtesy of the saxophones, the cooing of the hen by the flutes and the chirping of the chicks from the oboes. Jeanty's polka "Pauvres et Pauvres" (The Poor and the Poor) (1901) is a "social satire criticizing the exploitation of the small by the great" (Herissé n.d.). Written at the behest of an elite women's charity organization dedicated to "comforting their unfortunate brothers," "Pauvres et pauvres" "nails to the pillory the 'Great' poor who are always looking out for themselves" (Herissé n.d.).

Perhaps the most interesting example of Jeanty's interest in the cultural practices of ordinary Haitians came in his méringue, "Zizipan." A "méringue evoking the celebrations of yesteryear," "Zizipan" refers to a processional band that marched in the streets of Port-au-Prince during the Easter seasons of the 1880s (Herissé n.d.). While both Herissé and Corvington refer to this practice as "carnivalesque," it is likely that Zizipan was in fact a Lenten processional band from a tradition known as Rara. Despite its resemblance to Caribbean carnival traditions, Rara is a distinct cultural celebration that has close ties to Haitian traditional religion. In the late nineteenth century, Rara was associated with the more rural sectors of the population and was seen as a "genuine" or "authentic" peasant tradition. According to Corvington, "at the time, Georges, the king of *Oual-Ouadi* [or Rara] from the plain [of Léogâne] introduced his band to the city and established his quartier general in La Saline" (Corvington 1993, 334). As a title for a popular méringue, "Zizipan" therefore referenced a current lower-class Haitian practice that was well known by both elite and working-class audiences.

Artists like Occide Jeanty and Oswald Durand used their respective creative genres as contact points with rural and working-class Haitians. Music and poetry evoking scenes from barnyard to religious procession allowed bourgeois audiences to connect themselves selectively to aspects of lower-class Haitian culture without risk of social contamination. In turn, bourgeois writers used narrative forms including poems, personal experience narratives, and experiential programs to compose descriptions of important Haitian artists. These descriptions referenced cultural values that resonated with elite and lower-class Haitian audiences alike.

Bourgeois writers also borrowed from Vodou religious imagery to underscore Jeanty's importance as a cultural hero. Narratives about Jeanty's importance as a national figure, his bravery under duress, as well as the inspirational power of his musical compositions, also contained references to Jeanty's divine inspiration, specifically through what appears to be possession trance. Haitian journalist Félix Herissé collected several personal experience narratives about Occide Jeanty during the course of his research on Haitian classical music. Most of the narratives focused on Jeanty's creative process, drawing attention to his prodigious talent, especially his ability to compose quickly. One such narrative focused on "La Rentrée à Jerusalem," a processional march composed by Jeanty for the Musique du Palais National for the annual Fête Dieu parade. According to Herissé in a rather elliptical narrative, the following exchange occurred between Jeanty and the members of his military band:

Occide was resting for some time without having composed a thing. His musicians said to him:

"What, General! You've prepared nothing for us to play!"

"Wait, it is not yet time."

And the musicians tried to uncover the mystery. Why this silence?

Sometime later, they tried to cheer him up.

"Wait, I told you" [Jeanty replied].

One day when they were together, Occide looked at nature and saw everywhere the red flowers of the flamboyant tree. He went into a meditation: all of a sudden, he threw, with a festoon of basses, these red garlands of the flamboyant, the signal of Fête Dieu.

Occide translated the human sentiments into an aspect of nature. (Herissé n.d.)

In this literally flowery description of the creative process, Jeanty's "festoon of basses" is figuratively strewn by the composer in a burst of creative energy. Despite the fact that Jeanty was essentially a government employee hired to compose pieces for official state functions, his inspiration could neither be hurried—"Wait, it is not yet time"—nor coerced by his expectant musicians. According to this account, Jeanty's work transcends the political moment and acts as a conduit from the forces of nature to the realm of the soldier.

Jeanty's artistic genius was frequently attributed to divine inspiration or intervention; he was himself a medium for the musical arts. In the following narrative by Marat Chenet, Jeanty achieves an ecstatic state of inspiration. Jeanty visits Chenet after mulling over ideas for a "grand work":

Occide Jeanty arrived at my school. I was playing the piano and I stopped.

"I don't play in front of artists," I said to him.

"Continue. You will inspire me."

He asked for a pencil and went to the balcony, bringing some sheets of music paper from his pocket. After some time, I looked through the corner of the door. One could only see the whites of his eyes in an ecstatic fix. Suddenly, he whistled in the air and began pointing the pencil in all directions, as though he were a painter; he was distributing the parts to all the voices. (Herissé n.d.)

The parallels between this story and a description of a Vodou possession are compelling. First, Jeanty's musical possession trance occurs while listening to music. Although not a strict requirement for spirit possession in a Vodou ceremony, music is often present as an inducement for the spirits to enter the bodies of devotees. Second, as in a Vodou spirit possession, Jeanty assumes the look of a worshipper mounted by a spirit, rolling his eyes back in his head in a physical manifestation of trance, moving his arms to music that comes from his inspirational source. Jeanty's experience is a graphic example of the performative aspect of possession trance. During his trance, he assumes the artistic role of painter (or better, perhaps, conductor), serving as a distributor for the musical voices he hears. The idea of "possession-performance" is particularly appropriate here since Jeanty is depicted as a medium for divine inspiration, while his personal and professional attributes make him a well-suited individual for such a trance. While Haitian elite writers borrowed ideas from Vodou to describe Jeanty's musical inspiration, they also drew heavily on his background as a soldier to reinforce his authority and to connect him with the legacy of Jean-Jacques Dessalines.

DEFENDING THE NATION MUSICALLY: "1804" AND THE POLITICS OF PERFORMANCE

Like Ogou and Dessalines, Jeanty is often associated with the protection of Haitian sovereignty offered by the military. Unlike today's Haitian military, which is designed to police the Haitian population, the military in Jeanty's early career was still a defensive force, poised to protect the country from foreign invaders. Despite the Haitian army's inability to keep foreign forces from intervening in Haitian political affairs—witness the Batsch and Lüders incidents—Haitians perceived their army as a bulwark against colonialism. In addition, Haitian militarism extended to the predominantly rural sectors of the country, with each regional center boasting its own militia loyal to the local military leader.

Jeanty had risen to the rank of general in the Haitian army by the time U.S. troops landed in Port-au-Prince in 1915. Unlike many of his fellow generals, who were given their ranks as compensation for political favors, Jeanty was a career soldier, having started his association with the Musique du Palais National as a ten-year-old cornetist at the rank of corporal. Since his entire career was spent in Port-au-Prince and Jeanty's father was also a well-regarded soldier-musician, he rose quickly in the military ranks and was a well-known public figure by the beginning of the twentieth century.

Jeanty was very active in the musical life of Port-au-Prince before the U.S. occupation. According to Ciceron Desmangles, a physician who was in his nineties when I interviewed him in 1988, the Musique du Palais National performed band concerts frequently on the Champs de Mars, the public park space directly in front of the National Palace. Dr. Desmangles recounted the following description of a typical afternoon performance on the Champs de Mars:

> Every Thursday or Sunday, there was a concert at the National Palace. Everyone brought their own chairs. All the palace musicians had red coats and blue trousers; they wore the colors of the country. Then the

moment arrived; everyone came to the place just in front of the palace. Everyone came, there were many, *many* people. Our father and mother took us to the Occide Jeanty concert. They were a well-trained band with quality musicians whom everyone liked very much.[2]

Families would either "promenade" in the park before band concerts or wait expectantly for public screenings of silent films after sunset. The Musique du Palais National was a regular feature at the Champs de Mars performances; they also performed at local churches during religious festivals. In addition, the Musique du Palais National performed regularly at the Théâtre National (Corvington 1993, 330).

When the United States Marines landed in Haiti in 1915, the Haitian military was reorganized into the Gendarmerie d'Haiti, and in 1928 was renamed the Garde d'Haiti (McCrocklin 1956, 177). During the U.S. occupation, the new Haitian army was used primarily to quell protests and other political disturbances by Haitian citizenry. While the enlisted members of the new Garde d'Haiti were drawn indiscriminately from the Haitian population, Haitian officers were selected by U.S. Marines in order to ensure their allegiance to the occupation government. Haitian military officers who supported a "nationalist" agenda were suspect in the eyes of their U.S. overseers and were dismissed from the army. Some of the ousted Haitian officers took up with the *kako* movement, a renegade military force devoted to resisting the U.S. occupation with a combination of guerrilla attacks and sabotage. The best known kako leader, Charlemagne Péralte, a former lieutenant from the Léogâne district, led the kako resistance until his capture and execution in 1919.

Jeanty left the army in 1916. Although secondary sources disagree as to the reason for his departure, the stories told about his leaving the army give glimpses of the personality that would make him the subject of legend. Dumervé (1968, 127) claims that Jeanty was incensed at the fact that he was demoted from general to lieutenant by the U.S. command and that Jeanty resigned his commission rather than accept such an indignity. Jeanty's family, however, argues that the newly installed Haitian president, Sudre Dartiguenave, had personal problems with Jeanty and removed him without cause (Jeanty n.d.). Herissé (n.d.) provides a colorful explanation for the antipathy between Jeanty and Dartiguenave. Before Dartiguenave assumed the presidency, one of his daughters fell into a swoon upon hearing Jeanty's bugle solo during the annual Fête Dieu parade. She told the startled Jeanty that she would kiss him, much to the chagrin of the president. To make matters worse, one day Jeanty was allegedly rehearsing near the National Palace when Dartiguenave passed by. Jeanty ignored the president and kept rehearsing the group, despite the custom of saluting the head of state with an "aux champs" or field salute. "Occide gave him the following explanation for his silence: 'Since [the days of] Hyppolite, when the band rehearses, it doesn't stop to salute the president'" (Herissé n.d.).

Upon leaving the army and the directorship of the Musique du Palais National, Jeanty taught solfège at the Lycée Pétion and assumed the directorship of a small band from Petit Goâve, a small port city about sixty kilometers west of Port-au-Prince. On 10 February 1917, Jeanty directed his new band in a concert at Port-au-Prince's Théâtre Rex (Dumervé 1968, 127).

In 1922, Jeanty was reinstated to his position as director of the Musique du Palais National by President Louis Borno. Between 1922 and the end of the U.S. occupation in 1934, Jeanty resumed his regular duties as leader, conductor, and composer for the band. It was through his public performances with the Musique du Palais National that Jeanty created his most lasting impression as a defender of the Haitian nation. By performing pieces that had extramusical programs referring to Haitian political resistance, the Musique du Palais National, with Occide Jeanty conducting, became a symbol of Haitian resistance, albeit in musical, not military terms.

In his study of the military in Haiti, Michel Laguerre stresses that there is a difference between what he calls the overt military resistance of the kako forces—"the kakos of action"—and the "kakos of discourse," or that "segment of the population at large who shared the anti-American posture of the rebellious kakos and sided with them in their public speeches and writings" (Laguerre 1993, 70). I contend that, as a "kako of discourse," Jeanty contributed in his own ways to the rhetorical resistance to the U.S. occupation. His "Cacos en Caqui" (Kakos in Khaki) was a drama with music that included several satirical skits poking fun at the United States. Jehan Ryko, whose real name was Alphonse Henriquez, provided the words for "Miss Ragtime," one of Jeanty's tunes for the play. During his performances of the piece, Henriquez dressed himself as a kako, donning "boots with spurs; khaki trousers stuffed in the boots; an officer's coat held back with a belt; revolver at his side; a kako's red handkerchief at the neck; an officer's hat with a tassle" (Ryko n.d.).

"Miss Ragtime" parodies an American woman trying to speak Haitian Kreyòl. Driving her car or riding on her horse, the woman mixes English and Haitian Kreyòl in ways characteristic of foreigners who cannot be bothered to learn the language:

> Cé moi, cé moi, cé moi qui rélé miss Ragtime
> Cé moi, cé moi, cé moi qui passé tout ma *time*

A *driver* tout le time en auto, en auto:
A *rider* tout le time à cheveau, à cheveau.
(Ryko n.d.)

It's me, it's me, it's me who's called Miss Ragtime
It's me, it's me, it's me who passes all "my time"
"A driver" all the time in a car, in a car
"A rider" all the time on a horse, on a horse.

The song includes several English words which are included in a pronunciation key: "time = taïme; driver = draïver; rider = raïder" (Ryko n.d.). The Haitian singer performs a piece imitating a foreigner imitating a Haitian.

In a handwritten note on the back of the music for "Miss Ragtime," Henriquez (in his Jehan Ryko character) explains:

Miss Ragtime mété femme américaine nan bétise. Ou di femme américaine cé bouzin; femme américaine boué tafia; femme américaine volé; Cé pa bien! (Ryko n.d.).

Miss Ragtime ridicules American women. You say American women are prostitutes; American women drink moonshine; American women steal. That's no good!

As Nina Yuval-Davis and Floya Anathias have observed, women are often the focus of nationalist rhetoric and may serve as "symbolic signifiers of national difference" (Yuval-Davis and Anathias 1989, 7). In this case, Henriquez and Jeanty employ a well-worn tactic of insulting a political enemy through the disrespect of that nation's women. Miss Ragtime not only likes to drive around in her car, she practices "petit kissing" and "delicious loving," attributes of the "bouzin" or slut whose disregard for the social conventions of polite Haitian society make Miss Ragtime no better than a common prostitute. Perhaps the most condemnable aspect of Miss Ragtime's ditty is that she is completely unaware of the scrutiny Haitian audiences give her. She is, like the U.S. Marines who walk the streets of Port-au-Prince, deluded with her own notions of privilege and power. As Haitian audiences laughed along with Henriquez and Jeanty in their denunciation of the U.S. through its women, "Miss Ragtime" confirmed in the minds of Haitian audiences that the U.S. occupation could be resisted in public, performative ways.

Jeanty's most famous composition, "Dessalines ou 1804: Marche Guerrière" (Dessalines or 1804: War March)—known to Haitian audiences as "1804"—was another example of a work that, through performance, became an unofficial anthem of Haitian resistance and political

Example 2.1. Occide Jeanty, "1804," mm. 1–24

autonomy until the end of the occupation in 1934. Despite the fact that "1804" was written in commemoration of the centennial of Haitian independence in 1904 and not specifically written as a political protest march, Haitian audiences associated the march with the Haitian struggle for independence during the colonial period. The march became an anthem of anti-American resistance for Haitians and continues to have revolutionary connotations for Haitian audiences. Written accounts of the period, as well as several interviews I conducted with Haitians who remembered

Occide Jeanty, recounted how when "1804" was played by the Musique du Palais National with Occide Jeanty directing, Haitian audiences spontaneously rioted in the streets of Port-au-Prince, voicing their anger and frustration at the United States' occupation of their country (see ex. 2.1).

Previously, active resistance to the American regime was confined to the countryside, where armed bands of kakos engaged the U.S. Marines in small skirmishes. The U.S. military presence, which was initially embraced by bourgeois Haitians, had met little open resistance in Port-au-Prince, so the urban response to "1804" was especially significant. During the latter part of the occupation, Jeanty was forbidden to play "1804" with the band during their popular Sunday concerts in the Champs de Mars. Jean Brierre (1909–92), a Haitian poet and friend of Jeanty's, recalled how "1804" stirred audiences during the occupation:

> Occide Jeanty was a big influence on me because he was a leader in the resistance against the American Occupation. Each time Occide Jeanty directed the group from the National Palace, he had this piece "1804." The crowd was electrified! When Occide played "1804," the crowd was extraordinary; the crowd demonstrated so much that they forbade the performance of "1804."[3]

When I asked Brierre if the ban on "1804" was enforced with other military bands, he replied no. "They could play it anywhere," he recalled, "but Occide was not allowed to perform it on Sunday nights on the Champs de Mars." Other bandleaders could perform the piece with impunity; only Jeanty was forbidden to lead the march.

Several writers tried to explain the power that "1804" seemed to hold over Haitian audiences. Jean Brierre wrote the longest tribute in verse to Jeanty in his *Aux champs pour Occide sur un clavier Bleu et Rouge* (Field Salute for Occide on a Blue and Red Keyboard, 1960). This 43-page poem, an "hommage to Master Occillius Jeanty" outlines Jeanty's entire career. The title of the poem refers to the field salute or "aux champs" usually accorded an important political figure and drapes the piano in the blue and red of the Haitian flag. Brierre told me that "Occide was considered [as important as] a head of state" and that the poem was intended to give praise to Jeanty for his patriotism and bravery.[4] Whereas the first three sections of the poem evoke the musician's life from his Haitian beginnings in "Dans nos bois" (In our woods), to his time in Europe in "Paris," to his return to Haiti and the beginnings of his composing career in "Moisson" (Harvest), the last three sections focus on Jeanty's most political compositions: "Les Vautours de 6 Décembre," "Les Imprécations" [de Dessalines], and "Mil huit cent quatre" (1804).

For Brierre, Jeanty was not only a praiseworthy colleague and friend; he was the embodiment of the spirit of the revolution. Brierre depicted Jeanty as holding a baton that "tempered suddenly and multiplied into a quiver of arrows" (1960, 28). Claiming that Haitians had been waiting for one hundred years for "a man who would harmonize the tragedy" of Haitian history (39), Brierre casts Jeanty as Dessalines incarnate, a courageous defender of Haitian independence. Through his triumph over adversity, Jeanty, like Dessalines, ultimately earned the respect and admiration of his colleagues, especially fellow artists and patriots.

Another Haitian poet, Frédéric Burr-Réynaud (1886–1946) wrote an experiential program about "1804" in the form of a poem. Burr-Réynaud was a lawyer and journalist who served as a deputy to the legislature from Léogâne, a small city thirty kilometers west of Port-au-Prince (Saint-Louis and Lubin 1950, 618). His poem, "Hommage à Occide Jeanty: 1804," first published in 1933, begins with a recollection of a recent performance of the work. Upon hearing the march, the narrator experiences "a shudder that shakes our souls and our bodies," which makes him remember the "love, the glory and the hopes" of "our [Haitian] hearts" (Burr-Réynaud 1933, 8). The "cheers of the crowd" salute the venerable Jeanty and act as a form of consolation for the "forgotten injustices" he experienced.

Journalist Félix Herissé penned program notes for Jeanty's "1804" that linked the musical gestures of the march to the struggles of General Dessalines against the French army. Herissé's program turns the historical event of Dessalines's bravery into a performative act that demands that Haitian listeners position themselves in the struggle for independence. As Haitian listeners commemorate the first Haitian Revolution by listening to "1804," they are performing a second Haitian Revolution against the forces of the U.S. occupation. According to Herissé's notes, each musical phrase in "1804" corresponds to important events in the Haitian Revolution. For example, Herissé claims that the break strain of the march evokes Dessalines's war cry, "Dessalines pa vlé ouè blan, touyé yo!" (Dessalines doesn't want to see whites, kill them!) (Herissé n.d.)

Whereas Burr-Réynaud's poem focuses on the personal, emotional response of the poet himself to a particularly moving performance of "1804," Herissé's program links musical gestures with the scenes of war; the basses call upon the troops to "charge" the enemy while the trombones imitate the moans of wounded Haitian soldiers. Both Herissé's program and Burr-Réynaud's poem, however, come to their dramatic climaxes when they recall Dessalines's battle cry "Dessalines doesn't want to see whites." In both the program and the poem, Jeanty reenacts the revolutionary struggle between Haitians and French forces. Both Dessalines and Jeanty call for the expulsion of the white invader, thus symbolically linking the two Haitian soldiers by their struggles in preserving the integrity of the Haitian nation. In both Herissé's program and Burr-Réynaud's poem, Jeanty is able to accomplish what the Haitian military could not: a symbolic defeat of the forces of white oppression.

Haitian audiences have continued to assign "1804" extramusical characteristics. When heard by a Haitian audience today, "1804" can elicit dramatic, visceral responses from sympathetic listeners. In an interview in 1988, Frantz-Gerard Verret, son of Haitian composer Solon Verret, described the physical sensations a Haitian might feel when listening to a performance of "1804." "When one [a Haitian] hears ["1804"], all his head hair stands on end, all the hair on his arms stands up. He thinks we are not going to accept an invasion that will return us to slavery."[5] Verret added that sensitivity to the programmatic message of "1804" was something that had to be learned and experienced by audience members. He told me, "When you [Largey] hear ["1804"], you don't hear it the same way I hear it."

What Haitian audiences hear, however, has been conditioned by the social and political contexts in which "1804" has been played. As Brierre pointed out, the performance of "1804" was not generally prohibited during the U.S. occupation; only Jeanty was forbidden to play it. It was the combination of personality, musical work, locale, and timing—Jeanty directing "1804" on the Champs de Mars on Sunday evenings—that created a volatile performance situation. As Thomas Turino has observed, "the affective potential of music is constantly utilized, and in some cases manipulated, for a variety of highly significant social ends including the mobilization of collectivities to create or defend a nation" (Turino 1999, 244). The power of "1804" as a musical sign was derived not only from its symbolic linking of resistance to the U.S. occupation with the war for independence, but also from the emotional response *expected* of Haitian audiences upon hearing the work. Burr-Réynaud's poem describes:

> Marches, war songs and Eighteen-hundred-and-four
> Where the splendor of the glorious past returns
> And which moves the crowd, at the end of the blueish evening,
> With wild shouts in memory of the ancestors.
> (Burr-Réynaud 1933, 8)

Even during a military occupation of their country, Haitian audiences were able to imagine themselves resisting political oppression; the "wild shouts" of contemporary listeners connect them with cultural values of independence, rejection of colonialism, and resistance against the reimposition of slavery.

Messages embedded in a performative display are, at least in Haiti, dependent upon audience members' abilities to understand and appreciate them. As Averill (1997) has pointed out, many Haitian performative genres send messages—or *voye pwen* (throw a point)—to Haitian audiences. As I have argued elsewhere, the power of a pwen lies in its ability to engage listeners in current situations by recontextualizing cultural ideas through performance (Largey 2000, 240). According to Averill, "the pleasure that a group takes in singing along with a pwen is not in receiving a critique in its entirety but in deciphering the critique and combining it with the unspoken, shared community knowledge of what has occurred" (Averill 1997, 17). Associated with the densely layered meanings of Vodou songs, pwen are often used in Haiti in rhetorical situations where direct confrontation or aggression would be too dangerous. During the U.S. occupation, songs critical of the occupation government allowed Haitian audiences to share subversive ideas through the consumption of performative practices that required "insider" cultural knowledge. In the case of "1804," Haitians could symbolically reenact the struggle for Haitian independence as long as their enthusiasm remained within the bounds of behavior acceptable to the U.S. Marines. The performance of "1804" with Occide Jeanty directing the Musique du Palais National was a simulacrum of Dessalines's historic battle with foreign forces. As Brierre pointed out, the combination of the inflammatory music and the patriotic bandleader made it impossible for Haitian audiences to control themselves when Jeanty performed the work on the Champs de Mars in Port-au-Prince.

Pwen, however, are not limited to singular insider interpretations. Part of the pleasure of interpreting a pwen lies in audiences' abilities to assign new meanings to cultural performances. According to Haitian pianist and music educator Micheline Dalencour, "1804" was rumored to contain musical quotations from different military regiments in the Haitian army.[6] Provincial bands had their own identifying themes that they used to excite local crowds. According to Dalencour, Depestre Salnave, a flutist and music teacher at the Institution de Saint Louis de Gonzague, told his students that each musical theme in "1804" represented Haitians from all parts of the country, bringing the people together thematically as well as emotionally. Salnave added that the "war cry" tune in "1804" was associated with the Sixth Demi-brigade, the military unit closest to Dessalines in the Haitian war for independence. According to Salnave, the "war cry" theme should properly be sung to the words "Dessalines doesn't want to see whites, kill them" (see ex. 2.2).

Example 2.2. Occide Jeanty, "1804," mm. 40–44

Ultimately, it is less important that Salnave's musical etymology for the war cry is accurate than it is to note that Jeanty's music continues to provide a focus for Haitian nationalist sentiments. Other Haitian writers sought to align Jeanty not with the heroes of Haitian independence but rather with the luminaries of the European art music tradition. In an article commemorating the death of Jeanty, Rémy Volvic imagined the composer as the rival of the great international composers of the day:

> The American, the European have implanted an exotic music among us. The Haitian seemed not to know that, just like BEETHOVEN, STRAUSS or MASSENET, he could be endowed with musical genius. He needed a savior who could draw out his ignorance: Occide JEANTY arrived. His studies, his méringues completely filled with local spirit; his waltzes, "Les vautours de 6 Décembre" [The vultures of 6 December], "Tichat" [Little cat], "Zizipan," "1804," "Les imprécations de Dessalines" [Dessalines's curses], reinvigorate the patriotic spirit and can be favorably compared with the musical productions of any race. He has immortalized himself. His work constitutes one of the clearest proofs that Apollo, contrary to the long-held popular belief, scattered six lights and the harmony of his lyre on the black as well as on the white. (Volvic 1949, 2)

Jeanty, by virtue of his musical abilities and his patriotic commitment to his country, is likened to a "savior," or *messi,* ready to resist the political and musical invasions of Europe and the United States. Not only is Jeanty the equal of European musical luminaries, he surpasses them by way of his commitment to musical activities "filled with local spirit." Just as Apollo, the Greek god of war, shared his musical talents with black composers, perhaps Ogou, the Haitian warrior spirit, shared his loyalty and bravery with Jeanty in defense of the nation.

Although the concept of recombinant mythology may be applied to situations outside Haiti, it is important to remember that recombination must always be examined in specific historical and cultural contexts. In Haiti, the fusion of the historical figure of Emperor Dessalines and the mythological figure of Ogou Desalin came at a period of national strife in which President Hyppolite sought to capitalize on the patriotic potential of Jean-Jacques Dessalines's story. The result of Hyppolite's effort was a mythological narrative that associated Hyppolite with not only Dessalines's spirit of resistance but also with the emperor's fatal mistake in not appreciating the responsibilities of power.

When Occide Jeanty wrote band music before and during the U.S. occupation of Haiti, his invocation of Emperor Dessalines in such pieces as "Les Imprécations de Dessalines" and, especially, "1804" allowed Haitian audiences to experience the thrill of Haitian nationalist resistance without having to resort to combat. Seen through the lens of recombinant mythology, Occide Jeanty used his military and musical power toward nationalist ends, treating musical performance as a type of "possession-performance" in which the insights of an ancestral past were juxtaposed with the reality of Haitian life. Jeanty's image has been "traditionalized" by Haitian audiences who have used historical, as well as folkloric, ideas to place him in the historical past, while equating him with the heroes of Haitian independence, in his own time as a defender of the Haitian state, and in their present time as a symbol of resistance against oppression.

~3~
AFRICANS AND
ARAWAKS

The Music of Ludovic Lamothe
and Justin Elie

Jean Price-Mars's *Ainsi parla l'oncle* challenged elite Haitians to include African culture, specifically the Vodou religious tradition, as part of their image of the Haitian nation. While elite Haitians of Price-Mars's era could not deny that some of their ancestors were from Africa, they looked to French culture as the basis of Haitian elite cultural identity. By denying their ancestral connections to African culture and privileging their cultural ties to Europe, elites were guilty of willfully disregarding one of the important components of their cultural heritage.

The question of Haiti's cultural roots was not as simple as Price-Mars suggested, however. Rather, debates about Haitian cultural roots have dealt with three cultural antecedents—Africans, Native Americans, and Europeans—who existed in relation and even competition with each other. Before Haitian independence in 1804, European culture dominated social life; African and Native American populations were not understood to have cultural practices. During the colonial period, most Europeans thought that enslaved Africans were better off for having been removed from their non-Christian home contexts and saved from eternal damnation (Cohen 1980). Colonial Europeans did not think much better of Native American cultures. Europeans thought that Quisqueya, the Arawak name for the island, was a cultural *tabula rasa*. Christopher Columbus, who first encountered Arawak people in 1492, claimed that they possessed neither language nor culture, two preconditions for recognizing Native Americas as people in their own right (Knight 1978, 10–11).

After the elimination of the Native American population of the island, however, European colonists held up Native American populations of the Caribbean—including the Taínos, the Guantanebeys, and the Caribs—as contrasting examples to newly enslaved Africans:

> The Caribs, once replaced by the transplanted African, were then idol-
> ized as the "golden Carib," to be contrasted with the black slave, whom
> Edward Long, a Jamaican planter and most severe of colonial histori-
> ans, compared to the orangutan. If the Caribs were a repository of An-
> tillean innocence, then the Africans became the exemplum of waste,
> treachery, and barbarism. (Dayan 1995, 190)

As Europeans consolidated their control over the Caribbean, Africans
were placed at the bottom of the social hierarchy, below the exterminated
Native American population.

While Europeans idolized Native Americans in the colonial period and
romanticized them after their elimination, people of African descent,
especially mulattoes, appropriated Native American identity as a way
to distance themselves from the African side of their heritage. Light-
skinned persons of color saw Native American identity as an alternative to
either African identity (which was too socially limiting) or European
identity (which was carefully regulated by white colonials). Many light-
skinned Haitians claimed Native American ancestry to circumvent laws
that discriminated against them according to race. Enterprising mulatto
colonists could purchase legal papers that attested to their Native
American roots (James 1963, 42). After Haitian independence, however,
Native American and African identity changed in relation to the new
Haitian nation. While European cultural standards remained important,
especially for the French-identified members of the light-skinned ruling
elite, the identification with things African and Indian grew steadily during the nineteenth century and was not simply a crass move by blacks to
appropriate Native American identity to raise their status.

As the cases of Haitian composers Ludovic Lamothe and Justin Elie
will show, Native American and African as well as European cultural ideas
have been used to negotiate Haitian cultural identity. Such a negotiation
is always partial; since Haitian independence, no single cultural strain has
ever dominated nationalist discourse for long. At different points in
Haiti's history, the emphasis on a particular cultural history has often
been a sign of a larger, politically charged situation in which participants
selectively identify themselves with a particular cultural group. Despite
this shifting rhetorical terrain, Haitians have, since independence, moved
away from a singular European-oriented cultural aesthetic. Through a selective use of Haiti's multiple cultural influences, composers laid claim to
more than one historical lineage.

In this chapter, I argue that Justin Elie's and Ludovic Lamothe's interest in associating Haitian musical identity with Native American, African,

and European cultures reflected not only their position as cosmopolitan members of their elite class, but also their refusal to embrace European-derived musical aesthetics as the only measure of artistic achievement. By composing art music that explored alternative origins for Haitian music, Elie and Lamothe could claim a unique Haitian identity while selectively maintaining connections to the musical traditions of Europe.

Yet, Elie's and Lamothe's ideas about how to draw upon the inspirational potential of Native American and African music were constrained by transnational assumptions about non-European cultures in the early to mid-twentieth century. Audience expectations for Indian and African music were shaped by contemporaneous developments in the popular entertainment industry. As audiences developed a taste for these so-called exotic musics, the music industry favored musical compositions that reinforced rather than challenged stereotypical depictions of Indian and African people, and Elie and Lamothe obliged those tastes to a degree.

It would be a mistake to consider the work of Elie and Lamothe purely in terms of their desire to appeal to a cosmopolitan audience, however. While both composers were interested in success with foreign listeners, their insistence on constructing what they considered to be a Haitian musical style went beyond their desire for popularity. Indeed, the "success" of both composers cannot be measured by either the sales of their sheet music or the incomes they generated by composing and performing their works. Rather, both Lamothe and Elie adapted themselves to their respective musical markets: Lamothe in Haiti and Elie in the United States.

The opportunities available to Lamothe and Elie in Haiti and the United States were shaped by the exigencies of art music performance and by the expectations of their respective audiences. Composers of "art" music need performance venues, artists to perform their works, and steady incentives to compose. Lamothe, whose compositions were written entirely for piano, found a small but consistent audience in the piano parlors and salons of middle- and upper-class Haitian homes. Lamothe was limited by Haitian elites' low tolerance of materials from the peasant culture, especially Vodou, yet he managed to write several works that drew upon Vodou inspiration. Elie, whose aspirations leaned toward larger, orchestral works, found that moving out of Haiti was the only way he could secure performances of his music.

Elie, who left Haiti to seek his fortune in the United States, found that predominantly white audiences expected music that closely adhered to the exoticized stereotypes generated about Haiti, and about black and Native American cultures in general. His efforts to compose "serious" works during his time in the United States were met with solicitations to compose music with Haitian themes that exploited the more sensational aspects of Haiti's African and Indian heritages. Gender also played a crucial role in rendering this music exotic both in Haiti and transnationally.

This chapter argues that Lamothe and Elie made efforts to connect themselves to Haitian cultural resources through two different but related strategies. Through his efforts to incorporate lower-class musical styles, including the music of the Vodou ceremony into the classical repertoire, Lamothe engaged in what I term a "vulgarization" of Haitian music. Elie, on the other hand, tried to "classicize" Haitian music by using themes that evoked a distant, mythological past. Both composers were interested in conveying the power of Haitian music to audiences at home and abroad.

LUDOVIC LAMOTHE AND THE "VULGARIZATION" OF HAITIAN MUSIC

Ludovic Lamothe's prominence as a composer of méringues presents a striking example of a Haitian elite crossing class boundaries by means of a popular and political musical genre. Born in Port-au-Prince, Lamothe (1882–1953) was a member of a distinguished Haitian family. He was the son of Virginie Sampeur (1839–1919), a highly regarded poet. Before her marriage to Ludovic's father, Sampeur was married to poet Oswald Durand, author of the Haitian Kreyòl poem "Choucoune." Lamothe's father, Tacite Lamothe, was a pianist, and his grandfather, Joseph Lamothe, was also a proficient instrumentalist.

Educated at the Institution de Saint Louis de Gonzague in Port-au-Prince, Lamothe developed a reputation for technical facility on the piano and compositional prowess at an early age. Like other highly regarded Haitian composers, Lamothe's discovery by the musical authorities of his day was the subject of a widely known folkloric account. According to the legend, Occide Jeanty, leader of the Musique du Palais and foremost musician of his day, was walking down the rue des Miracles when he heard a brilliant rendition of a march he had written for President Hyppolite. The piano was a wretched instrument, its strings in need of a tuning and some repair, but the music was remarkable. Peering into an open window of the house, Jeanty saw ten year-old Ludovic Lamothe performing his work with gusto (Herissé n.d.; Pradel 1912).

Lamothe traveled to Paris in 1910 on a scholarship raised by German merchants residing in Haiti. In Paris, Lamothe studied with Louis Diémer at the Paris Conservatory and held a recital at the Cercle des Annales. Lamothe returned to Haiti in 1911, where he supported himself by

Figure 3.1. Haitian composer Ludovic Lamothe seated at the piano.
From his musical album titled *Musique de Ludovic Lamothe* (1955).

giving piano lessons and performing in private recitals in his home, usually on Sunday afternoons (see fig. 3.1).

Toward the end of his career, Lamothe was plagued with financial
difficulties, and, on 9 February 1944, he was evicted from his home of
more than thirty-six years. His popularity among elite music lovers
prompted a fund-raising campaign. Elites who led the effort included the
historian Jean Fouchard, poet Camille Lhérisson, and writer Philippe
Thoby-Marcelin. They opened an account at the Banque Nationale in
Lamothe's name and published the names of contributors to the account
each day in the local papers. Within a few months, the fund drive raised
$4,248.94, which was used to make a downpayment on another home for
Lamothe (Herissé n.d.).

Lamothe's precarious finances were due, in part, to the difficulty of
making a living as Haiti's foremost pianist-composer. Lamothe had only
two compositions published outside Haiti during his lifetime: the méringue
"La Dangereuse," published in Hamburg, Germany by Musicalien
Druckerei (n.d.) and the "melodie" for voice and piano titled "Billet,"
printed by Imprimerie Roeder in Paris (n.d.). Most of Lamothe's works,
however, were released by the composer in Haiti and were copied and
printed at his own expense.[1]

Lamothe can hardly be blamed for not publishing more music during
his career. In Haiti, the business of selling sheet music has always been

a difficult one. With a relatively small number of musically literate consumers to purchase musical scores, Haiti developed an informal sheet music economy in which composers themselves took on the responsibility of writing, copying, and distributing their work to their public. As a result, while only a few of Ludovic Lamothe's piano works were published during his lifetime, his music circulated among his loyal clientele. As Haitian organist and physician Jean-Claude Desmangles reported, Lamothe was famous for his Sunday afternoon salons in which musicians and aficionados gathered to hear Lamothe play his own works.[2] Desmangles also noted that Haitian musicians have been in the habit of keeping their own albums of published and hand-copied scores for personal use. Desmangles himself, as well as the amateur musicologists Constintin Dumervé (1968) and Félix Herissé (n.d.), all assembled collections of Haitian sheet music that contained pieces by Lamothe.

While contemporary Haitian musicians consider Lamothe's compositions *mizik savant* or "art music," most of his piano pieces were drawn from Latin American dance genres popular in the early twentieth century, including the danza, the habanera, and the méringue, as well as the European-derived valse and gavotte. These dance forms have not generally been included in the Western art music canon. Indeed, musicologist Carl Dahlhaus has called such popular music forms "trivial music," a designation that implies a judgment of their aesthetic and formal properties (Dahlhaus 1989, 312). For Dahlhaus, the music of the dance hall, while psychologically uplifting for the assembled crowd, could not sustain the formal analysis necessary for legitimate art music. Dahlhaus's negative opinions about such repertoire, while not based on empirical evidence, nevertheless reflect a widely held attitude that dance music, especially pieces that were not part of the eighteenth-century European repertoire, was unworthy of the music scholar's attention.

In Haiti, however, the relationship of so-called art music to popular music does not conform to Dahlhaus's aesthetic hierarchy. In the late nineteenth and early twentieth centuries, certain Haitian dance forms were understood to be both art music and popular music. The formal characteristics of musical genres were subordinated to the specific ways in which audiences used such genres. As Peter Wade has observed about similar musical processes in Colombia, musics that cross class boundaries are often "created in complex processes of interchange, class mediation, and appropriation that worked in ambiguous spaces between country and city, between social classes, and, not infrequently, between the national and international" (Wade 2000, 8).

As a musical genre that appealed to upper- and lower-class Haitians, the méringue ranged in style from formal parlor settings to political protest songs. While elite audiences enjoyed méringues lentes, or slow méringues, in their salon recitals, they also consumed popular méringues in sheet music form that evoked the sounds and sentiments of the street. In Haiti, elites used the French term "vulgarisation" (which translates as "popularization" in English) to refer to the infusion of elite parlor music with lower-class musical elements. Popular méringues that crossed over to an elite audience were referred to as "vulgarisations," a term that maintained the class divide as it brought Haitian listeners together.

One of the most important "vulgarisateurs" of the méringue was Haitian music publisher Fernand Frangeul (1872–1911). Born in Port-au-Prince and trained from a young age as a musician, Frangeul performed in the Musique du Palais as a trumpet player. Frangeul was an avid collector of printed music; he began a music library as a young man and amassed a collection of piano method books and musical instruments. Eventually, Frangeul ordered a music printing press from France so that he could produce sheet music locally (Dumervé 1968, 186). His publication list featured several méringues, gavottes, and military marches by Haitian military musician Occide Jeanty, as well a version of the popular "Choucoune" by Haitian composer Mauléart Monton and poet Oswald Durand. Frangeul also published music written by foreign composers who were popular in Haiti, including several pieces by Ford Dabney, the U.S. bandleader who was hired by President Nord Alexis in 1904 to provide music for official Haitian functions (Dauphin 1980, 59).

Many of the works in Frangeul's catalogue were considered part of the art music repertoire of any Haitian pianist. In addition to these parlor pieces, Frangeul's catalogue included works that were labeled "popular méringues with words." These compositions were either newly composed works inspired by Carnival themes or transcribed street songs that praised or critiqued important people in Haitian society. Such "popular méringues" were known by a variety of terms. Averill notes that in the early days of the Haitian republic, street songs that either praised or criticized political figures were known as *mereng koudyay* (French: méringue coup d'jaille) for their spontaneous, energetic quality (Averill 1997, 220).

Since *mereng koudyay* did not rely solely on written dissemination, printed songs were often just transcriptions of music already in popular use. Most of Frangeul's popular méringues, for example, were listed as "published and arranged" by Frangeul himself; the publisher did not take credit for writing the song. A journalist at *Le Nouvelliste* observed on 19 May 1912, a year after Frangeul's death: "As soon as a méringue was in vogue, he notated it in music. He went thus, a passerby, his ear attentive to our [Haitian] tunes—happy and old songs which brought joy to our fathers and which give us pleasure" (quoted in Dumervé 1969, 187).

Frangeul's popular méringues included lyrics that commented on political and social issues of the day. His catalogue contained such songs as "Tippenhaoua Coté Ouyé" (Tippenhauer, Where Are You?) and "Tippenhaoua Mandé: Coté Co-dd Laà" (Tippenhauer Asks: Where's the Rope?), two songs about the German official Rudolph Tippenhauer who was convicted of defrauding the Haitian government in 1902 but who never served his sentence (Heinl and Heinl 1979, 326); as well as "Salomon Bon Vieilla" (Salomon is a Good Old Fellow), about Haitian president Lysius Felicité Salomon (1879–88) (Dumervé 1968, 190). Frangeul also published "Antoine Simon Dit Ça" (Frangeul 1910), a "sung méringue" which recounted Simon's successful military action to seize the Haitian presidency from Pierre Nord Alexis. As Nord Alexis's regime (1902–8) was losing its influence in Haiti, Antoine Simon, a regional general from the southern Haitian city of Les Cayes, plotted an invasion of Port-au-Prince.

In this song, well-known Haitian political figures are called by their contemporary nicknames: President Nord Alexis is known as "Tonton Nord," while his influential and infamous wife—whose official nickname was Mère Alexis—is known to the Kreyòl-speaking masses as Cécé. In the following stanza, Simon rattles the confident Nord Alexis with a successful military advance on Anse-à-Veau on 27 November 1908:

Voyé palé Tonton Nord	Tonton Nord went to talk
Oua dit l'rouété cò-l'nan ça	You say he'll throw his body into this
Antoine Simon pas pé joué	Antoine Simon isn't afraid to play
S'il pas rouéta l'a moura	If he doesn't stop, [Nord] will die.
("Antoine Simon" 1910, 3)	

Like many Haitian political songs, this lyric invokes the "pwen" (point) song style described in chapter 2, in which singers place themselves rhetorically in the song. In the second line, the song switches from third to second person as the singers remind themselves of Nord Alexis's former resolve to stop Simon's insurrection. In the third line, Simon's tenacity—he "isn't afraid to play"—leads to the eventual downfall of Nord's regime. While the score of the song does not indicate any official sponsorship on the part of the Simon government, this version of events would have been agreeable to the new president, especially in his dealings with his political adversary.

The music itself also conveys a sense of popular connection, with its use of the five-note pulse or "quintolet" (also known as the cinquillo in Spanish). As we will see in chapter 5, Occide Jeanty championed the use of the quintolet as the best notation for rendering the méringue rhythm.

Example 3.1. Fernand Frangeul, "Antoine Simon Dit Ça"

An - toin' Si - mon dit ça, rhoï!_____ Qui ba - gay' ci - là Mes-sieu? Les -

prit cher con - nin mal, rhoï!_____ Qui ac - tion ci - là Mes-sieu? Cé

toutt bon cé pas jouett, Rhoï_____ Qui pa - ròl' ci - là, Mes-sieu?

Frangeul's liberal use of the quintolet figure, as well as his vernacular use of Haitian Kreyòl in the song text, gave his méringue a look and a sound that conformed with elite expectations for street songs (see ex. 3.1).

In Haiti, songs of political praise and protest comment on the consequences of political power. While political songs may serve both sides of the political continuum, they are most often set in the Haitian Kreyòl language to give the impression that they reflect popular support for a particular issue. In the case of "Antoine Simon," the song text is critical of Simon's political adversary, Nord Alexis. However, the song itself—composed in December 1909 and published on 15 October 1910 during Antoine Simon's administration—came well after the fall of Nord Alexis's government, thus making the song's oppositional stance toward the former president moot. By recounting the president's heroism in overthrowing a corrupt regime, the song serves as an after-the-fact political endorsement of Simon.

Although the popular méringue in Haiti is usually associated with pointed political critique which "Antoine Simon dit ça" seems to lack, the song does reflect a Haitian lower-class sensibility with its praise for a leader who was well known as a supporter of Vodou and whose folksy manners were the butt of many Haitian elite jokes (Heinl and Heinl 1979, 348). The popularity of such méringues among the lower classes does not explain, however, why Frangeul would transcribe and harmonize such melodies and publish them in piano-vocal scores, since only literate people with money to spend would purchase such music. The presence of these popular méringues in the music collections of Haitian pianists points to a connection between Haitian working classes and elites that bears further examination.

By looking at méringue as a musical genre that crossed class boundaries in early twentieth-century Haiti, it is possible to refute Dahlhaus's characterization of such repertoire as "trivial" and to reevaluate the social importance of popular piano music. Composers such as Lamothe were working at a time when pianists expected Haitian popular music to uplift them musically and enrich them culturally; the méringue was, to borrow a contemporary term, a "crossover" genre that appealed to more than one social group. As a genre that not only served different class strata in Haiti but also allowed cross-class performance of social and political issues, the méringue was an important source of interclass contact in early to mid-twentieth-century Haiti.

Lamothe's repertoire included several types of méringue, from the most formal, elite-oriented forms to the méringue of the street. While Frangeul merely transcribed songs from the street, not claiming credit for their composition, Lamothe wrote original compositions that reached across class boundaries.

On the elite end of the musical spectrum was Lamothe's "La Dangereuse," a *méringue lente,* or slow méringue. With its slow tempo, restrained dynamics, and gentle expressive style, the *méringue lente* was the preferred style of elite salon recitals. "La Dangereuse" is a typical Haitian *méringue lente* with its characteristic quintolet or cinquillo rhythm. In most slow méringues, the quintolet rhythm moves back and forth from treble to bass registers. In "La Dangereuse" however, the cinquillo rhythm is mostly in the left hand, giving the treble part a tranquil, vocal character (see ex. 3.2).

Example 3.2. Ludovic Lamothe, "La Dangereuse," mm. 1–30

Significantly, most *méringues lentes* included few dynamic markings, suggesting that even elite Haitian musicians were expected to know the proper interpretation of the style without having to be told. In "La Dangereuse," there are only three dynamic markings in the entire piece: measure 17 has a crescendo, while measures 25 and 96 have a *subito piano* marking. With its lilting melody, active (but not impossible) left hand part, and its characteristic rhythm, the *méringue lente* was popular with elite audiences. Musicians like Lamothe performed *méringues lentes* in private recitals or in Sunday afternoon salons in which friends and family members insulated themselves from the pressures of everyday life in a cultured enclave.

Lamothe also composed méringues that appealed both to elite and working-class audiences. By writing works that reached out to different class strata in Haiti, Lamothe gave elite Haitians opportunities to imagine themselves as participating in Haitian cultural life without having to join the lower class crowd in the street, especially during Carnival. As Gage Averill notes, "although it is often said that Haitian carnival is a time when classes mix freely and in mutual tolerance, there are powerful limits on the extent of interaction" (Averill 1994, 221). Carnival has historically been a contested event with elites trying, albeit unsuccessfully, to control lower-class behavior, mostly through financial sponsorship. During the U.S. occupation, despite the Haitian government's best efforts, Carnival celebrants had repeated clashes with occupation forces.

By aligning themselves with the anti-occupation sentiments of the Carnival crowds in song, Haitian elites could participate in political resistance against the occupation by performing *méringues de Carnival* or Carnival méringues in the privacy of their private piano parlors. Perhaps the best example of this was Lamothe's "Nibo," which won the 1934 Port-au-Prince city council competition for the best Carnival méringue (Dumervé 1968, 247; Corvington 1987, 312). Carnival méringues were intended to get people on their feet to dance, sing, and participate in the celebration of one of Haiti's most important national holidays.[3] According to an article in *Le Nouvelliste* in 1934, "Nibo" was enjoyed by all strata of Haitian society:

> The author, in an inspiration that one could call unbridled, appears to truly have expressed the *ohé! ohé!* [carnival refrain] of the reveling crowd. The rhythm is erotic and inclines, in the first measures, to the most frenetic joy. We repeat that this is not a personal opinion; rather it is supported by the delirium that this captivating composition achieved with the public on the evening of Mardi Gras. Everyone, old and young, from the most serious to the most careless, was tingling with excitement [*avaient des fourmis dans les jambes;* literally, had ants in their legs, used here to suggest a compulsion to dance]. (quoted in Averill 1997, 51; his translation)

In the context of Haitian Carnival, the success of Lamothe's "Nibo" was dependent on people's of all classes ability to recognize the melody and dance appropriately.

Like most Carnival music, "Nibo" gave participants an easily recognizable melody and several opportunities for them to punctuate the song with gestures and shouts. The first theme in "Nibo" contains two sforzando chords following a motif of two eighth notes and a quarter note at a *piano*

Example 3.3. Ludovic Lamothe, "Nibo," mm. 1–8

dynamic. The sforzando chords on A minor (m. 2) and B major (m. 4) call upon participants to move dramatically with the music (see ex. 3.3). Unlike "La Dangereuse" which maintained a steady quintolet rhythm throughout, only measure 6 of "Nibo" has the syncopated "quintolet variation" associated with the Haitian méringue.

In the second theme, which is played at a fortissimo dynamic, the right and left hands in the piano part alternate unsyncopated duple measures with a complete quintolet rhythm (see ex. 3.4). Carnival méringues are noteworthy for their recognizable phrases and their ability to generate excitement from the crowd. In "Nibo," Lamothe eschewed the more complicated, contrasting development section of "La Dangereuse" in favor of a dramatic and endlessly repeatable musical phrase that could be easily memorized and subsequently performed by street crowds.

While the musical structure of "Nibo" is unremarkable, its social and political meanings for Haitian audiences are noteworthy. The occupation of Haiti by U.S. military forces was scheduled to end on 21 August 1934, approximately six months after the 1934 carnival. Since the massacre of

Example 3.4. Ludovic Lamothe, "Nibo," mm. 33–40

Haitian civilians at Marcheaterre in 1929, Haitians had agitated for the end of the occupation in increasingly violent demonstrations. With the election of the transitional president Eugene Roy in 1930—and the removal of the unpopular president Louis Borno—the *désoccupation* of Haiti began in earnest. When Sténio Vincent assumed the presidency later in 1930, the Haitian government regained control of most of the functions of the state. For instance, the Haitian legislature was allowed to pass laws without U.S. approval. By the beginning of the 1934 carnival, the timetable for the U.S. evacuation had been set and Haitians looked forward to the departure of occupation forces. In this context, "Nibo" was understood as an anticipatory anthem for the celebration to come in August 1934.

The enthusiastic reception of "Nibo" by Haitian audiences is all the more important since, unlike most popular méringues, "Nibo" was published without words. As with most "point songs" in Haiti, however, the meaning of a song is negotiated between the composer and audience in a specific historical context. The more specific the context, the less focused the words need to be in order for the message or "point" of the song to be received. In Haiti, audiences are adept at filling in meanings for songs, especially when there is a clear adversary in a rhetorical exchange. Haitian crowds adopted "Nibo" as their oppositional anthem since it was clear to Haitians of all economic strata that the U.S. occupation of Haiti was coming to an end. The success of "Nibo" as a Carnival méringue was due to its ability to express Haitians' political opposition without provoking the wrath of the occupation forces.

From the seasonal Carnival song to the music of the piano parlor, Lamothe's méringues targeted heterogeneous Haitian audiences through a "vulgarization" of elite repertoire. However, Lamothe's use of lower-class Haitian music was not only designed to bring elites and lower-class Haitians together against the U.S. occupation and to celebrate the departure of U.S. occupation forces. Lamothe was also interested in turning to the roots of Haitian music, specifically the African side of Haitian culture, to compose a national musical style that would signal Haiti's arrival as an independent, African-identified nation.

"CAN WE HAVE A NATIONAL MUSIC?"

In response to his own rhetorical question posed in an article titled "Pouvons-nous avoir une musique nationale?" (Can we have a national music?) (Lamothe 1935), Lamothe turned his attention to the Haitian méringue and the songs of the Vodou ceremony. By stressing the common African ancestry of both the méringue and Vodou ceremonial music, Lamothe believed that he could overcome the limitations each genre had as a potential national music representing the Vodou Nation. On one hand, the méringue was certainly "universal" in its widespread appeal as a pan-Caribbean dance genre, but was insufficiently "unique" to qualify as an unambiguously Haitian genre. Songs from the Vodou ceremony, on the other hand, were "unique" in that they were associated solely with Haitian traditional religion, yet they were difficult to translate musically into a "universal" format.

Lamothe recognized that the méringue was related to other quintolet-based Caribbean dance styles. He wrote that "the méringue today, our national dance, in spite of the untimely intrusion of the vulgar foreign dances (one step, fox trot, etc.) is plainly of Spanish origin and is called the 'Habanera'" (Lamothe 1935, 11). Lamothe even used the labels "danza" and "habanera" interchangeably in his piano sheet music collection (Lamothe 1955, 63).

Although later Haitian writers would make claims for the méringue as the "national dance of Haiti" by postulating the existence of a unique Haitian style (Fouchard 1973/1988b), Lamothe was not concerned to point out the national origins of the méringue because he believed that similarities within quintolet-based dance music styles were a result of their common African ancestry and that the African roots of the méringue were key to establishing a Haitian national music. In his 1935 article, "Can We Have a National Music?" Lamothe wrote: "It is certain, however, that the rhythm of [the Haitian méringue], thanks to the contributions of ancient African dances, underwent modifications not encountered elsewhere [in the Caribbean] that hindered the spread of this unique musical style." (Lamothe 1935, 11).

Jean Price-Mars's exhortation to turn to African-based music as the origin of Haitian culture appealed to Lamothe. Lamothe used ethnographically inspired language to link the musical productions of Haitians to their African forbears:

> The black has a reputation of being naturally talented in music. The peasants often get together in the countryside or they organize dances accompanied by songs, and it is not rare to find gatherings [assemblées] of more than two hundred country people taking part in a wake or in a wedding feast. They pass the night singing and all the invited contribute to the celebration, some with the songs, others with the drums. (Lamothe 1935, 9)

In this passage, Lamothe described peasant cultural activities—from the *fèt chanpèt* or country dance to the all-night *veye* or wake—that always included music. Lamothe's brief description accurately depicted the importance of musical activities in rural settings.

Ethnographically inspired language does not always constitute ethno-graphic insight, however. While Lamothe clearly had a deep appreciation for the cultural power of African-derived music, some of his generaliza-tions about the musical affinities of African and Haitian people echoed the racialist discourse prevalent at the turn of the century. In "Can We Have a National Music?" Lamothe expressed his disappointment with the cur-rent state of Haitian music:

> How is it that we, incontestable descendants of Africans, love music to an extraordinary degree, yet there is not a single recorded instance of singing involving two-part harmony? How has this natural faculty been allowed to atrophy? Under what influences? (Lamothe 1935, 11)

For Lamothe, African musical abilities were eroded in the Haitian popu-lation as a result of slavery, poverty, and ignorance. Rather than value the contemporaneous musical practices of the Haitian lower classes, Lamothe assumed a devolution of Haitian musical style from a pure African source.

Lamothe believed that the characteristics of a national music were determined not only by the origins of a country's musical materials but also by how those materials were transformed into a "universal" product suitable for consumption outside the nation. In order to compose music that drew upon Haiti's Vodou heritage, Lamothe thought he needed to transform Vodou music by translating it into classical musical notation. Lamothe believed that the difficulties Haitian composers faced in promoting their music abroad stemmed from this problem in musical translation. He complained that "our airs nicely express a collective sen-sibility, but they don't have, it seems, that communicative value to leap over our borders, in spite of the incontestable talent of their authors and the efforts made to acclimate them overseas" (Lamothe 1936, 5). Despite composers' efforts to make their music accessible, Haitian music lan-guished overseas as a musical curiosity. Lamothe likened the fate of ex-ported Haitian music to that of a delicate tropical flower: "Our music is like certain hothouse plants [which are] very rare and beautiful, but when transported to another soil, are unable to survive" (Lamothe 1936, 5).

One of the principal impediments to making Haitian music appealing to foreign audiences was the question of musical notation. While Haitian music was easily learned by local audiences familiar with Haitian perfor-mance practice, it presented a problem to performers who relied solely on written music. Lamothe reported a similar problem encountered by com-poser Cécile Chaminade, who wrote that it was impossible to interpret a Columbian dance rhythm properly from notation, while any Colombian musician familiar with the style could replicate the rhythm with ease. Lamothe said "the same disagreement arises with our Haitian airs; that is why all the efforts of our composers ought to tend to simplify our music in order to make it clearer, easier, unless we never want it played by foreigners" (Lamothe 1935, 11).

Lamothe did his best to keep his own musical notation of Haitian music relatively easy for foreign interpretation. His best known meringues— "La Dangereuse" and "Nibo"—were written in a duple meter and relied on relatively uncomplicated variations of the quintolet rhythm. His approach differed from other Haitian musicians who felt that the use of duple meter did not adequately convey the rhythmic complexity of the méringue. For example, Justin Elie's *Méringues populaires* (1920) and Eugène de Lespinasse's "Do-Do Méia" (n.d.) featured alternating 2/4 and 5/8 meters to give their méringues a unique look.

Finding a suitable rhythmic notation for foreign musicians was only part of the solution to the problem of promoting Haitian music abroad, however. According to Lamothe, the composer was responsible for transforming music with local cultural significance into art that transcended a particular culture. For Lamothe, this musical transformation would ideally involve a conservation of the important cultural traits of the music while elevating the music to a "higher" plane. Lamothe cited Chopin and Tchaikovsky as examples of composers who successfully integrated the national styles of their respective homelands into their compositions. Lamothe recounted an anecdote in which Tchaikovsky incorporated a country song he heard into one of his compositions:

> The taste of a composer allows him alone to use a folkloric motive. It is thus how Tchaikovsky, on a day without inspiration, did something all the illustrious composers understand by working on the slow movement of his famous string quartet while he heard a beautiful melody sung in the street. He wrote it immediately and incorporated it into his quartet, where it remains in the richest of settings. Is it the talent of the unknown artist or the genius of Tchaikovsky that made this an eternal work? (Lamothe 1937, 35)

Lamothe's example brings the unlettered, unknown artist into a relationship with the art music composer who, according to his taste, sets the raw material of folksong into an "eternal work" of classical music.

For Lamothe, "national" artists were in a perpetual search for musical materials that would give their works cross-class appeal within their nation state and would appeal to audiences outside the nation as examples of a universal art music repertoire. Lamothe himself turned to the musical

Example 3.5. Ludovic Lamothe, "Sous la Tonnelle," mm. 1–19

performance practice of Vodou ceremonial music—including rhythmic patterns and musical structure—in an effort to bring Haitian elite and lower classes into a relationship with each other and, in so doing, present a unified cultural front for foreign audiences.

Lamothe's Vodou-inspired piano music set rhythmic elements from ceremonial contexts in works with a distinct pianistic sensibility. In "Sous la Tonnelle" (Under the Arbor), the left hand provides a "dahome" rhythm from the Rada *nanchon* or denomination of Vodou spirits in the form of a steady sixteenth-note triplet ostinato beneath a lyrical melody (see ex. 3.5). A tonnelle (tonnèl) is a spiritual shelter or bower, constructed for Vodou ceremonies to keep rain off participants. Herskovits described it this way:

> The *tonnelle,* which is merely a flat brush roof supported by a number of upright posts, must be built strongly enough to withstand the assaults of those possessed, who not only lean heavily on the supports, but sometimes climb through the brush roof to lie for a time on the cross-beams which form the base for this flimsy covering. Its ostensible aim is to protect the participants from what is known as *neige* or "snow," as the heavy dew is called, but, as might be expected, the structure as well has a ceremonial purpose. (Herskovits 1937, 180)

For Haitian audiences, the title "Sous la Tonnelle" clearly identifies this piece as being related to the Vodou ceremony. As Constintin Dumervé said about "Sous la Tonnelle": "All the bases of this music are linked to Vodou and the three shrill little notes heard just before the final chord represent the symbol: 'A bobo' [Ayibobo]" (Dumervé 1968, 246).[4]

The title of Lamothe's piano piece "Loco" (Loko) refers to a spirit in the Rada *nanchon* or denomination of spirits who are responsible for agricultural prosperity and are associated with "coolness." In "Loco," the insistence of the triplets in the left hand against the predominantly duple rhythms of the right hand set up a rhythmic tension evocative of the Vodou drum battery (see ex. 3.6).

Usually in a Rada ceremony, the small, high-pitched drum—called either *boula* or *kata*—carries the triplet ostinato pattern. Vodou initiates, called *ousi,* participate in the ceremony by going into a light possession trance and dancing to the percussive music. In the ceremony, the largest drum, *manman* or mother drum, determines when the ostinato will *kase* or "break." Breaks in the rhythmic ostinato serve to push dancing *ousi* deeper into possession trance. After a brief interlude in which dancers wait for the return of the principal beat from the mother drum, the dancers resume their counterclockwise dance formation. "Loco" uses a rhythmic break in measure 23 that evokes the *kase* of the Vodou dance. The triplet ostinato that breaks at measure 23 resumes in measure 39 and carries the piece to three solemn chords in the final measures.

In "Sobo" (see ex. 3.7), Lamothe combines several Haitian rhythms from the quintuplet-based "banda" dance associated with the trickster spirit Gede to a modified quintolet rhythm reminiscent of "Nibo." In all three examples—"Sous la Tonnelle," "Loco," and "Sobo"—the left hand of the piano part acts as a percussion battery. The right hand plays more of a melodic role, imitating the vocal line of the Vodou song.

Example 3.6. Ludovic Lamothe, "Loco," mm. 1–31

From the locale that inspired "Sous la Tonnelle" to the Vodou spirits
Loko and Sobo that were both associated with Dahomean spiritual
antecedents, Lamothe's Vodou-inflected pieces reflected his belief that
Haitian composers should write music that demonstrated links with
Haitian and specifically African culture. While Lamothe recognized

Example 3.6. (*continued*)

Native American influences on Haitian music—he called the *tambour maringouin* or mosquito drum an Arawak invention and labeled the *lanbi* or conch shell the "hunting horn of Haiti" (Lamothe 1935, 9)—his response to his own rhetorical question, "Can We Have a National Music?," seemed to emphasize the African side of Haiti's cultural past.

Example 3.7. Ludovic Lamothe, "Sobo," mm. 1–21

JUSTIN ELIE AND THE "CLASSICIZATION"
OF HAITIAN MUSIC

While Ludovic Lamothe looked to Africa and specifically to the Vodou ceremony as sources for his musical compositions, Justin Elie drew on Native American music for his creative inspiration. Elie wrote several pieces that

Example 3.7. (*continued*)

used Indianist musical motifs and descriptive programs that put Native Americans at the center of Haitian musical life. Unlike Lamothe, whose audience was primarily drawn from Haiti, Elie developed his career in the United States. Eager for music that used Indian themes, audiences in the U.S. expected music about Indian life to conform to their own ideas about Native American culture.

Elie's experiences in the United States illuminate the different expectations of Haitian and U.S. audiences. During his time in Haiti, Elie's depictions of Native American music and culture were romanticized to a degree, but they were also resistant and progressive, especially as they depicted Native Americans fighting against foreign domination. When Elie moved to the United States, however, his musical depictions of Native American culture were marketed as reactionary stereotypes characteristic of the U.S. Indianist movement.

At the height of his career, Justin Elie (1883–1931) enjoyed the most prominent international reputation of all the Haitian composers; this reputation was fostered by his frequent trips abroad from his student days on. Born in Cap Haïtien, Elie received his early education in Haiti, studying with pianist Ermine Faubert from 1889 to 1894 and enrolling briefly at the prestigious Institution de Saint Louis de Gonzague in Port-au-Prince. In 1895, he traveled to France and enrolled at the Cours Masset, a preparatory school for the Paris Conservatory. After gaining admission to the Paris Conservatory in 1901, he studied with Antoine François Marmontel and Charles Wilfred Bériot for piano, Émile Pessard for harmony, and Paul Vital for composition (Dalencour 1983; Herissé n.d.).

Upon his return to Haiti in 1905, Elie participated in several musical soirées at the elite social clubs of Port-au-Prince, including the Cercle Port-au-Princien and the Cercle Bellevue (Durand 1983, 1). On 29 April 1905, Elie participated in a "grand recital" at the Asile Français in Port-au-Prince. The recital featured many of the prominent Haitian artists of the day, including the leader of the Musique du Palais, Occide Jeanty, the singer Madame F. Faubert, the violoncellist Edouard Laroche, and the violinist Ferdinand Fatton. A journalist at the time described the event this way:

> And now the place of honor for the evening; M. Justin Elie . . . reveals himself to be a master of the piano. On the program, one finds the Sonata in Bb of Chopin, "La Campenella" of Lizst and a "Grande Valse de Concert" written by the artist. (quoted in Dalencour 1983, 4)

Elie maintained an active musical schedule for the next two years. He participated in recitals with other Haitian artists, including pianist Ludovic Lamothe and violinists Philippe Elie and Georges de Lespinasse (Durand 1983, 2). On January 1908, the newspaper *La Lanterne* reported that Elie performed in a benefit concert for the victims of a fire (Dalencour 1983, 4).

From 1905 to the end of 1908, Elie traveled around the island of Hispañola, visiting the Haitian towns of St. Marc, Gonaïves, Port-du-Paix, Jacmel, Jérémie, and Les Cayes, as well as the capital of the Dominican Republic, Santo Domingo. Unlike Ludovic Lamothe, Elie traveled extensively in the Caribbean. He undertook a concert tour in 1909 and 1910,

Figure 3.2. Justin Elie pictured on the cover of his publication for
piano solo titled "Nostalgie."

featuring works by European composers, and visited Jamaica, Puerto
Rico, St. Thomas, Curaçao, Venezuela, and Cuba.

Elie's concerts were especially well received in Jamaica. On 3 February
1909, in Collegiate Hall in Kingston, Elie performed a sonata, a nocturne,
and an étude by Chopin, a "Grande Polonaise" by Saint-Saëns, as well as
the "Rhapsodie Hongroise" and "La Campanella" by Lizst. He was
assisted by Carlota Millanes, a Mexican soprano who sang several arias
from Verdi's *La Traviata.*[5]

In March 1909, Elie traveled to Cuba for two months. He performed a
recital that was reviewed in the Havana newspaper, *La Lucha:*

The admirable interpretation of this guest of Havana allows us to believe the authenticity of the lofty praise in the Parisian press about Justin

Elie by the music critic from the *Figaro,* Gabriel Fauré; and by critic and composer André Wormser; as well as the former director of the Conservatory Théodore Dubois; and the brilliant author of *Samson et Dalila* [Camille Saint-Saëns]. (quoted in Dalencour 1983, 5)

In Cuba, he met Cuban pianist Ernestine Lecuona (1882–1951), a former classmate from the Paris Conservatory and a composer of salon music. Lecuona's younger brother, Ernesto, would later write works that drew upon the musical resources of the Cuban countryside (Moore 1997, 129–30, 135–40).

As Ludovic Lamothe left Haiti in 1910 to study in France, Elie returned to Haiti to develop his career as a pianist and composer. The years between Elie's return to Haiti and his departure for the United States in 1922 saw profound changes in his homeland. In 1915, when the U.S. began its nineteen-year occupation, many Haitian elites thought that the military intervention would restore civil order to a society that had become increasingly violent and anarchic. As Haitian president Sténio Vincent observed several years after the end of the occupation, many Haitian elites originally acquiesced to the presence of U.S. troops:

> There was, among the Haitians, a sort of discreet understanding to excuse the intervention, hoping that it would liquidate the chaotic situation that existed in the country, substituting an organized life of peace and work. The most intransigent patriots, those who were obstinately refusing to accept the *fait accompli,* came to consider it as a necessary evil, albeit temporary, faced with the evidence of the results. (Vincent 1931, 278–79, quoted in Bellegarde-Smith 1985, 23)

Eventually, however, the segregationist attitudes of the U.S. occupation forces wore on Haitian elites. Upper-class Haitians were routinely excluded from social functions with U.S. military personnel; the American Club, a social organization for expatriate Americans, was closed to Haitians of all social classes. Haitian social clubs like the Cercle Bellevue gradually closed their doors to U.S. citizens in a retaliatory move (Schmidt 1995, 137).

As some members of the Haitian elite traded social snubs with officers in the U.S. military, many Haitian peasants were waging a war of resistance against the Marines. Peasants resented the U.S. occupation forces' use of *corvée* or forced labor gangs that effectively enslaved poor Haitians in order to build up a crumbling Haitian road system. In 1918, Haitian peasant insurgents called *kakos,* led by Charlemagne Péralte and Benoît Batraville, began a year-long guerrilla war. While the *kako* resistance was short-lived—Péralte was killed by U.S. Marines in 1919 and Batraville the following year—the movement demonstrated that Haitian resistance could make occupation forces consider Haitian points of view. The use of *corvée* was halted in 1919 as a result of the *kako* resistance.

While some elites continued to curry favor with occupation officials, others actively resisted the occupation through the arts, literature, and ethnography. Justin Elie's *Méringues populaires* (1920) were a set of six dances published by R. de la Rozier Co. in New York City that set a tone of resistance toward the U.S. occupation, albeit in a form that only Haitian audiences would recognize. "Méringue No. 6" was based on "Totu pa gen dan" (Totu has no teeth), a song made popular by Auguste de Pradines, popularly known as Candio or Kandjo as it is spelled in Haitian Kreyòl (Dauphin 1980, 56). Born in France, Kandjo became famous in Haiti for his topical méringues. According to Averill,

> Kandjo fashioned a career that mixed bitter social satire . . . patriotism, and tender local themes . . . on a musical platform that combined French chanson, Haitian *mereng,* and Haitian traditional-style melodies. With his knack for capturing popular sentiments, he won for himself a devoted audience that spanned urban and rural environments (he sang at many rural *fèt chanpèts*) and all social classes. (Averill 1997, 50)

Elie's use of a song by a well-known and beloved social satirist in a parlor-style méringue was a subtle but important gesture of defiance. Unlike Lamothe's "Nibo," which was written when the end of the occupation was in sight, Elie's *Méringues populaires* were penned at the height of the occupation, before Haitian elites were actively involved in anti-American demonstrations and well before Price-Mars's call for a nationalist music based on the songs of the Haitian countryside.

Elie was one of several Haitian intellectuals who, even before the indigenous movement, decried European characterizations of Haitians as backward and uncivilized. While Haitians thought that Africa in the early twentieth century was in a state of turmoil, they were aware that Africa had, at one time, boasted civilizations that surpassed those in Europe (Nicholls 1979, 130).

One civilization that captured the imagination of Europeans and Haitians alike was that of Egypt, whose control by Great Britain made it a preferred travel destination for European tourists. As geographer Derek Gregory observes, "by representing Egypt as an anachronistic space in which past and present existed *outside* the space of the modern, [travel writers] claimed to open an imaginative (and extraordinarily presumptuous) passage into an ancient land" (Gregory 1999, 137). For Haitian intellectuals, Egypt provided a glorious civilization for the ancestral imagination that was centered on the African continent rather than in Europe.

By making a connection to an Egyptian past, Haitians laid claim to an aristocratic lineage. The ancient, heroic civilization of the pharaohs provided an alternative to the degraded views of African culture and the association of Africa with slavery. In adopting ancestral Egypt as a part of their cultural origins, they also recast Vodou as a religious practice with roots in a powerful culture respected by Europeans.

By connecting Vodou to the heritage of the pharaohs, Haitian intellectuals were engaging in a nationalist project that Partha Chatterjee has called a "classicization of tradition." Classicization is the use of historically and geographically distant ideas to link current practice to an esteemed "classical" past. Chatterjee has claimed that many nationalist movements in developing countries have conceptualized culture as divided into two spheres, the material and the spiritual (Chatterjee 1993, 73). While bourgeois citizens of such countries readily adopt the material values of Western culture, they simultaneously assert a jealous guardianship of their own culture's spiritual values. For Haitians, claiming Vodou as a part of their "spiritual culture" involved connecting it to a classical past in order to purge Haitian traditional religion of its lower-class associations.

Chatterjee has also asserted that the establishment of a "classicized" tradition has an important gendered component. The material, worldly component of tradition has often been associated with "outer" male spheres of power and authority while the spiritual dimensions have been connected to the "inner" female sphere of the home:

> The world is external, the domain of the material; the home represents one's inner spiritual self, one's true identity. The world is a treacherous terrain of the pursuit of material interests, where practical considerations reign supreme. It is also typically the domain of the male. The home in its essence must remain unaffected by the profane activities of the material world—and woman is its representation. (Chatterjee 1993, 120)

If Vodou was to give spiritual succor to the Haitian elite, it needed not only a connection to a heroic past but also a domesticated narrative that gendered national identity as female.

For Justin Elie, Cleopatra provided an ideal dramatic subject to link Vodou with a "classicized" past. Elie wrote the music for a "poème musical en 4 tableaux" called *Cléopâtre* in 1917. The lyrics for the drama were penned by Louis-Henri Durand, a customs official and amateur poet who also wrote the libretto for Elie's *Aphrodite* in 1914. Elie's *Cléopâtre* featured Queen Cléopâtre, her distant lover Antoine, and the court snake charmer, Chalcidas. Cléopâtre, separated from her lover Antoine for four years, worries that Octavia, Cléopâtre's rival, will supplant her as queen.

Octavia enlists Chalcidas, a Roman snake charmer, to secretly poison Cléopâtre. Chalcidas's plot is revealed by his lover, Mirlitza. Cléopâtre sentences Chalcidas to death but relents when she hears that Antoine is returning to her.

While the plot of Elie's *Cléopâtre* loosely follows the plot of several other versions of the drama including those of Jules Massenet (*Cléopâtre*, 1914), Victor Masse (*Une nuit de Cléopâtre*, 1885) and Xavier Leroux (*Cléopâtre*, 1890), the music links the ancient world of classical Egypt to the sounds of contemporary Haiti. In an experiential program for the work, Haitian journalist Placide David claimed that "Justin Elie helps himself with great advantage to 'vaudouesque' airs, to give this impression of mysterious dread" (David 1934, 3).[6] According to David, each tableau opens and closes with "vaudouesque" music. In the first tableau, Cléopâtre longs for her beloved Antoine:

> Her "vaudouesque" theme presently unfolds and unrolls fluidly, alertly, subtly like her vagabond thoughts that wander among the monuments of Alexandria, silent proof of its former prosperity. This sad and melancholy melody, remarkable for its purity and its simplicity, follows its course after a pure design and charges the noble elevation of the romanticism of Justin Elie. (David 1934, 3)

Here, "vaudouesque" music connects the wandering thoughts of Cléopâtre with the former grandeur of the Egyptian capital and the rising artistry of the composer. In the second tableau, "cabalistic themes of a vaudouesque incantation" set the somber mood for Cléopâtre's clandestine meeting with Chalcidas (David 1934, 4). Music that evokes the Vodou ceremony thus sets the general mood of the drama and serves as catalyst for important dramatic moments.

While the music to *Cléopâtre* has not survived, the "musical poem" made a lasting impression on Haitian audiences. Not only did David's experiential program link the classical drama to "vaudouesque" airs, but other critics identified Elie's music as either being specifically drawn from the Vodou ceremony or directly inspired by an ancestral Egyptian connection. Haitian composer and critic Franck Lassègue described Cléopâtre as "scènes voudoesque" (Lassègue 1929, 30), while Volvick Ricourt's poem, "Hommage à Justin Elie," pictured Elie receiving his creative inspiration at the foot of the Sphinx (Ricourt 1933, 8).

While *Cléopâtre's* connection to the practice of Vodou implicitly pervades the work, other pieces by Elie were explicitly inspired by Haitian traditional religion. Two of Elie's Vodou derived works, "Scènes

Vaudouesques" and "Deux Poèmes Vaudouesques," were written while Elie was beginning his composing career in Haiti (Durand 1983, 2). Elie also wrote two works for solo voice that made reference to Vodou ritual. His "Hymne à Damballah" uses *langaj* or Vodou ritual language derived from praise songs for Damballah (Danbala), the Vodou spirit associated with snakes, and his consort Aïda (Ayida). His "Chant des Hounsis" refers to the song of an *ousi*, the ritual assistant in the Vodou ceremony.

Invocations of Egypt and Vodou each had their limitations. On the one hand, despite the potential appeal of Vodou as a representation of the "spiritual" side of Haitian nationalism, overt depictions of the Vodou ceremony or invocations of ritual language were still problematic for Haitian elite audiences in the early twentieth century. On the other hand, links with a mythic Egyptian past were sufficiently regal for elite tastes, but they lacked a direct, visceral connection with Haitian culture. This created a dilemma resolved by the incorporation of an alternative indigenous spirituality into Haitian classical music. In the nineteenth century, Haitian intellectuals turned to the Native American heritage of their island for "classical" inspiration. But Indian influences were officially commemorated much earlier when, after the 1804 revolution, the government changed the name of the former colony from Saint-Domingue to Haïti, which means "mountainous land" in Arawak.

As nineteenth-century writers recounted Native Americans' struggle against the Spanish invaders, they identified the natives' struggle with their own current political situation. In 1822, Haitian forces invaded the eastern half of Hispañola that was held by Spain. In the ensuing twenty-two year occupation of Santo Domingo—which was to eventually become the Dominican Republic—Haitians liberated Spanish slaves and became the first occupation army headed by blacks. Dominican resentment toward Haitians and Haitian fears of Dominican reprisals fueled impassioned nationalist writing on both sides.

Haitian historian Emile Nau (1812–60) became one of the most outspoken advocates of a Haitian historiography that gave Native Americans a prominent place in the development of Haitian culture. Nau identified three important cultural activities that could be associated with national identity: music, language, and defense of the nation.

In his *Histoire des caciques d'Haiti* (1894/1963), Nau paid particular attention to the musical and cultural products of the Arawak people. Nau described the "sacred hymns sung in honor of the caciques by their subjects, as well as funeral songs sung in commemoration of their dead leaders" (Nau 1894/1963, 1:43). According to Nau, music was an important feature of Arawak ceremonial life.

Nau was also one of the first historians to challenge the conquistadors' claims that the Arawak people lacked both language and culture. In his chapter entitled "De la langue et de la litterature des aborigenes d'Haiti," Nau called the Arawaks' language "sonore et gracieuse" (sonorous and gracious), and claimed that despite dialect differences between the five caciques, the Arawak peoples shared a language which came from the same "souche mère" (family tree) (Nau 1894/1963, 2:60).

Nau was also partially responsible for linking important Native American historical figures with the history of Haiti as an independent nation. By claiming that Native Americans embodied the values of a nationalist consciousness even before the existence of a Haitian state, it was possible to include Native American heroes in the history of pre-colonial Haiti, thus "classicizing" Haitian culture by connecting it to a primordial Native American (as opposed to African or European) culture.

Since the entire Native American population was killed by the Spanish invasion, later generations of Haitian historians were able to imbue the Indians with nationalistic characteristics that combined the best qualities of elite Haitian culture: patriotism in defending Haitian soil from foreign invasion and a cultured comportment that attested to their ruling competence. According to Nau, Native American societies were ruled by royal families who controlled their dominions through benign despotism. In the *cacique* or kingdom of Xaragua (which was located in what is now southern Haiti and was headquartered in present-day Léogâne), the royal family was led by Caonabo, a fierce male warrior and his wife, Anacaona, a beautiful and talented ruler whose royal demeanor commanded great respect among her people (Nau 1894/1963, 1:118).

As Lora Romero argues in her study of domesticity in the United States, nationalist narratives often rely on gendered roles to reinforce contemporary identification with the past:

> Even when nationalism acknowledges women as the mothers of the nation, it disjoins violence and nurture through figures of gender difference. Although deployed differently in masculinist and womanist nationalisms, gender difference works toward the same end for both: a means of imagining pure oppositionality. (Romero 1997, 69)

Nau described Caonabo and Anacaona as political threats to the Spanish colonial government. Caonabo, one of the most persistent combatants with the Spanish, was captured by a ruse in 1494 and put on a ship to Spain where he died en route (Nau 1894/1963, 1:91). Anacaona, unaware that Caonabo was captured, organized a tribute to Governor Nicholas Ovando consisting of elaborately dressed singers and dancers performing "nationalistic airs" for the occasion (Elie 1944, 195). Ovando took advantage of the opportunity to butcher the assembled crowd, killing Anacaona as well as the rest of the women and children gathered for the performance.

Anacaona was posthumously endowed with the attributes valued by generations of Haitian elites. According to one account, Anacaona's funeral confirmed her status as member of a royal bloodline:

> Anacaona's body was colored with white and red flowers . . . a fine cotton cloth, woven from different colors. . . . On her head, neck, and arms, she had a garland of natural red and white flowers that exhaled their perfume. In her bearing and in her attitude, one could well see that she was a princess. (Elie 1944, 196)

Nau's nineteenth-century depiction of Anacaona as a Native American princess who was murdered by Spanish colonists identified her as a defender of Haitian soil in the face of foreign intervention.

Haiti's tempestuous relationship with its Spanish-speaking neighbors in the Dominican Republic made a twentieth-century interpretation of Anacaona's struggle against the Spanish even more appealing to Haitian audiences than in the nineteenth century. Nau's depiction of the Arawaks—and especially Anacaona—met elites' need for a regal line that was derived from neither Europe nor Africa. Arawaks were portrayed as a cultured, musical, and poetic people who were the original inhabitants of the island. Although they had no biological ties to African-descended Haitians, Arawaks remained as powerful symbolic ancestors.

Justin Elie showed an interest in Native American themes early in his career, only twenty years after the 1894 publication of Nau's history of the Arawak caciques. Between 1910 and 1922, Elie wrote "Chant du Barde Indien" based on a text by Honduran poet Joaquin Bonilla. He also set Haitian poet Jean-Joseph Vilaire's "La Mort de l'Indien" (1916) to music. In this poem, a Native American hangs his hammock in the woods and breathes his final breath.

> He came to be in an immense forest,
> To mingle his soul without remainder with nature.
> With his dashed hopes and the ills that he endures,
> He leaves this earth without a single regret.
> (Vilaire 1950a, 237)

The noble warrior, sensing the end of his time on earth, prepares himself for his reunification with nature. Vilaire's "Indien" accepts his fate without question; the peaceful Arawak subject is inseparable from the land. As Vilaire showed in another poem titled "Caonabo," however, Native

Americans could also be selfless defenders of Haitian soil. In the poem, Vilaire depicts the struggle of the proud Arawak warrior who has been captured by the Spanish, yet refuses to give up his anticolonialist struggle:

O proud Caonabo! Lift yourself from under your chain
And your manacles, which form a pile
So heavy, which would tire the muscles of twenty arms.
Without reeling, hold yourself firm and straight like a chain.
(Vilaire 1950b, 237)

Elie eventually set Vilaire's poem to music in his "Chant de Guerre de Caonabo."

Whether depicted as peaceful autochthons or fierce freedom fighters, precolonial Native Americans gave Haitian elites ways to imagine their ancestors as both royal and resistant. But the inspirational value of Native American resistance was not limited to romanticized accounts of Arawak history. During the U.S. occupation, armed peasant groups called themselves *kakos* after the *caciques* or warlords of aboriginal Haiti.

ARAWAKS ABROAD: TRANSPLANTING THE NATIVE AMERICAN ROOTS OF HAITIAN MUSIC

When Justin Elie moved from Haiti to the United States in the early 1920s, he brought along romanticized impressions of African and Native American influences on Haitian culture. These impressions, however, were at odds with the overtly sensationalist images of both African and Native American peoples in the United States. In moving to the United States, Elie's Native American-based compositions lost their Haitian nationalist underpinnings; his publications with Carl Fischer, Inc. conformed to the Indianist stereotypes prevalent in the U.S. entertainment industry. In many ways, Elie was freer to oppose the United States occupation of Haiti than he was to resist the sensational and exploitative themes of U.S. popular culture.

Eager to make a career of music composition, Justin Elie left Haiti on 12 September 1922 and moved to New York City. Although he regretted leaving Haiti to pursue his career, the Haitian musical scene was ill equipped to further Elie's musical interests. The major music ensembles in Haiti were military wind bands, including the Musique du Palais, under the direction of Occide Jeanty, and the Musique de la Garde, directed by Théramène Ménès. As state-sponsored musical ensembles, military wind bands played repertoire for governmental functions; Elie's preference for piano compositions, vocal works, chamber music, and larger orchestral repertoire did not coordinate well with the ceremonial duties of the band composer.

Elie had reason to believe that he had made an excellent choice in moving to the United States. His wife, Lily, joined him in New York in February 1923 and the two of them performed frequently in recitals that included Elie's own compositions. On 22 November 1923, Elie performed a concert for the Alliance Française de New-York at the Waldorf-Astoria Hotel. In a program that included works by Erik Satie, Puccini, and B. Godard, Elie and soprano Suzanne Galien performed three of his own vocal works: "La Mort de l'Indien," "Quelque Chose Sanglote En Mon Âme," and "Plaisirs d'Amour." [7]

Elie and his wife also joined the Music and Art Lover's Club, an association of professional and amateur musicians designed to bring audiences and artists together. The program for the club's "Gala Concert" of 12 March 1923 states:

> One does not merely sit and critically watch or listen at an assembly of this remarkable association; one sits among, one mingles with the artists. Association with them is one of the pleasantest forms of social contact it is possible to imagine.[8]

The program advertised a recital the club sponsored at Carnegie Hall that included vocalists, pianists, violinists, and dancers. Elie provided piano accompaniment for a dancer listed as "Hasoutra" as she interpreted Elie's pieces, including "Hymne et Danse à Legba," "Danseuse des Nuites," "Danse de Nonun," and "Danse des Zémès." An undated report from the *New York Musical Advance* described her as follows:

> Mlle Hasoutra, formerly of the Opera-Comique and recently of the Winter Garden in New York, has become known by her Javanese dancing. She also made a thorough study of the old Carribean [sic] Indian tribes, their legends, customs, gestures and character, for these dances were written especially for her by Mr. Elie. Her interpretation of these works is essentially original and absolutely authentic. (Anon. 1923b)

Miss Hasoutra's promotional materials assured New York audiences that they were being treated to an artistic experience that connected them with the Caribbean. As a composer who was born and raised in Haiti, Justin Elie did not need the same rhetorical legitimation as Mlle Hasoutra; his status as a "young Haytian composer" gave him the necessary credentials to claim a cultural connection to Caribbean music.

During his first few years in the United States, Elie regularly programmed pieces of his own composition that used Vodou-inspired themes, including his "Légende Créole" for violin and piano that was based on the Haitian song "Zonbi Ban-n Mannan" (Herissé n.d.). In July 1923, Elie also composed the music for *Voodoo Moon,* a dance piece that featured his artistic partner, Gilda Gray, who had worked previously as a dancer in the Ziegfield Follies. Gray was also the owner and principal dancer for the dance and supper club, Rendez-Vous, located on West 45th Street in Manhattan, where *Voodoo Moon* received its first performance.

While the music for *Voodoo Moon* has not survived, the production was reviewed in the New York newspapers at the time. While some accounts referred to *Voodoo Moon* as a "ballet," the work was actually a series of choreographed dances intended as "after theater" entertainment ("Voodoux at the Rendez-Vous" 1923). One article referred to *Voodoo Moon* as a "divertissment [*sic*] aboriginal" in an effort to capitalize on the exoticism of a French-influenced "aboriginal" art ("Gilda Gray" 1923). A review in the *Evening Telegram* depicted Gray's dancing costume this way: "In her brilliant costume of flame-colored feathers, with armlets and head-dress of writhing serpents, she looked for all the world like a voo-doo priestess of the 15th century" (Anon. 1923a). *Voodoo Moon* was billed as an exotic spectacle that would expose the audience to an ancient yet titillating culture.

Exactly what culture *Voodoo Moon* was designed to portray was unclear from the press releases and reviews for the performance. Audiences were assured that Elie's credentials as an interpreter of "the Voodoo" were beyond reproach. One source claimed that Elie "spent fifteen years in a study of the primitive music and dances of his native country" ("Gilda Gray" 1923). At the same time, audiences were told that "voodoo" was the product of Native American culture. Religious practices associated with enslaved Africans were not included in descriptions of *Voodoo Moon's* inspirational sources. The *Evening Telegram* review is typical:

> Justin Elie, the young Haytian who composed the music and directed the ballet for this novel entertainment, spent years of study of the traditional rites of his forefathers. In "Voo-Doo Moon," written especially for Miss Gray he has preserved all of the beauty and primitive appeal of the ancient Indian chants. (Anon. 1923a)

In the same article, the author explained that the "Vaudou" of Elie's composition was directly traceable to the Native American inhabitants of Haiti and that the practices which were associated with black people and known as "voodoo" in 1923 were, in fact, a corruption of the "original" Indian culture of the island:

> The history of the Vaudou (voodoo) is, in a measure, the history of ill-fated Hayti. The original inhabitants, we are told, were a peace-loving, indolent nation, whose sole enjoyment was dancing to the beating of

drums. After its discovery by Columbus and subsequent enslavement by the Spaniards, the few remaining aborigines fled to the mountains where clandestine meetings were held. Here, while dancing and singing, the leaders went about sowing the seeds of revolt, at the same time invoking the help of their gods to free them from the invaders. It is this dance which Miss Gray presents and not the voodoo of recent times which is an outgrowth of negro importation when the Indians were practically exterminated. (Anon. 1923a)

In this account, Africans stole "voodoo" from Native Americans and used it for their own devices. Even more telling, the view of the "indolent" Indians of Haiti contrasted sharply with contemporaneous newspaper accounts of black Haitians who, resisting the U.S. occupation of their country, were often depicted as barbarous savages. In addition, this account takes the runaway slave phenomenon known as *mawonaj* (marronage) in which African slaves escaped the plantations and made communities in the rugged mountains and turns it into a runaway Indian narrative.

As Justin Elie found, audiences in the United States during the 1920s were hungry for entertainment that posed Native Americans as original, ancient, and authentic cultural actors. Native Americans had been the focus of dramatic and musical works in the United States since the 1830s. As Indian populations were gradually subjugated during the nineteenth century, their depictions in popular culture transformed from "laughing-stocks" to more noble characters by the end of the century (Pisani 1998, 221). By the end of the nineteenth century, Native Americans had been the subject of several musical works, including white composer Robert Stoepel's *Hiawatha* (1859) with a text based on Henry Wadsworth Long-fellow's 1855 poem, *The Song of Hiawatha*, and Afro-English Samuel Coleridge-Taylor's popular *Hiawatha's Wedding Feast* (1898).

As Michael Pisani has shown in his study of musical depictions of Native American culture in the late nineteenth and early twentieth centuries, composers who wrote Indian-themed works relied mostly on a collection of stock musical devices that Pisani has termed the "ready made toolbox of exotica" (Pisani 1998, 229–30). Such musical motifs include the use of sustained fifths, "rude or peasant" rhythms, exaggerated dynamics to imitate percussion, pentatonic scales, doubling melodies at the fourth or fifth scale degree, and "the three-note descending 3–2–1, usually given out in the rhythm two sixteenths and an eighth or two eighths and a quarter (short-short-long); this rhythm becomes an exotic feature in itself; even when the three pitches vary, it serves as a typical across-the-board device specifically used for Indians" (Pisani 1998, 230).

With the growth of ethnographic studies in the late nineteenth century, and particularly the development of phonographic recording technology, composers saw opportunities to present Indian work that was more musically connected to Native American culture. Ethnographer Alice Fletcher and composer John Fillmore promoted the use of ethnographically collected Indian musical materials in musical compositions; Fillmore's pieces set Native American melodies to Western harmonizations. In addition, Arthur Farwell (1872–1951) founded the Wa-Wan Press in order to publish and promote harmonizations of Indian melodies.

Among the more renowned of the composers who used Native American motifs was Edward MacDowell, whose *Second Orchestral Suite ("Indian")* (1895) contained themes that were drawn from Theodore Baker's 1882 thesis on Native American music (Pisani 1998, 231). As Tara Browner points out, "though MacDowell was clearly interested in Native cultures (his curiosity about Indians led him to Baker in the first place), he saw Indian melodies as exotic raw materials that expressed shared universal human emotions, not as products created from a specific musical tradition with its own aesthetics" (Browner 1997, 270). As a result, MacDowell also relied heavily on the "toolbox of exotica" that characterized much of the Indianist music of the period.

By the 1910s, harmonized Indian melodies drawn from ethnographic sources fell out of favor with U.S. audiences. Instead, music based on Indian themes tended toward "fanciful compositions in which transcribed Indian music provided the foundation for a fantasia" (Pisani 1998, 246). Despite the efforts of composers like Arthur Farwell, Charles Wakefield Cadman, and Charles Sanford Skilton to write music that portrayed Indians in a sympathetic light, audiences demanded an "exotic Indian" and flocked to those entertainments that delivered that image: silent films, popular songs, and light opera (Pisani 1998, 248). Popular entertainments had been promulgating Indian musical clichés since the debut of Stoepel's *Hiawatha* in 1859; by the 1910s, examples of exoticized Indian music had "made their way into the silent movie music collections for movie-house accompanists, such as the Sam Fox volumes of the 1910s and the encyclopedia of Erno Rapee (1924)" (Gorbman 2000, 236).

By the 1920s, exoticism and ethnographic verisimilitude were viewed as complementary characteristics in Indianist musical compositions. With the advent of ethnographic research in the late nineteenth century, composers used ethnographic rhetoric to bolster their efforts to bring hitherto undervalued musical materials to a concert-going audience. While audiences demanded the musical clichés they had come to expect from popular entertainments, there was a concomitant desire to connect Indian musical activity to scholarly, ethnographically based research.

When Justin Elie arrived in the United States, music publishers were looking for opportunities to capitalize on consumer interest in exotica at home and abroad. Elie's status as a conservatory-trained and Caribbean-born pianist-composer made him an attractive prospect for a music-publishing career. Before emigrating from Haiti in 1921, Elie had already established professional contacts with the music industry in the United States. These contacts netted him a contract from the QRS Music Company, a firm that produced piano rolls for player pianos. On 1 March 1921, the company sent Elie a letter confirming a verbal agreement to pay the composer a royalty of $.04 per roll for five rolls of compositions.[9] Upon his arrival in the United States, Elie negotiated a contract with Carl Fischer Music, Inc. to publish his music manuscripts.

Elie's first compositions with Carl Fischer were his "Haitian Legend" (Légende Créole) for violin and piano (1921), "Prayer at Eventide (Prière du soir) Invocation No. 2" (1922) for chamber orchestra, and the piano compositions "The Echo (Ismao-o!): Ancient Mountain Legends, No. 1 (Les Chants de la Montagne No. 1)," "Nostalgia (Nostalgie): Ancient Mountain Legends No. 2 (Les Chants de la Montagne No. 2)," and "Nocturne: Ancient Mountain Legends No. 3 (Les Chants de la Montagne No. 3)" (1922).[10]

In "Haitian Legend," Elie uses not one but two distinctively Haitian musical motifs most often associated with Haiti's African heritage. The piece begins "lento e lamentoso" with a plaintive theme in the violin. The first theme is characteristic of the Haitian *complainte*, a melody in a minor key that bears some similarity with African American blues. Often, the lyrics for the *complainte* bemoan the physical or spiritual condition of the singer (see ex. 3.8). At measure 51 marked "allegro vivace," Elie inserts a lively, major-keyed melody based on the Haitian children's song "Zonbi Ban-n Mannan," in which singers describe the capture of a chicken and its metamorphosis into soup (Dauphin 1981, 24–25) (see ex. 3.9). For the remainder of the "Haitian Legend," the plaintive first theme is answered by the playful second theme, giving the listener an aural impression of two different, but characteristic Haitian musical genres.

"Prayer at Eventide" (1922) was a work for chamber orchestra that did not have a specific program linked to either African or Indian cultural ideas, yet Elie used techniques drawn from the "ready-made toolbox of exotica" Pisani describes as typical in the works of Indianist composers in the United States. The opening melody is in parallel fourths and fifths,

Example 3.8. Justin Elie, "Haitian Legend," mm. 3–11

while the bass voices provide a drone in fifths. The melody uses a pentatonic scale (see ex. 3.10).

The *Ancient Mountain Legends, nos. 1–3* ("The Echo," "Homesickness," and "Nocturne") were pieces for solo piano that Carl Fischer promoted as evocative, exotic music of a distant, forbidding land though it contains virtually no evidence of Indian musical traits. The first piece, "The Echo (Ismao-O!)," is a short work that features a simple, descending melodic line in 6/8 meter. The second piece, "Homesickness (Nostalgie)," is a harmonically static work that contains arpeggiated figures in the

Example 3.9. Justin Elie, "Haitian Legend," mm. 51–54

Example 3.10. Justin Elie, "Prayer at Eventide," mm. 1–4

right hand over two-measure phrases. The third, "Nocturne," is a contemplative piece with a conservatively harmonized melodic line.[11]

Despite their relatively prosaic harmonic and rhythmic vocabulary, *The Ancient Mountain Legends, nos. 1–3* were reviewed in the musical press as examples of Elie's skills as a collector and arranger of ancient Indian music. Music reviewer George Melville wrote:

> *The Ancient Mountain Legends,* published by Carl Fischer, Inc. and built on genuine primitive themes, are all pregnant with the mysterious romanticism of the native tribes of Latin-America. In this set, Mr. Elie has developed these themes with a characteristic harmonization, however keeping the full value of the original mood of the songs. (Melville n.d.)

Here, exoticism and mystery are used as selling features for musical works that are in fact indistinguishable from many of the parlor pieces for piano from the period.

Melville went on to explain how the process of transferring so-called primitive music to a more cultured setting required important changes in the inspirational source material. For example, the modern composer was thought to be better served by using Western instruments rather than relying upon the original "aboriginal" ones:

> The personal investigations conducted by Mr. Elie among the Latin-American Indians have taught him the impossibility of using only native instruments in order to convey all the impressive effects of their worship ceremonies, songs and dances. The limitation of the American Indian instruments does not allow them to express the true magic effect of their mysterious music. (Melville n.d.)

Here, Melville markets Elie as a "modernist" composer who put the sounds of the past to work in pieces that "express the true magic effect" of exotic music by making the absurd claim that European instruments are more suitable for Native American music than the indigenous instruments that first performed the music.

Novelty and exoticism were attractive qualities not only to capitalist promoters but also to more scholarly writers interested in Native American music's ability to revive a moribund tradition (cf. Lott 1995). In December 1923, Dr. Conrad H. Ratner published an essay titled "Justin Elie, and the Revival of the Music of the Natives of Latin America." Ratner identified the "native music" of Latin America as an inspirational repository for a new, American form of musical composition:

> Among the wide range of novelties imported to enrich our musical world, there has as yet been no representation introducing us to the native melodies and rhythms of Latin America. Perhaps it is because of the difficulty of producing something veritably native. The fairly total submergence of native music by the influences of European civilization has caused even the informed to doubt the practicability of discovering it and presenting it in all its indigenous richness and mystical beauty. The Latin Americans, themselves, due to their assimilation of European ideas, have entirely lost sight of the native element in their chants. The serious investigator must always be on guard lest he be deceived by acquired European tendencies even in an Aztec phantasy played in Mexico by a Mexican fanfare or by a dance of Inca rendered by a Peruvian orchestra. (Ratner 1923)

According to Ratner, orchestras throughout the Americas were perpetuating a European-oriented attitude toward their indigenous musical traditions. Only a trained ethnographer with a developed artistic sensibility could rescue a legitimate Latin American musical heritage from oblivion.

Ratner identified Elie as a pathbreaking ethnographer of Native American culture and exaggerated Elie's experience with and exposure to Native American music in order to legitimize Elie's work as a composer:

> Justin Elie, the Latin American composer, who studied at the Conservatory of Paris, has devoted ten years to concentrated investigation among tribes, living among them, at times at the very risk of his life, leading the simple and picturesque existence of a people so capricious, carefree and degenerate. He was urged on to specialize in this study by a love of the exotic in music and by the unique chants of the natives, full of melody and marvelous rhythm, at once paradoxical and disjointed. (Ratner 1923)

Ratner's view of Elie as an experienced and adventuresome ethno-grapher—for example, his claim that Elie spent "ten years among the natives . . . at the very risk of his life"—was tempered by his acknowledgment of the composer's education at the Paris Conservatory. Despite the fact that Elie's work in the Caribbean was as a touring pianist and not an ethnographer, Ratner alleged that Elie had done work specifically among Native American groups. Moreover, by naming Inca and Aztec civilizations as worthy of musical investigation in the earlier passage lamenting "acquired European tendencies" in Latin American music, Ratner implied that Elie drew his artistic inspiration from Peru and Mexico, places that Elie never visited.[12]

While Ratner made a case for Elie's ethnographic credentials, he si-multaneously reinforced the exoticized cravings of U.S. audiences. In the following description of the folk music from which Elie drew his inspira-tion, Ratner employed the same sensationalist rhetoric used to depict Gilda Gray's costume in *Voodoo Moon*:

> Imagine a graceful, supple yet well sinewed body, sparely clad, bizarrely painted, fervidly, aye religiously pouring forth its soul in fluent, beauti-ful and expressive gestures; imagine too, a high-pitched, lusty voice, zealously chanting a melody, asymmetrical, with rhythm, but little rhythm; now plaintive, now majestic, always sincere and intense; add to that the imperfect flute, ambling on like a jester, nonchalant, indepen-dent, weaving in utter disregard of the melody; let it all be accompanied by three drums, each beating out its own accent quaintly, yet in remark-able unison, lending color, emphasis and height, and you have an en-semble most fascinating in its picturesqueness, mysticism and romantic wealth—an ensemble entirely characteristic of the Latin American aboriginal. (Ratner 1923)

Ratner's portrayal of Elie as an ethnographer of the exotic brought Elie the recognition he sought in the press. It also encouraged him to write spectacular works that appealed to an audience hungry for exoticized dis-plays of foreign cultures.

In 1928, Elie composed *Babylon: A Suite of Four Orientalist Sketches* (1928a), a work in which he collaborated a second time with *Voodoo Moon* dancer Gilda Gray. The theme of the work was equally as sensationalist as *Voodoo Moon*, though its exoticism was transported to an "orientalist" setting. The first three movement titles evoked a sexualized portrait of a female character or role while the final movement, "Orgie," implied a sex-ualized finale for the suite. The first movement, "Odalisk," depicted the

Example 3.11. Justin Elie, "Queen of the Night," mm. 1–6

odalisque, a female slave or concubine in an Oriental harem, a favorite exotic focus for European painters. In the second movement, "Bayadère," the exoticized female subject was an Indian dancing girl; in both cases, female types provided entertainment for predominantly male audiences.

In the third movement, the "Queen of the Night," Elie relied on stock techniques that Pisani identifies as common to Indianist composers. The opening melody is supported by parallel chords followed by the sustained fifths in the left hand from measures 7–20. The pentatonic melody strongly suggests an E minor tonality, especially with the B major chord at the end of the first melodic statement (see ex. 3.11). In addition, in measures 41–42, the chromatic motion in the inner voices gives the melody an Orientalist zing (see ex. 3.12).

The best example of the transformation of a Native American inspirational source into a sensationalized U.S. Indianist vision is in Elie's *Kiskaya: An Aboriginal Suite for Orchestra* (1928b). As the subtitle implies, the piece is meant to invoke the music of aboriginal peoples, especially the cultures of Central and South America. According to the unattributed program notes that were published along with the score, Elie's interest in aboriginal music came from extensive personal experience:

> In the orchestral suite by Justin Elie we find musical evidence of the composer's extensive research into the lore of the Aboriginal tribes of the Western Hemisphere. Mr. Elie has been especially interested in the Indians of Central and South America, for it was in that part, perhaps, that the highest type of culture existed. At any rate, the folk-songs of the

Example 3.12. Justin Elie, "Queen of the Night," mm. 41–42

Aborigines have proven immensely adaptable to modern orchestra treatment. (Elie 1928b, 1)

The notes go on to laud Elie's musical translation of "truly primitive" music of Latin America:

> Kiskaya, which was written while the composer was under the immediate influence of his Indian research, may well be considered as a unique and original work, reflecting, as it does, the past glories of Indian civilization. Mr. Elie has brought to musical literature an idiom which, when not shamefully misinterpreted, has been entirely overlooked in the past. He has accomplished the very difficult task of creating music that embodies the truly primitive and has shown to what a great extent the musical instincts of the Latin American native were developed. (Elie 1928b, 1)

In addition to exaggerating the extent of Elie's travels (as noted earlier, he traveled to the Caribbean, but made only a brief concert appearance in Venezuela), the author of the program notes obscures the specifically Haitian inspiration for the suite by erroneously identifying the setting of *Kiskaya* as somewhere in western Brazil, despite the title's clear reference to the Native American name for Hispañola, or Quisqueya. The program notes also refer to Quechua-speaking natives, a ruling "Inca" and his family as well as cave-dwelling oracles in the Brazilian jungles.

In *Kiskaya*, Elie emphasized the Native American connections Haiti had with its Latin American neighbors at the expense of the African roots of Haitian culture. Just as audiences saw Elie's *Voodoo Moon* as an endorsement of an Indian origin for Haitian traditional religion, they embraced *Kiskaya* as an authentic representation of the ancient music of Haiti, a music that was not derived primarily from West and Central Africa. Elie even borrowed programmatic ideas from his previous work, including his song "Le mort de l'Indien" to emphasize the Native American roots of the *Kiskaya* suite. The imaginary Indian world of *Kiskaya* also evoked the "classicization" impulses of earlier Haitian writers, especially those interested in the royal lineage of Anacaona and her Indian warriors.

Kiskaya was promoted as an example of how ethnography and artistry could work together to produce a musical product that informed as well as entertained. The music of *Kiskaya* was not based on melodies or rhythms collected in ethnographic fieldwork; it was a product of the artistically crafted imagination of the composer. Reviewers were eager, however, to attribute Elie's music to an ethnographic source as a way to give his pieces an added authority and an exotic appeal.

The first movement, "In the Temple of the Sun God" (Dans le Temple du dieu Soleil), is a calm ceremonial invocation to an Inca deity. The program notes depict the setting:

> It is the day of the "Intip-Rayme" . . . a feast of the Sun God . . . a great celebration is held in the Sun God's Temple . . . the Inca himself and the Royal Family take part. A llama is sacrificed to please the God. After the ceremonial, a long cortège proceeds to the place where there are dances and libations. (Elie 1928b, 1)

Marked *Andante tranquillo*, the movement's introduction opens with horns and strings playing open fifths while the oboe contributes a descending triplet figure. The clarinet answers the oboe one octave lower with a dotted-eighth-sixteenth-note figure. The introduction's principal theme, a diatonic outline of G major by the English horn and flute, is stated in eighth and quarter notes and is supported by bassoons, horns, and strings.

The lyrical quality of the principal theme is abruptly altered at the *L'istesso tempo*, where the upper strings play *pizzicato* (plucked) offbeats over a dotted eighth-sixteenth-note figure in the violoncelli and bassoons. An "Indian drum" and the stereotypical Indian melody reinforce each other, providing additional rhythmic interest while the oboe and trumpet play a variation on the principal theme (see ex. 3.13). As the movement comes to a close, the orchestral texture thins very quickly, leaving only the violoncelli and bassoons on the syncopated bass line and the "Indian drum" to fade quietly into the final *pianissimo* chord.

Heavily accented afterbeats in the brasses and winds and a steady, rhythmic drive give the second movement, "Dance to the Sun God" (La Danse du dieu Soleil), a brash, exciting character:

> A dance is consecrated to the God . . . It asks him to bless the tribes with victory . . . The drums, commencing softly, beat more and more furiously. The Quechuas dancers, dressed in flaming, gorgeous costumes made from the plumes of tropical birds, dance to the barbaric music. In their fanatical zeal to please the Sun God, they become more and more excited. At the end of the dance, some of them fall dead to the ground. (Elie 1928b, 1)

In measures 1–4, Elie uses motives that evoke Pisani's "toolbox of exotica": the drumbeats for the dance appear in the violoncelli and basses, as well as in the bass and "Indian" drums. The tempo marking, "allegro barbaric, ma non troppo," along with the accented afterbeats in the violin and trumpet (m. 3), indicate an incessant, driving quality to the opening, which is

Example 3.13. Justin Elie, "In the Temple of the Sun God," mm. 34–38

relieved only with the entrance of the horns at measure 13 (see ex. 3.14). Later in the movement, at measure 46, the flute has the following melody based on the méringue (see ex. 3.15). The méringue rhythm appears several times in the score, usually in the upper melodic voice, much as it would appear in a piano arrangement of the popular Haitian dance.

The third movement, "Procession of Shadows" (Le Défilé des Ombres), is an adagietto with cadenza-like solos for flute in the opening measures (see ex. 3.16). This movement borrows its narrative from Elie's earlier song, "Le Mort de l'Indien," which was based on the poem by Jean-Joseph Vilaire in which a Native American warrior goes off to the forest to die:

> In the last hours of the day, the Aborigine lies under the trees . . . Falling leaves flutter downward . . . They remind him of the days before the conquest . . . In the white clouds of the horizon he reads the tragic passing of his vanishing race. (Elie 1928b, 1)

Unlike Vilaire's other poem, "Caonabo," in which the warrior fights against the chains of slavery and does not concede victory to the Spanish even in the face of death, the Aborigine in "The Procession of Shadows" is conquered in both mind and body. While Vilaire's poem presented the

Example 3.14. Justin Elie, "Dance to the Sun God," mm. 1–12

Indian's death as a blending of human and natural elements, "The Procession of Shadows" casts the Aborigine's situation as a metaphor for the eventual disappearance of Indians in the Americas.

Finally, the fourth movement, the "Dance of the Cave Man" (Danse de l'Homme des Grottes), relies on an insistent rhythmic pulse and heavily accented chords, especially in the brass parts. The activities described in

Example 3.15. Justin Elie, "Dance to the Sun God," mm. 44–46

Example 3.16. Justin Elie, "Procession of Shadows," mm. 1–3, flute only

the program for the movement resemble those of Vodou, yet they are located in the jungles of Brazil, not the mountains of Quisqueya:

> Among some tribes in Brazil, sorcerers and medicine men predict the
> future in oracles. These oracles are always preceded and followed by
> cabalistic rites and dances. The cave men live hermit lives. They wear
> hideous masks, amulettes and fetiches. (Elie 1928b, 1)

Still, reviewers were willing to embrace this fanciful assembly of randomly
chosen Native American groups and rhythmically enticing music and
credit Elie with successfully uniting the modern and ancient. One reviewer wrote:

> Justin Elie is one of the foremost of Latin-American composers, a great
> world musical figure, perhaps one of the most ultra-modern and at the
> same time most delightfully ancient minds in the entire domain of mu-
> sic today. For Elie is modern in treatment, while his thematic musical
> material is over 5,000 years old, with themes drawn from the great days
> of the Mayas, the Caribs, the Aztecs, the Toltecs. (Somers n.d.)

Somers not only credits Elie with writing beautiful music, but also describes Elie's mind itself as having both ancient and modern qualities. For
Somers, "The Dance of the Cave Man" both surpassed contemporary
compositional practice and invoked Native American cultures:

> His "Cavemen Dance" is more advanced in syncopated effect than
> Gershwin's "Rhapsody in Blue"; its rhythms are comparable to those of
> Ignor [sic] Stravinsky; its mood is that of the native tribes who came from
> Atlantis to Mexico, when Atlantis was a great midocean island, whose
> glories have long since been clothed in myth and legend. (Somers n.d.)

Despite this appeal to the mythical quality of contemporary Native American culture, Somers insists on labeling "Dance of the Cave Man" the result of Elie's face-to-face encounter with Indian people in the Americas:

> "His country" is Haiti, but Elie studied at the Paris Conservatory. An
> investigation of 10 years was given over by him to the study of primitive

music; he lived with the primitive tribes, heard their chants, learned their instruments, and transcribed their rituals and ceremonials. His "Dance of the Cavemen" is the result of that study. (Somers n.d.)

Despite the fact that Elie did not "live with primitive tribes," and that "Dance of the Cave Man" was not based on any specific ethnographic content, the piece was marketed and interpreted as an ethnographically based art work, adding to its value in an Indian-crazed U.S. market.

Elie was able to parlay his success with *Kiskaya* into other employment opportunities as a composer. In May 1931, Elie negotiated an arrangement with the National Broadcasting Company to provide, conduct, and arrange music for a weekly radio program called "The Lure of the Tropics" on radio station WEAF in New York City ("Programs for Today" 1931). His compositions were also heard frequently in concerts by the United Service Orchestra, a radio orchestra that by 1931 had given fifty-three concerts of music by Latin American composers ("Service Orchestra Is Lauded" 1931). In addition, Elie provided music for silent films. Ray Hart, conductor of the Rialto Orchestra, used one of Elie's pieces as an overture to the 1925 film, *The Phantom of the Opera* (Somers n.d.). Elie also arranged other composers' works for silent films; Paramount Studios, for example, asked Elie to make an arrangement of Tchaikovsky's *Fifth Symphony*. According to Elie's daughter, Elie was asked to "make the music fancier" for the film-going audience and Elie was "heartbroken" at having to tamper with what he considered to be a "classic" composition.[13]

Unfortunately, the work that might have secured Elie's name in the memories of concert-going audiences in the United States was never published. His *Fantaisie Tropicale* (1930) is a single-movement work for piano that was first performed on 13 July 1930 by Bolivian pianist Lolita Cabrera in a concert sponsored by the General Electric Company (Dalencour 1983, 14).

Built in short, two-measure phrases that return with a great degree of regularity, this work (in C minor) is episodic, with four major themes being explored through a variety of pianistic techniques. It opens with a ponderous four-measure statement of the first theme in the orchestra, which roots the work in a minor mode and a relatively low tessitura. The piano responds with a series of chords that begin in the uppermost register and culminate in a rhythmic descent reminiscent of Grieg's *Piano Concerto in A Minor*. The piano and orchestra trade the opening theme, whose every appearance is made distinct with either stark octaves or expansive harmonies. The second theme appears first in the orchestra, invoking the syncopated feel of the Haitian méringue. A third theme also exploits the five-note pulse of the méringue quintolet. A fourth, more lyric theme provides a restful harmonic backdrop for the acrobatic piano part. It is developed through a series of variations, each successively more demanding for the performer. Later, this lyric theme is blended with the opening motive in an imitative (*fugato*) style in the orchestra. With two cadenzas at the end, the *Fantaisie Tropicale* closes with an exciting and technically demanding flourish.

In spite of its technical and artistic merits, *Fantaisie Tropicale* was never published due to Elie's sudden death on 3 December 1931 of a cerebral hemorrhage.[14] His body was sent to Haiti where it was buried at a ceremony officiated by Elie's friend and fellow musician, Occide Jeanty.

Moving to the United States undoubtedly gave Elie opportunities that he would not have had in Haiti. He performed regularly as a pianist in New York City; his music was performed with relative frequency and was warmly received in the U.S. musical press; he also worked in radio and silent film. In comparison with Ludovic Lamothe, who was known principally for parlor music—with its informal performances and small audience—Elie was able to work as a composer, arranger, conductor, and performer of his own works in a variety of concert settings. Unlike Lamothe, however, Elie's success as a musician was tied to his ability to navigate the artistic world of the United States, in which black composers were pushed toward writing works that identified them with exotic peoples and locales. While Elie brought an interest in Native American culture with him when he moved from Haiti to the United States, he was more concerned with entertaining audiences than with presenting himself as an expert on Indian music. Ironically, in the context of U.S. Indianist movements that valued "authentic" sources, Elie's compositions were promoted as the artistic result of ethnographic fieldwork, not as the creative musings of a composer exploring the cultural resources of his native country.

Ludovic Lamothe and Justin Elie turned to the music and culture of their homeland to create a Haitian musical legacy. Lamothe tried to harvest the unique and universal qualities of Vodou songs and the méringue respectively to create a Haitian "national music" with limited success due to his isolation from international audiences. Elie's artistic vision was constrained by audience expectations and by employment restrictions based on his race. Elie was, like the U.S.-based African American composers of his day, expected to conform to white racial expectations, particularly a penchant for the exotic.

~4~
VISIONS OF VODOU
IN AFRICAN AMERICAN
OPERAS ABOUT HAITI

Ouanga *and* Troubled Island

amulet

In 1928, African American composer Clarence Cameron White
(1879–1960) and librettist John Frederick Matheus (1887–1983)
made a six-week trip to Haiti in search of musical materials for an opera.
Their work, entitled *Ouanga*,[1] chronicled the rise and fall of Jean-Jacques
Dessalines, one of the leaders of the 1804 Haitian Revolution. White
finished the score to the opera in 1932 after receiving a Julius Rosenwald
fellowship to study in Paris with Raoul Laparra. The opera was first performed in concert version in 1932 in Chicago, but was not staged until
1949 when the Harry T. Burleigh Musical Association gave a performance of the work in South Bend, Indiana. In 1950, the opera received
a performance by the Dra-Mu Negro Opera Company in Philadelphia,
and in 1955 the opera was staged at Xavier University in New Orleans.
In 1956, the National Negro Opera Company performed concert versions of *Ouanga* at the Metropolitan Opera and at Carnegie Hall in New
York City.

In 1931, Langston Hughes (1902–67) visited Haiti for a six-month
vacation and wrote several articles based on his experiences, as well as
sketches for a play that would eventually be called *Emperor of Haiti*. Like
Matheus's libretto for *Ouanga*, Hughes's play depicted the exploits of
Jean-Jacques Dessalines and ended with Dessalines's murder at the hand
of his political rivals. In 1936, Hughes was approached by composer
William Grant Still (1895–1978) for a libretto; Hughes offered Still his play
about Haiti and by 1938 a version of the drama, renamed *Troubled Island*,
was nearly ready for production. After Still spent ten years searching for
a production venue for the opera, *Troubled Island* opened in 1949 with
Laszlo Halasz at the New York City Center of Music and Drama.

In spite of the early recognition accorded *Ouanga*, which won the David
Bispham medal in 1932 and was performed at the most prestigious

U.S. venue for opera, *Ouanga* has gone unperformed since 1956. *Troubled Island* fared even worse, receiving only three performances. Their spotty performance histories are not surprising; many dramatic works for the musical stage have suffered similar fates, and those by black artists have been discontinued with alacrity (Baker et al. 1978). What makes *Ouanga* and *Troubled Island* important for this study is the extent to which they embody a felt connection between Africa, the United States, and Haiti.

An analysis of *Ouanga* and *Troubled Island* as products of diasporic cultural processes subverts prevailing discourses about Africans in the diaspora. As Paul Gilroy points out, black diasporic culture has most often been described in totalizing ways that range from essentialist positions that avoid differences of time and place to the nationalist conceptions of Africans only in relation to particular nation-states. The problem with both essentialist and nationalist positions is that they provide little discursive space to explore the interconnectedness of the black experience while remaining cognizant of different national and political contexts. Gilroy characterizes both these positions as being more concerned with "roots" (associated with origins and essence) rather than the more fluid and malleable "routes" (associated with movement) (Gilroy 1993, 19).

White, Matheus, and Hughes made trips that were part research expedition, or "musical pilgrimage" as White termed it (White 1929, 505), and part tourist vacation. As such, their journeys demonstrate the ways in which people in the African diaspora forged ties with each other across political and linguistic boundaries through a form of cultural tourism (Clifford 1997). However, White, Matheus, and Hughes were not simply cultural voyeurs intent on exploiting Haitian culture for their personal gain. Each artist was committed in his own way to bringing Haiti's plight during the U.S. occupation to the attention of an African American audience. By turning to the elite artistic model of opera as a vehicle to address common concerns among black people, these African American artists engaged in what I term "diasporic cosmopolitanism."

The Haitian Revolution makes a perfect focal point for diasporic cosmopolitanism because of its symbolic significance to blacks in Haiti and the United States. *Ouanga* and *Troubled Island* are important for their dramatizations of the Haitian Revolution, whose symbolic importance to Haitians and African Americans cannot be overstated. The first time black people established a nation-state based on the abolition of slavery was understandably important, yet the Haitian Revolution was not historically valued to the same degree by dominant historiography as the contemporaneous eighteenth-century revolutions in France and the United States. Michel-Rolph Trouillot suggests that the Haitian Revolution's relative unimportance to historians until recently is a function of its challenge to eighteenth-century logic. The Haitian Revolution was, according to Trouillot, unthinkable for most white historians:

> The unthinkable is that which one cannot conceive within the range of possible alternatives, that which perverts all answers because it defies the terms under which the questions were phrased. In that sense, the Haitian Revolution was unthinkable in its time: it challenged the very framework within which proponents and opponents had examined race, colonialism, and slavery in the Americas. (Trouillot 1995, 82–83)

When white historians did think about the Haitian Revolution, they focused on those parts of the chronicle that were imaginable to them, that is, how whites wished black protagonists to be. For example, most of the literature in English inspired by the Haitian Revolution has tended to feature Toussaint Louverture, one of the first leaders of the slave insurrection. Louverture—a free, literate coachman on the Breda plantation—eventually became a general in the insurrectionary army. He was taken prisoner by a ruse in January 1802 and sent to the Joux Prison in eastern France, where he died shortly before the declaration of Haitian independence in 1804. White historians' accounts of Louverture's dramatic persona emphasized his willingness to collaborate with his rivals, his belief in the plantation system, and his mercy toward individual slave owners.

Ouanga and *Troubled Island,* however, focus on the story of Jean-Jacques Dessalines, the Haitian general who led Haiti to independence and who was himself born a slave. During the nineteenth century, most U.S. accounts of the two Haitian generals compared Dessalines unfavorably with Louverture. While Louverture embodied "stability and forgiveness," Dessalines was "the sinister figure representing a long line of violent, vengeful rulers" (Hunt 1988, 91). Historian Alfred Hunt describes an 1848 article in which Louverture was pitted against Dessalines:

> In this fictional and emotional account, Dessalines captured Toussaint's former master after Toussaint had helped him escape. Toussaint pleaded for his former master's life, but Dessalines replied, "He must perish because he is white. His color is his guilt." Dessalines then killed the planter, and a grief-stricken Toussaint resigned from the army. Dessalines was then accused of betraying Toussaint to the French, and of ordering that all whites be slain. He was finally assassinated by his own men, who rejoiced that "the tyrant is no more." ("Dessalines and Toussaint L'Ouverture" 1848; quoted in Hunt 1988, 91)

In this account, Dessalines embodied ferocity, cruelty, and vengeance, qualities most feared by whites in the United States. By comparing Dessalines with Louverture, white writers were able to emphasize those qualities that made Dessalines so fearsome and, by contrast, to bring out those traits in Louverture that were considered positive.

By choosing a dramatic subject whose reputation as a fierce defender of black sovereignty pitted him against the white oppressor, Matheus and Hughes positioned their respective libretti as alternatives to the narrative of Louverture's tragic legacy. Dessalines, whose revolutionary battle cry was "koupe tèt, boule kay" (cut heads and burn houses), invoked the idea of black national identity without assuaging white audiences.

White fear of Haiti had deep roots. As the only republic founded on a successful slave revolt, Haiti has long symbolized the threat of black rebellion. Nineteenth-century white American writers, fond of stressing Haiti's so-called exoticism and primitivism, depicted Haiti as a degenerate and dangerous place, an example of what could happen if black people were given equal rights with whites. In the twentieth century, works such as John Houston Craige's *Black Baghdad* (1933) and *Cannibal Cousins* (1934) continued the earlier trend by giving lurid secondhand accounts of religious practices that included human sacrifice and cannibalism.

For African American writers, however, Haiti has served primarily as an inspirational example, representing courage in the face of adversity, strength to overcome the yoke of colonial domination, and the assertion of an African-based culture as a valuable and potent heritage. Most of the inspiration of Haiti's history came from the country's successful struggle for independence from France. Haitian armies, led first by Toussaint Louverture and then by Jean-Jacques Dessalines and Henri Christophe, defeated Napoleon's troops with a combination of guerrilla tactics and tropical disease, and, in 1804, Haiti proclaimed its independence.

Haiti was not, however, an unambiguous symbol of black resistance against white imperialism. While the story of the revolution and the victory of poorly armed slaves over the most powerful army in Europe gave hope to African Americans before emancipation, the subsequent treatment of Haiti by its former European colonizers, as well as by the United States, showed African Americans that the price of freedom included eternal vigilance against white oppression. Despite the fact that General Dessalines's armies defeated the French forces during the Haitian war for independence, France sued the new Haitian republic for war damages, forcing the decimated national treasury to pay 150 million francs, effectively wiping out Haiti's meager financial resources (Nicholls 1979, 65).

In addition, political strife in Haiti during the nineteenth century eroded the inspirational value of the Haitian Revolution in the minds of African Americans. Fourteen of twenty-six Haitian presidents before 1915 were ousted in coups d'état (Paquin 1983, 270–71).

African American intellectuals had a difficult time reconciling the positive values of Haitian anticolonialism with the country's tumultuous politics (Plummer 1982, 127). Its religious practices were also a stumbling block since Vodou was considered by white and black Americans as little more than a superstition that compounded the political problems of the country. Their view of Vodou was not so different from that of Haitian elites prior to the revaluation of Vodou in the early twentieth century.

As Haitian intellectuals struggled to understand their relationship with the cultural practices of the Haitian rural underclass, African American artists and writers became interested in Haiti as a symbol of black distinctiveness in the Americas. Literary critic J. Michael Dash has noted that the view of Haiti as a repository for African cultural traits made Haiti the focus of a new, negrophilic form of cultural representation:

> Haiti features as a theme, a referent for racial and cultural stereotypes that satisfied ideological and exotic needs among many adherents in the New Negro Movement of the 1920s and 1930s. Haiti became overvalued because of its earthiness, its exuberance, its spirituality. It was the most persuasive illustration of a racial *Geist,* invoked by many black intellectuals of the New Negro Movement. (Dash 1988, 55)

Unfortunately, the very traits of spontaneity and sensuality that were extolled by African American writers were interpreted by white writers as a sign of Haitian barbarism and bestiality, albeit as an antidote to white intellectualism. White, Matheus, Hughes, and Still eschewed these overtly racist depictions of Haitian culture, believing that their works would help dispel negative associations about Haiti.

While *Ouanga* and *Troubled Island* have similar plots, they differ in several respects. In *Ouanga,* a Vodou priest punishes Dessalines with a magic curse or *ouanga* for turning his back on the Vodou heritage of his newly founded country. Vodou's prominent role in Dessalines's downfall reflects elites' interest in and ambivalence toward Haitian peasant culture. What is most significant about *Ouanga* is that it dramatically juxtaposes elite and peasant musical ideas in ways that challenge simplistic critiques of the opera as sensationalistic. *Ouanga* was the first opera to feature a range of Haitian musical genres that transcended class boundaries. While White's renderings of Vodou ceremonial music relied on notions borrowed from Haitian elites, *Ouanga*'s use of Vodou as the catalyst of Dessalines's downfall was revolutionary because it credited a religious practice associated with the lower classes with tremendous political power.

In *Troubled Island,* Vodou is an important dramatic device but is less prominent than in *Ouanga.* Hughes, whose political sensibilities inclined him to reject black elites' view of Haitian peasant culture, recast Dessalines's story as a critique of racial and class prejudice within black society. In *Troubled Island,* the dark-skinned Dessalines is betrayed by his light-skinned army officers and his white wife, Claire Heureuse. Whereas *Ouanga* depicts the struggle of the Haitian Revolution as dependent upon the Haitian people coming to terms with their Vodou heritage, a heritage that is simultaneously important yet threatening to the new nation, *Troubled Island* presents Vodou primarily as spectacle. Rather than depict Vodou as a factor in the historical conflict, the opera uses Vodou to add cultural flavor to a more deeply rooted class conflict. Both operas reflect the efforts of African American artists to translate the inspirational story of the Haitian Revolution to a broader diasporic audience even as they reveal the limits of cultural tourism.

During the nineteenth century, middle-class African American travelers joined the ranks of tourists in search of new experiences, refreshment from their routines, and rejuvenation from the pressures of everyday life. As Carla Peterson has shown in her study of African American women speakers and writers from the northern United States, African Americans "on tour" not only wrote about their travel experiences but also used writing as a means to critique social injustice and to identify themselves with their subjects (Peterson 1995, 88–118).

As tourists, African American travelers like White, Matheus, and Hughes enjoyed some of the status accorded foreigners when traveling abroad, yet they were frequently excluded from the privileges accorded white travelers.[2] Their "hybrid" status (Peterson 1995, 9) as members of an educated African American elite who were still subject to the same inequities and injustices as their poorer and less educated brothers and sisters put White and Matheus in a complex position. They were real participants in an ongoing effort to contribute to the "racial uplift" of all African Americans regardless of class association. Their efforts to draw on the historical example of the Haitian Revolution and its subsequent defeat of European colonial power could be viewed as an anticolonialist critique that holds up Haiti as an African liberation from European domination. However, as educated African American artists turning their attention to the historical and artistic significance of Haiti, they repeated many of the commonly held Haitian elite misconceptions about lower-class Haitian culture, especially about Haitian Vodou.

RESEARCHING *OUANGA*

For both White and Matheus, travel was a logical extension of their previously formed interest in the artistic and cultural life of Africans in the United States and elsewhere. Their connections with other parts of the African diaspora were formed in their student days, when both men were introduced to the accomplishments and hardships of their fellow African-descended artists. Like many aspiring African American composers of his generation, White followed the career of Samuel Coleridge-Taylor, the famous Afro-English composer who wrote *Hiawatha's Wedding Feast* (1898). Coleridge-Taylor first visited the United States in 1904 at the behest of the Samuel Coleridge-Taylor Society of Washington, D.C., an organization formed in 1901 by Arthur Hilyer to promote music by and for black people. Black American musicians considered Coleridge-Taylor a fine example of a composer who, despite personal hardship due to racial prejudice in his native England, managed to enjoy a successful career. During his United States tour, Coleridge-Taylor met Clarence Cameron White and encouraged the young White to pursue his dream of becoming a composer. White eventually went to London to study with Coleridge-Taylor for three years. After his work with Coleridge-Taylor, White became interested in the folksongs and spirituals of African Americans. Coleridge-Taylor's inspiration to turn to the "folk music of the American Negro" came, interestingly enough, from his reading of W. E. B. Du Bois's *The Souls of Black Folk* (1903). White's interest in black folk music was thus the product of a trans-Atlantic fertilization of ideas.

White's travel to Europe and his subsequent interest in the music of the African Americans in the southern United States is reminiscent of the principal character in James Weldon Johnson's *The Autobiography of an Ex-Colored Man*, first published in 1912. Johnson's narrator—who is unnamed in the book—discovers an affinity with the music of southern black people after an extended tour of Europe. Upon hearing a white performer turn the music of "rag-time" into a classical-sounding piano composition, Johnson's narrator longs to return to the United States to prove his abilities as a translator of black music for a wider audience. He states:

> I made up my mind to go back to the very heart of the South, to live among the people, and drink in my inspiration firsthand. I gloated over the immense amount of material I had to work with, not only modern rag-time, but also the old slave songs—material which no one had touched. (Johnson 1927, 471)

Upon his return to the United States, White pursued his interest in African American folksong, writing *Bandana Sketches* (1918), *From the*

Cotton Fields (1920), and *Forty Negro Spirituals* (1927). He became increasingly interested in providing folksong material for other composers to fashion a new "American School of Composition" based on black folk idioms (White 1927, 81). Haiti provided a ready source for White's musical needs. It was very close to the United States and could be visited at a reasonable cost. Haiti was also considered to have more African cultural retentions than any other country in the Americas. Its largely rural population made it a logical choice for research into folk music traditions.

Haiti also had a long history that was well known to many African Americans. John Matheus recounted how he first heard the story of Haitian general Toussaint Louverture from a Stubenville, Ohio publisher of a Garveyite newspaper called *The Equator:*

> I was still in what was called grammar school when I heard for the first time Wendell Phillips's panegyric to Toussaint L'Ouverture, Haitian general, statesman, and hero. I was wonderfully impressed. . . . It was Fleetwood Walker who told me the story of Toussaint L'Ouverture who always opened the ranks of the enemy and never lost a battle. I began to read about him in all the books available to me. The Haitian Revolution gradually unfolded. (Matheus 1972, 429)

But to understand the use Matheus and White were to make of this inspiring history, we must recall the politically complex relationship between Haiti and the United States, particularly during the era of the U.S. occupation.

The invasion of Haiti on 28 July 1915 by the United States Marines helped focus African American attention on the plight of their Haitian neighbors. Among other displays of military muscle, U.S. Marines put groups of peasants and political insurgents on labor gangs called *corvée,* forcing them to work on public works projects. With the suspension of the Haitian constitution in 1918, Haitians were reminded of their subordinate status during the colonial period under France (Plummer 1982).

During the first few years of the occupation of Haiti, African American groups became increasingly critical of the military intervention. James Weldon Johnson, field secretary of the National Association for the Advancement of Colored People (NAACP), made a trip to Haiti in 1920 to assess the effects of the occupation on Haitians (Plummer 1982, 132). Johnson used his influence at the NAACP to press the Harding administration to include black representatives in commissions to Haiti for the investigation of abuses by the United States forces. Despite pressure from the NAACP, President Harding appointed only one black member to the committee: Napoleon Marshall, a captain in the United States Army.

Captain Marshall and his wife, Harriet Gibbs Marshall, invited Clarence Cameron White to visit them in Haiti toward the end of their tour in 1928. White knew Harriet Gibbs Marshall from his days at the Washington Conservatory of Music and School of Expression in Washington, D.C. Gibbs Marshall, the first black music graduate from Oberlin College (1889), was the first director of the Conservatory and brought White there to head the string department (McGinty 1979; Terry 1977).

During their time in Haiti, the Marshalls were socially and politically marginalized. As the only black member of the investigative commission, Capt. Marshall was excluded from most social functions and was forbidden to enter the segregated American Club, a privilege usually allowed to U.S. military officers (Plummer 1982, 135, n. 54). Perhaps as a result of their exclusion from U.S. social functions, the Marshalls became very active in voluntary associations within Haiti, forging friendships with their Haitian hosts. Harriet Gibbs Marshall worked with Haitian women and served as the Vice President for the Organization of Haitian Women (Marshall 1930, 5).[3]

After their departure from Haiti, the Marshalls became outspoken critics of the occupation and began the Save Haiti Committee, an organization whose purpose was to send 50,000 signatures to President Herbert Hoover to demand the withdrawal of United States troops. White became a member of the Save Haiti Committee upon his return to the United States, raising funds for educational projects and teachers' salaries.

White's and Matheus's visit to Haiti in 1928 thus came at a turbulent time in Haitian-United States relations. African American organizations were becoming more vociferous in their condemnation of what they considered to be an unjust and inhumane military campaign against Haiti. Groups like the NAACP were also using Haiti as an analogue to their own situation in the United States, likening the disenfranchisement of poor Haitian voters to the fate of poor black people in the southern United States. As educators, White and Matheus felt a special responsibility to bring the story of the Haitian people to audiences in the United States and to promote a change in U.S. foreign policy towards Haiti.

Ouanga was a collaborative effort by White and Matheus, but the work was first envisioned by J. "Fred" Matheus after he joined the faculty of the West Virginia Collegiate Institute, a historically black college located in the town of Institute, just outside Charleston, West Virginia. Matheus joined the romance language faculty in 1922, and White came in 1924 to teach violin in the music department.

Matheus had been interested in Haiti before his acquaintance with White; he had even written a story about Toussaint Louverture (Matheus n.d.). Originally, Matheus intended to write a one-act play about Haiti, set in the present. The play was to be a comedy entitled *Tambour* (French for "drum") to be set in Haiti during the United States occupation of the country. White intended to contribute incidental music to the drama in the form of a *méringue*, a dance form enjoyed by elite Haitian audiences since the nineteenth century.[4] As their talks about collaborating progressed, Matheus and White realized that they lacked background about the proper execution of Haitian dance. Matheus later recalled:

> In our dialogues Mr. White and I knew that an outstanding feature for the success of the opera would be the dances. Choreography must supplement group and solo singing. There would be arias and choruses, drums, rhythmic motion and frenzied dancing. We must catch an authentic local color. It became imperative that we go to Haiti in person. We could hear the songs, see the dances, catch the spirit of the African mood. (Matheus 1972, 433)

On 7 August 1928, White, Matheus and White's son William sailed to Port-au-Prince from New York City aboard the Ancon, a ship on the Panama Railroad Steamship Line.

Upon their arrival in Haiti, White and Matheus met with Captain Napoleon Marshall and Harriet Gibbs Marshall. As *chargé d'affairs* for the United States government, Marshall was in a position to introduce White and Matheus to a significant number of Haitian dignitaries, including the former Haitian president François-Denis Légitime and the current president, Louis Borno. The Marshalls also facilitated their visitors' contact with members of the Haitian elite, especially those people who were working on projects that were not under the auspices of the occupation government. Matheus reported that he and White met the editors of most of the important Haitian newspapers, including *Le Nouvelliste* and *Le Temps*. One of the editors refused to speak English, stating "Moi, je ne parle jamais cette langue de cochons!" (I never speak that language of pigs) (Matheus 1972, 435–36). Fortunately, Matheus's background as a French professor allowed the pair to conduct their visits in a language more amenable to their Haitian hosts.

Although Matheus and White were officially in Haiti to collect material for their opera, White took the opportunity to perform a violin recital on 8 September 1928 at the Théâtre Parisiana in Port-au-Prince as a way to raise money for local charities. The proceeds from the recital went to the Comité de Secours pour les Sinistrés du Département du Sud and to the Association des Femmes Haitiennes pour l'Organisation du Travail ("Générosité" 1928). White performed several works, including two pieces by Samuel Coleridge-Taylor: the "Ballade in C minor" and his "Danse Africaine." White also performed several of his own compositions, including an adaptation of an African American work song ("Chanson du Travail"), a piece inspired by the Louisiana bayou country ("Sur le Bayou"), and two pieces with programmatic links to African or black identity ("Chant Nègre" and "Danse Nègre") ("Le concert de M. Cameron White" 1928; "Le récital du compositeur White à Parisiana" 1928).

As a result of his generosity, White was lauded in the Haitian press. Flattering reviews referred to his physique as well as his playing ability. Other references to White's education, his fame as a composer, his talent on the violin, and his light skin color served to identify him as a person of good *formation,* a French word used by Haitians to refer to a person's breeding and social standing. White was, by virtue of his training, appearance, and vocation, an honorary member of Haiti's upper class. According to one newspaper account:

> Mr. Cameron White has a handsome, sympathetic, round and good head. Crinkling hairs that are graying. A generously smiling face, but one that contracts and hides his smile when he plays the violin. Elegant, well dressed. [He has] the torso of a singer. The body of a baritone. He leaves the impression that one has seen him somewhere. Better still, that one has joked with him. ("Le concert de M. Cameron White" 1928)

While Matheus and White were able to move easily within the social circles of the Haitian elite, they were most interested in observing the musical habits of Haitian lower-class rural workers or *abitan* who were, in White's and Matheus's views, the keepers of "the spirit of the African mood" and the focus of their research. Their access to people in the lower socio-economic strata of Haitian society, especially those who practiced Vodou, was limited. Haitian president Borno was vehemently anti-Vodou and used the Haitian army to stamp out Vodou activity throughout the country (Heinl and Heinl 1978, 485). Vodou ceremonies attended by tourists and United States military officers tended to be staged representations of worship services and stressed the more spectacular varieties of possession trance. Captain Marshall arranged for White and Matheus to attend a staged Vodou ceremony or "voodoo show" and helped White negotiate a price for a pair of ceremonial drums to be used in the opera's premiere ("Clarence Cameron White Returns from Haiti" 1928).

Despite the fact that White and Matheus were in Haiti to gather information about music associated with rural life in general and the Vodou ceremony in particular, they left little record of their contact with members of the rural underclass. White did, however, keep a photograph scrapbook of their trip in which he pasted pictures taken during their tours around the country. White's photographic documentation consists entirely of tourist snapshots. Most of the photographs were of buildings, such as the Cathedral of Saint Marc, statues of the figures of the Haitian Revolution, namely Toussaint Louverture and Jean-Jacques Dessalines, or of individuals White and Matheus visited, such as the Marshalls and the George Price family (White 1928). They also visited the Citadelle Laferrière, one of the most frequently visited tourist sites in Haiti. Built in the early nineteenth century by the emperor of northern Haiti, Henri Christophe, the Citadelle was intended to defend the new Haitian republic from a reinvasion by French forces. The fortress sits on the summit of the mountain called "Bishop's Bonnet" and takes several hours to reach on foot. White had a picture taken of himself at the Citadelle while sitting atop a donkey, the preferred mode of tourist transportation to and from the fortress even today.

White, his son William, and Matheus all returned to the United States aboard the steamship *Luna* and arrived in New York City on 24 September 1928. Matheus managed to finish a draft of the libretto in 1929 that was tentatively called *Cocomacaque: A Drama of Haiti* (Matheus 1929b).[5] *Cocomacaque* begins with a musical prologue by the spirit of Toussaint Louverture, the Haitian general who was captured by the French and imprisoned in France. Toussaint's song chronicles the African experience in the Americas from the first slaves landing on the shores of Saint-Domingue, or colonial Haiti, to the inevitable slave uprising. Dessalines's assassination, foreshadowed in the prologue, is attributed to his abandoning the "sacred Laws," a reference to the *lwas* (French "*loas*") or spirits of the Vodou religious tradition. There were several versions of the opera, one in 1932 titled *Ouanga!* (with an exclamation point) (White and Matheus 1932) and one in 1955 titled *Ouanga* (without punctuation) (White and Matheus 1955). This chapter focuses on the 1955 version because of its sharp focus on the importance of Vodou in the Haitian struggle for independence.

OUANGA AND THE DIVERSITY OF HAITIAN MUSICAL STYLES

The 1955 version of *Ouanga* demonstrates the importance of White's and Matheus's trip to Haiti to gather ethnographic materials. By incorporating the range of Haitian musical styles they encountered on their trip, their opera shows a mingling of cross-class musical forms, from the music of the Vodou ceremony to the Haitian parlor méringue.

Act I, scene I of *Ouanga* begins at a midnight Vodou ceremony on a mountaintop near Cap Haïtien. The worshippers call to the Vodou spirit

Legba to hear their prayer. The worshippers shout "Legba, ybo le a le o," a phrase in *langaj*, the coded ancestral African language spoken by Vodou initiates. Mougali, the *manbo* or female Vodou priest, enters and makes a direct plea to Legba to help alleviate the misery of the Haitian people, a misery she attributes to the "tyrant" Dessalines:

> Mougali.　O Legba! Serpent guardian, Hear us.
> 　　　　　We bring Thee gifts
> 　　　　　We bow before Thee, glorious One, All powerful!
> 　　　　　Thy stroke is like the lighting,
> 　　　　　Thy strength is like the hills!
> 　　　　　Accept the gifts Thy children bring,
> 　　　　　Show Thy pow'r, o hissing serpent.
> 　　　　　Drive the tyrant from our shores!
> Chorus (shouting).　At him we cast the magic word,
> 　　　　　The lightning word, the word of cursing.
> 　　　　　Ouanga! Ouanga! Ouanga! Ouanga!
> 　　　　　(White and Matheus 1955, 24–27)

The Vodou spirit Legba, the guardian of the crossroads and the intermediary between the material and spiritual world, is conflated with Danbala, a Vodou spirit associated with snakes. Mougali and the worshippers call upon Legba to "drive the tyrant" Dessalines from Haiti's shores and to put a magical curse or *ouanga* on him. Mougali and her followers end their denunciation of Dessalines with a chant (see ex. 4.1).

> Eh! Eh! Bomba Hen! Bomba Hen!
> Canga bafaté,
> Canga dokila.
> (31–33)

Dessalines enters and curses the Vodou practitioners:

> You lazy ones! You will not work!
> All night you dance in the moonlight.
> All day you sleep in the sun!
> Your fields are empty and barren.
> The freedom of Haiti is yours now,
> Accept the new law and cast away
> your enslaving folly!
> (33–35)

While Mougali and the Vodou followers call for a return to the sacred "loas" [lwa] or spirits of Haitian Vodou as the basis of the new Haitian

Example 4.1. *Ouanga* (1955), act 1, sc. 1, page 31

nation, Dessalines demands that secular laws, not "loas," should be the driving force of the new state.

Défilée, a slave woman who was once Dessalines's common-law wife, tries to stop Mougali from casting the ouanga on Dessalines. She argues that Dessalines will return to the way of the spirits if given enough time. Dessalines, impressed with Défilée's courage but not dissuaded by her reasoning, asserts that he is destined to lead his race to glory. Dessalines

Example 4.2. *Ouanga* (1955), "Silhouette 'Congo Dance,'" page 49

leaves and Mougali finishes casting the ouanga as the worshippers perform the "Bomba hen!" chant.

White's and Matheus's use of the "Bomba hen!" chant demonstrated their awareness of Haitian history. The chant was reportedly used at the 1791 ceremony of Bois-Caïman and was often attributed to Boukman Dutty, one of the important leaders of the slave revolt. White and Matheus probably saw the chant in Price-Mars's *Ainsi parla l'oncle* (1928/1983,

111). Price-Mars reproduced the chant from Moreau de Saint-Méry's *Description topographique, physique, civile, politique et historique de la partie française de l'isle Saint-Domingue* (Moreau de Saint-Méry 1797, 1:46–50), the earliest known published description of Vodou. As a representation of Vodou practices current during the Haitian Revolution, White's use of the chant is similar to Moreau de Saint-Méry's version.[6]

Between scenes in act 1, White included an instrumental entr'acte that featured a "Congo dance" at midnight on Bonnet d'Evêque (Bishop's Bonnet), as well as a Congo dance in "silhouette" for a cadenza of "three Voodoo drums, pebble shaker and struck steel bar" (pp. 49–51) (see ex. 4.2). These elements show White's efforts to incorporate the ethnographic insights from his and Matheus's trip to Haiti into the opera. The musical ensemble's instruments (three drums, shaker, and struck steel bar) are commonly associated with the Rada nanchon or denomination of spirits; the steel bar provides a rhythmic ostinato for the more rhythmically complex drum parts. This rhythmic "cadenza" also demonstrates some of the problems of reproducing a predominantly improvisatory and interactive musical genre with musical notation. The "voodoo drums" are notated on a single line, despite the fact that drum ensembles performing "Congo Dances" are usually performed with three drums playing independent musical lines. This example is not based on a "Congo Dance" from Haiti; it is a newly composed guide for percussionists unfamiliar with the drumming style. Still, White's effort to create a musical interlude with a connection to Haitian musical practices is noteworthy.

Act 1, scene 2, begins in 1804 in a clearing near a banana grove, just ten months after Dessalines's army drove the French forces from Haitian soil. Défilée hides in a nearby hut while Licité, a young dark-skinned peasant woman, meets Michel, a light-skinned soldier in the Haitian army and Licité's potential suitor. Michel announces that Dessalines will soon be crowned King of Haiti and that Vodou will be outlawed under the new regime. Défilée sings an aria expressing her love for Dessalines and her fear that the ouanga will retaliate against him. Dessalines enters and is moved by Défilée's love; she begs him to reconsider his position against Vodou. Dessalines expresses his fear that Vodou is coming between him and Défilée:

> For as a snake works its way beneath the ground,
> the Ouanga would try to coil itself
> about us and crush our hearts.
> Oh God! Save us both from dangers.
> (73–74)

Example 4.3. *Ouanga* (1955), "Ballet," act 2, page 98

Dessalines's aspirations to lead his country to glory overpower his desire to follow the path of Vodou; he asks Défilée to turn her back on the spirits and be his queen. She refuses and he bids her "adieu."

Act 2 begins in the public square of Cap Haïtien. Vendors hawk their wares with a chorus of street cries for everything from "café and sugar" to "calabash, sweet cakes, and gingerbread!" (82–85). As Mougali enters the

Example 4.4. Quintolet rhythm

square and asks the vendors for news, the sound of the cathedral choir in the background foreshadows Dessalines's upcoming coronation and his wedding to Claire Heureuse, a light-skinned woman from the upper class.

Dessalines's coronation and wedding not only marks the dramatic high point of the opera but also underscores Clarence Cameron White's artistic vision of Haitian cultural complexity. Dessalines's official status as emperor is reinforced by the visual and sonic support of the Catholic church. As Mougali and her supporters gather outside the cathedral, an offstage choir sings a Te Deum in the sanctuary. A second offstage choir praises the new emperor, singing "All Hail great Dessalines, All Hail." As both choirs exchange praises for the emperor, Dessalines, his new wife, Claire Heureuse, and a white priest named Father Brelle exit the cathedral and are greeted by the crowd. Dessalines tells the crowd that "happiness is now within our grasp; Peace will prevail with liberty!" (96–97).

A "ballet" ensues with a group of dancers performing to a Haitian *méringue lente,* or slow méringue, a favorite dance of the Haitian elite in the early twentieth century (see ex. 4.3). Like most Haitian méringues, the dance in *Ouanga* features the syncopated quintolet rhythm (see ex. 4.4). However, unlike most Haitian méringues in which the quintolet switches between the bass and treble registers, White's méringue quintolet remains in the bass clef for most of the dance. Perhaps this is due to the presence of vocal parts for the men's and women's choruses; most *méringues lentes* are purely instrumental. Nevertheless, the characteristic rendering of the quintolet rhythm was probably helped by White's familiarity with the music of the most renowned Haitian méringue composer for the piano, Ludovic Lamothe ("Le violoniste C. C. White" n.d.).

The méringue ballet is followed by a "Festival Dance," a duple meter quickstep at a considerably faster tempo (quarter note = 160) in which a second group of dancers performs for Dessalines and his entourage. The third dance group performs a "Dance Congo" in which a modified méringue rhythm is performed in 4/8 meter at a slightly slower tempo (eighth note = 126). The music for this "Dance Congo" is very different from the "Dance Congo" in act 1, indicating that White's use of the term "Congo" is simply a way to distinguish one specific dance as having lower-class, rural origins. All three dances—the méringue, the festival dance, and the Congo—demonstrate White's attention to ethnographic detail and his desire to include the diversity of Haitian musical styles in the opera.

As the dancers interrupt each other in a friendly competition, they each try to gain the attention of the emperor. Suddenly, Mougali and her entourage interrupt the festivities and tell Dessalines:

> Death to all who desert the faith!
> Death to him who turns against his loved one
> 'Gainst her who sings to him so sweetly in the palm grove.
> (pp. 109)

Dessalines shouts "seize the witch!" as Défilée rises to defend Mougali. Défilée channels the spirits as she condemns Dessalines to his fate:

> I am the aftermath that follows for him
> who sows the whirlwind.
> I am the scourge! The pestilence, The plague!
> . . . .
> Time was I loved him,
> Now, I go to chant his funeral dirge.
> (114–18)

Mougali, who has been hauled away by Dessalines's soldiers, is shot offstage. The church bell tolls and Dessalines tells the crowd that they are now truly free:

> Hear me, your bodies I have freed,
> ye are no longer slaves.
> I have killed once more to free your souls!
> (120–21)

Father Brelle, the white priest who presided over Dessalines's coronation, offers a benediction for the murdered Mougali as the choir sings "take to Thine arms the soul of poor Mougali!" (123). Both the spirits of Vodou and the Catholic hierarchy have turned against Dessalines, setting the stage for Dessalines's downfall.

Act 3, scene 1, takes place in the hut of the Vodou worshippers; the papaloi (Vodou priest) faces the altar. The worshippers sing the "Bomba hen!" chant from act 1 as they invoke the ouanga against Dessalines. They follow the historically based "Bomba hen!" chant with a more theatrically oriented "Voodoo death dance" in which the chorus hisses like snakes, singing "Ouanga's strong! . . . Hist! Potent charm! . . . hist! Ouanga kills! . . . Hist!" (130) (see ex. 4.5).

Dessalines enters the hut and expresses his remorse for killing Mougali. Dessalines reminds the papaloi that he, too, has the blood of Africa in his veins and that they share a common destiny. However, Dessalines demands that the "old ways" of Vodou be rejected in favor of a new world

Example 4.5. *Ouanga* (1955), act 3, sc. 1, page 130

order that Dessalines himself will rule. The papaloi and the mourners make a line "in the form of a huge snake" (139). As they cast the ouanga upon him, Dessalines is unable to move; his sword drops from his hand and he leaves the hut quickly.

Act 3, scene 2 takes place on the Red Bridge, with several of Dessalines's former soldiers lying in ambush for the emperor. Some of his men have told him to meet Défilée on the Red Bridge for a lovers' tryst; they tell Défilée the same story to ensure her role as decoy for Dessalines. Gerin, one of the soldiers, tries to convince Défilée to help him murder Dessalines. Défilée resists Gerin at first, but then resigns herself to watching Dessalines's inevitable fate. Dessalines arrives and recalls his and Défilée's earlier romance; Défilée begs Dessalines to return to his Vodou heritage. Dessalines relents to Défilée's request, but it is too late; his former soldiers ambush him and stab him with bayonets. She throws herself on the dying Dessalines and says "tell the Voodoo his dauntless soul has fled" (160–61).

White and Matheus wrote *Ouanga* to bring the Haitian Revolution and its tragic black hero, Jean-Jacques Dessalines, to an international audience. By choosing Vodou as the dramatic catalyst for their drama, White and Matheus showed that Haitian elites could not turn their back on the needs of the lower classes without disastrous results. The opera set Haitian elites and peasants in a drama that included their respective musical genres; méringues for Haitian elites and Vodou-inspired ceremonial music. *Ouanga*'s use of ethnographically based musical and dramatic materials provided a hopeful example to African American audiences that a black republic held in low esteem by most white Americans could nonetheless inspire important classical art.

As artists traveling abroad for musical inspiration, White and Matheus were lauded by the African American press as opponents of the virulently racist depictions of Haiti by white researchers. An editorial in the *Pittsburgh Courier* stated:

> Most, if not practically all, of the information about the lands populated by Negroes has been gathered by white men and women. . . . Customs and characteristics common to certain social strata the world around, are elevated to the position of Negro traits, particularly if they are considered discreditable. Thus we are always told that the residents of black countries are lazy, ignorant, immoral, superstitious, and so forth, as if that were not true of the residents of every country. Few countries are free of illiteracy, and none is free of laziness, immorality and superstition. When an African witch doctor prays for rain, that is superstition; when an American clergyman prays for rain, that is Christian faith. If a Haitian peasant sacrifices a goat and drinks the blood, that is voodooism; if a Nordic takes the Holy Sacrament, that is Christian devotion. We are led to believe by these white workers and travelers that everything these Negroes do is silly, as compared to the activities of whites who, of course, are always wise.
>
> Thus, it is a great pleasure to learn that two Negro professors from West Virginia Collegiate Institute have gone to Haiti for six weeks to study the life and musical spirit of the black people there. . . . Both are well equipped for the task, and while their aim is purely artistic and not political, we can confidently look forward to an unbiased study of these courageous island people. ("Studying Haitian Life" n.d.)

Other African American newspaper accounts extolled White's and Matheus's attempt to fuse Haitian "atmosphere" with an "entirely original creation musically" ("Clarence Cameron White Returns from Haiti" n.d.). To African American readers, White and Matheus were on a mission to restore some degree of dignity and respect to a people who had been maligned by white society in the United States.

White was interested not only in correcting American stereotypes about Haiti but in doing primary research on music of the African diaspora. By the time he and Matheus made their trip to Haiti, White had already published an article entitled "The Labor Motif in Negro Music" in which he called African American folk music a "vast storehouse" that could provide the classical composer ample inspiration (White 1927). He was concerned, however, that the folk expression of African Americans had been diluted to some degree by historical circumstance. White thought that establishing a truly original, American music based on folk music required more research on the musical antecedents of black American music; he believed that Haitian music provided just such a pure, unadulterated African music. After the 1928 trip, White wrote the following:

> When one goes into a virgin field in search of folk music "one seems to go back to the very beginning of things, long before literature existed." Fortunate it is to find in this day a few primitive folk who have not departed from naturalness and who still hold fast to racial characteristics. A visit to the island of Haiti proves even more enlightening in this regard than the folk songs and dances of our own Negro folk in the American Southland. (White 1929, 505)

White's choice of language to describe his mission is worth noting. His examination of what he calls the "virgin field" of Haitian folk music is conceived of not only as an exploration of musical materials but also as a trip to a primitive past "long before literature existed." This tendency to view Haitian peasants or *abitan* as geographically and temporally distant from modern urban culture is a common theme in Haitian elite discourse (Largey 1994, 105–6; Trouillot 1990, 81).

Indeed, White echoed many Haitian elites and U.S. travel writers who viewed the *abitan* as representatives of a more so-called "primitive" African-based culture. Clarence Cameron White used such literature, relying on American travel writer Blair Niles's *Black Haiti* (1926) for his data on Haitian history and falling prey to the same stereotypes as Niles. *Black Haiti* casts the Haitian peasant as an unreflective and ignorant savage, but a savage with a heart. White's own description of a typical Haitian peasant reflects this attitude:

> In Haiti there are two types of peasant, the peasant of the day and the peasant of the night, physically one and the same but mentally and emotionally two separate beings. The characteristically staid peasant by

day sheds his dignity under the moon and sings and dances with aban-
don to the barbaric pulsing of the "tambour." (White 1929, 505)

Matheus also indulges himself in Dionysian prose about his and White's
visit to a staged Vodou ceremony during their trip:

> We go through a gate. After an interval we hear for the first time the rhy-
> thmic beat of the famous drums. The percussion of the tom-toms sum-
> mons Africa, the Congoland, Krus, Basutos, Kaffirs, Zulus, the myriads
> of warriors, the women and the children. This is indelibly Africa's
> music. No white man can claim it. Rub-a-dub, dub! Rub-a-dub, dub!
> Wild, saturnalian cries. (Matheus 1972, 436)

Despite these brief flights of fancy, both White and Matheus were
committed in their own ways to dispelling negative associations of Haiti
by creating a drama that featured a protagonist with agency. White recounted that several producers urged him and Matheus to make the opera a comedy, thus making it conform to white audiences' expectations of
black musical theater of the day. He retorted that "most assuredly,
Ouanga was not 'funny'" (Matheus n.d.).

After White and Matheus finished *Ouanga*, their professional paths di-
verged; however, their interest in the music and culture of the African diaspora continued to develop. Thus *Ouanga* was a catalyst for further
trans-Atlantic connections. Later in his career, White took up the directorship of the School of Music at the Hampton Institute, where he suc-
ceeded R. Nathaniel Dett. At Hampton, White developed a course in
"The History of Negro Music" which traced the development of black
music from Africa through songs of slaves in the U.S. and the folk music
of the West Indies (White 1935).

Matheus maintained his connection with other parts of the black Atlantic in a more tangible way. In 1930, he went to Liberia with Charles S. Johnson as part of a delegation from the League of Nations to investigate allegations of slavery against the Liberian government. Their inquest resulted
in charges against several Liberian officials (Saunders 1987, 26). Later,
Matheus lived in Haiti from 1945 until 1946 when he served as the director
of English teaching for the Commission Coopérative Haitiano-Américaine
d'Education. Matheus himself presented biweekly educational radio
broadcasts in English on Haitian radio station HH3W, calling his program
"L'Anglais sur les Ondes" (English on the Airwaves) (Matheus 1946).

Matheus also wrote several works about Africans in the diaspora, including "Ti Yette" (1930), a play about a young woman and her brother
who travel from the United States to Haiti, "Coulev' Endormi" (Sleeping

Serpent) (1929c), a short story about a dancer in a Port-au-Prince bar, a poem entitled "Belle Mam'selle of Martinique" about a light-skinned Caribbean woman living in Paris (1929a), and "Sallicoco" (1937), a short story depicting the plight of Liberians enslaved in work gangs.

While Matheus's depiction of Haitian culture may have been shaped partially by misconceptions about Haiti and about Vodou in particular, he incorporated his experience in Haiti into his later work, expanding his creative focus to include people from all parts of the black Atlantic. In Matheus's story "Citadelle" (1974), André Solon, a Haitian bibliophile, realizes that it is his destiny to write the story of the Haitian Revolution to correct foreign misperceptions and to turn Haiti into a positive example:

> He would pen a masterpiece that would blast the vicious tales circulating in Jamaica, in America, in Europe, that Haiti was a decadent, a failure. Mais, non! She had an illustrious past. From African seeds of long lost tribes had blossomed statesmen, orators, scholars, poets. The world would know. They must hear. It was the inspired resolution of a reborn soul. (Matheus 1974)

Like Matheus's own work, Solon's history is intended to transform Haiti's past into a contemporary resource for the "racial uplift" of all members of the diaspora.

RESEARCHING *TROUBLED ISLAND*

Like Clarence Cameron White and John Matheus, Langston Hughes traveled to Haiti seeking artistic inspiration for a play he had started writing in 1928 about Haitian emperor Jean-Jacques Dessalines. Hughes wrote that "after I made my first notes for the play I decided that I needed to know the scenery and atmosphere of Haiti before actually writing the play" (Hughes 1949). After receiving the Harmon Award for his novel *Not Without Laughter*, he took his $400 prize and set sail for the Caribbean in 1931 with his new friend Zell Ingram, a student at the Cleveland School of Art. Hughes was disheartened in 1931; his relationship with wealthy white patron Charlotte Osgood Mason had ended due to artistic differences:

> She wanted me to be more African than Harlem—primitive in the simple, intuitive and noble sense of the word. I couldn't be, having grown up in Kansas City, Chicago and Cleveland. So that winter had left me ill in my soul. I could not put my mind on writing for months. But write I had to—or starve—so I went to sit in the sun and gather my wits. (Hughes 1956, 5)

Departing from Key West, Hughes and Ingram first visited Cuba, where they sought out places that were not frequented by U.S. tourists. During their visit to Cuba, Hughes noted the existence of what he termed a "triple color line" (10) in which white, mulatto, and black people were segregated in public. Hughes and Ingram, challenging the "whites only" policy at a Cuban beach, were arrested and brought up on specious charges. Only when Hughes and Ingram appeared before the Cuban judge—"a kindly old mulatto gentleman" (14)—were the charges dismissed and the beach owners forced to apologize for their wrongdoing.

Shortly after their experience at the Cuban beach, Hughes and Ingram set sail for Port-au-Prince, Haiti. Although they were supplied with letters of introduction from such American cultural luminaries as Walter White, William Seabrook, Arthur Spingarn, and James Weldon Johnson, Hughes and Ingram avoided contact with the Haitian elite, preferring to stay in modest hotels that were not patronized by tourists.

After a week in Port-au-Prince, Hughes decided that he and Ingram should travel north to visit Cap Haïtien and the Citadelle Laferrière, places Hughes had read about in Blair Niles's *Black Haiti* (Hughes 1956, 16). During their bus trip to Cap Haïtien, Hughes and Ingram were stranded in the coastal town of St. Marc for three weeks as they waited for the waters of a swollen river to ebb. Once over the river, the men resumed their trip north only to run out of gasoline in the mountains between St. Marc and Cap Haïtien. They spent the night trying to keep warm; Ingram nestled between sacks of rice atop the cargo truck while Hughes slept in an unused drainage pipe at the side of the road (18).

Hughes and Ingram eventually ended up in a small hotel in Cap Haïtien where they enjoyed a view of the ocean, cheap and plentiful food, and numerous acquaintances who accompanied them to bars and local nightspots. Hughes, who was interested in experiencing Haitian cultural life, went out of his way to attend events that were associated with the peasant class of Haiti, or, as Hughes described them, "the people without shoes." Hughes learned to distinguish different cultural activities through the drumming styles they used:

> Almost every night I could hear the distant drums far away on the plains
> across the bay, or possibly near at hand in some outdoor clearing at the
> edge of town itself. Not often were these drums playing for voodoo cer-
> emonies—as foreign visitors always seemed to believe. They were usu-
> ally playing for the conga, or pleasure dances of the peasants, who gath-
> ered to scoot barefooted back and forth across the ground, or circle in

one spot around each other in movements as old as Africa, to a rhythm
as old as the earth. (Hughes 1956, 21–22)

While Hughes romantically associated the dances of rural Haitians with
"movements as old as Africa," he was still aware of the different social
contexts in which rural Haitians used music. Hughes not only attended
"conga" dances, he once visited a Vodou ceremony, describing the songs
as "monotonous chants punctuated by long wails" (22). Hughes also visited a *veye* or a wake, in which participants celebrated the passing of a
neighbor with drinking, dancing, and games (23).

Hughes was simultaneously fascinated and repelled by the forms of
class prejudice he encountered in Haiti. He was especially attracted to situations in which he could test the boundaries of his elite Haitian host. After making several shopping trips into Cap Haïtien, the manager of the
hotel asked Hughes and Ingram to stop carrying their parcels home from
the market. Men of means, the manager told them, should have their servants carry their parcels, no matter how small.

Unlike White and Matheus, who mingled with the elite of Haitian society, Hughes actively avoided contact with the Haitian upper class:

I was afraid . . . that someone might recognize my name or know my
poetry, for I did not want to be lionized in Haiti, nor have my days filled
with invitations to dine with people who could not play drums. I wanted
to be lazy, lie on the beach as long as I liked, talk with whom I pleased,
go to cockfights on Sundays, sail with fishermen, and never wear a coat.
(Hughes 1956, 25)

For Hughes, Haiti was most enjoyable when experienced through activities associated with the lower-classes: cockfighting, "conga" dances, fishing, and drumming:

One day Zell and I sat on the inner balcony around the courtyard,
pounding away on two big voodoo drums we had bought, trying to learn
the play them with our bare fingers as the Haitians do. Just when we were
beginning to master a simple rhythm, the manager came rushing up the
stairs scolding in his patois French. "*S'il vous-plait, messieurs!* Kindly do
not play the drums! Please! It upsets the servants. They hear the drums
and they cannot work. Drums are not for gentlemen, anyway." (Hughes
1956, 26)

In their eagerness to flout Haitian elite conventions regarding lower-class
activities such as drumming, Hughes and Ingram were like most tourists
visiting Haiti. Their fascination with the social norms of Haitian elite

society (and their delight in transgressing the boundaries of acceptable behavior) marked them as outsiders watching a cultural drama of which they were not a part.

Hughes's touristic sensibility was most evident in his personal correspondence from the Haitian trip. In a letter to Carl Van Vechten on 27 May 1931, Hughes described a "conga" dance at which he and Zell Ingram "got tight on sugar-cane rhum, and Zell outdanced the natives (The snakehips was a new one to them)" (Hughes and Van Vechten 2001, 87). Hughes went on to describe the Haitian language as "marvelous—like Chinese—full of little tunes and half notes" (88). Haiti, like China, was an exotic locale that featured a language that was both obscure and entertaining.

One of the most important tourist activities Hughes enjoyed was visiting the Citadelle Laferrière, the mountaintop fortress built by Haitian ruler Henri Christophe. Hughes was impressed not only by the size and scope of the fortress but also by the political struggle it represented for black people:

> The Citadel is in ruins. But it is one of the lustiest ruins in the world, rearing its husky shoulders out of a mountain with all the strength of the dreams that went into its making more than a century ago. The immensity of the Citadel, towering on a mountain peak whose slopes would create a problem for modern buildings, is beyond belief. A hundred years ago, when motors and machinery were lacking, the transporting of its giant stones from the plain below, and the rearing of its walls, was one of the great feats in the history of human energy and determination. The fact that beauty as well as strength went into its making is cause for further wonderment, for the Citadel is majestic, graceful in every proportion, with wide inner staircases and noble doorways of stone, curving battlements, spacious chambers and a maze of intricate cellars, dungeons, terraces and parade grounds. (Hughes 1956, 26–27)

Hughes admired the fact that the Citadelle was built to protect the freedom of the first independent black state. He was also aware that the people who built the fortress were newly freed slaves, people who had much in common with the oppressed Haitian poor who Hughes encountered during his trip to Haiti. Hughes chose to identify the inspirational value of the Citadelle with the common laborers who built it, not the Haitian elites who planned its construction.

Despite his reluctance to mingle with the upper classes of Haiti, Hughes was interested in meeting Jacques Roumain, an elite Haitian poet who was also a founding member of Haiti's Communist party and who, according to Hughes "was one of the few cultured Haitians who appreciated native folklore, and who became a friend of the people without shoes" (Hughes 1956, 29). When Hughes and Ingram returned to Port-au-Prince, they paid a visit to Roumain at his home where they were warmly received. After their visit to Roumain, Hughes and Ingram returned to the boat they had taken from Cap Haïtien to Port-au-Prince. Sitting on the deck in filthy trousers and without a shirt, eating greasy sausage and drinking wine, Hughes was surprised to learn that Roumain had brought a delegation of Haitian officials to the boat in order to present Hughes with departing gifts. Hughes recounted this last encounter with Roumain, in which the Haitian poet was unfazed by Hughes's unkempt appearance, as an example of Roumain's dignity and refusal to bend to elite conventions of proper behavior (31).

When Hughes returned to the U.S., his accounts of his experiences highlighted the disruptive presence of occupation troops from the U.S. and the plight of the Haitian poor. In an article in *The Crisis* magazine titled "White Shadows in a Black Land," Hughes observed:

> The dark-skinned little Republic . . . has its hair caught in the white fingers of unsympathetic foreigners, and the Haitian people live today under a sort of military dictatorship backed by American guns. They are not free. (Hughes 1932, 157)

In another essay titled "People Without Shoes" (1931, 12), Hughes described Haiti as "a hot, tropical little country, all mountains and sea; a lot of marines, mulatto politicians, and a world of black people without shoes—who catch hell." In both cases, Hughes ingeniously twisted the paternalistic discourse of the occupation forces into a critique of U.S. policy.

During his time in Haiti, Hughes worked on the play that had initially inspired his trip. He finished the play in 1935, revising it slightly for its 18 November 1936 premiere at the Karamu Theatre in Cleveland under the title, *Emperor of Haiti: An Historical Drama* (Hughes 1936/2002; McLaren 1997, 101). Elsie Roxborough, a friend of Hughes's, attended the Cleveland performance and later produced a version of the play in Detroit on 15 April 1937 under the title *Drums of Haiti* (McLaren 1997, 101).

Encouraged by the play's modest success, Hughes became interested in bringing the story of *Emperor of Haiti* to a larger audience. In 1936, he began negotiations for a musical score for the play with William Grant Still, who was himself working as a film composer for Warner Brothers (Rampersad 2002, 336). In 1937, Still and Hughes signed a legal agreement to work together on an opera based on Hughes's *Emperor of Haiti* play; the opera would be called *Troubled Island*.

From 1937 until *Troubled Island* was finally performed by the New York City Center for Music and Drama in 1949, Still and Hughes faced great challenges in getting their opera produced.[7] The conductor Leopold Stokowski was an early supporter of the project and encouraged his successor at the City Center, Laszlo Halasz, to conduct the premiere of the work. Halasz conducted three performances of *Troubled Island* on 31 March, 10 April, and 1 May 1949.

CLASS CONFLICT IN *TROUBLED ISLAND*

Troubled Island attributes Dessalines's downfall to a mulatto conspiracy that takes advantage of the emperor's illiteracy and vanity. Unlike *Ouanga*, which attributes Dessalines's demise to his rejection of Vodou and its dark-skinned peasant followers, *Troubled Island* depicts the conflict between Dessalines and the light-skinned Haitian elite.

While *Ouanga* began before the slave uprising that brought Dessalines to power, the plot of *Troubled Island* begins in 1791 at the start of the Haitian Revolution with a group of slaves who meet at an abandoned sugar mill to distribute arms. Azelia, a slave woman carrying a basket of fruit, shows the assembled slaves that she has weapons concealed in her basket. Azelia's common-law husband, Jean-Jacques Dessalines, joins the conspiratorial meeting and is declared leader of the slave uprising. At Dessalines's urging, Martel, an elderly slave who was born in Africa, sings "Rememb'ring Africa," an aria that chronicles the enslavement of African people and their longing for their ancestral home.

A conflict brews between the dark-skinned slaves who toil in the fields and the mulattoes whose connections to French culture prompt them to act superior to the dark-skinned slaves. Congo, an African-born slave, warns Dessalines that mulattoes, given their class privilege and power, will turn a successful revolution into a second slave economy with mulattoes replacing whites as slave masters. Dessalines, recognizing that the success of the revolution depends on driving out the French, agrees to work with the mulattoes despite the warnings of his loyal dark-skinned followers.

As he prepares for the battle that will begin the Haitian Revolution, Dessalines calls to his all-black troops, identifying them by their African ethnic identities:

> Sons of Africa, join with me
> Tomorrow we'll be free.
> Senegalese, tall and proud like coconut trees
> And you that were from the coast of Calabar

Men from the Congo, join too,
The Congo drums will beat for you!
Ashanti men, be with us then
For Africa in Haiti now
Lifts her hand in freedom's vow.
(Still and Hughes 1949, 82)

In *Troubled Island,* Africa is both the homeland of black people and an imaginary refuge from the suffering and pain of the Americas. Putting aside their former regional identities in Africa, black people in Haiti join together to defeat their common enemy.

Just as Dessalines calls to the various African ethnic groups represented in slave society, so too does "voodoo" rally slave support for the uprising by calling out to various African-derived spirits. Once Dessalines finishes calling the African troops, the papaloi and mamaloi (the male and female Vodou priests) arrive, complete with Vodou drum battery and animals for the ritual sacrifice. The crowd calls first to Legba, the Vodou guardian of the crossroads, and then to other Vodou spirits like "Damballah wedo," "Ogun Balandjo," and "Nago Shango." After a vigorous Vodou invocation on the part of the chorus and dancers, the mamaloi sacrifices a rooster and anoints Dessalines with its blood (118). Later in act 1, "voodoo music" is used again to signal the slaves to begin the revolution in earnest. The stage directions state:

> With a great, booming sound, the signal drum in the [sugar cane] mill begins to throb. Little ways off yonder another drum takes up the sound, relaying its message to another, until the whole countryside resounds with the call of freedom. (128)

In *Troubled Island,* "voodoo" drums carry the message of the revolution to the slaves only after Dessalines removes his shirt and horrifies the crowd with the sight of the scars he received from repeated whipping at the hands of his slave master. The drama also fuses Dessalines's role in the revolution with that of Boukman Dutty, a slave leader who participated at the Vodou ceremony at Bwa Kayiman in which slaves took a blood oath to win the struggle for independence (Geggus 1991).

In act 2, which begins several years after the successful Haitian Revolution, the tensions between dark-skinned slaves and light-skinned children of colonial landowners develop into a class system demarcated by literacy. The illiterate Dessalines, dressed in his royal finery, dictates letters from his throne to his secretary Vuval, one of the mulattoes who joined the slave rebellion. Most of the letters are from newly wealthy black and mulatto

supplicants who request funds for their own enrichment; Dessalines re-
jects them angrily. One of the letters, however, is from a blacksmith in Gros
Morne who requests money for a teacher and a school. Vuval laughs while
reading the letter, noting that the letter is poorly written and that peasants
learning to read and write is a foolish notion. Dessalines, recognizing that
the helplessness of the slaves in this situation is similar to his own, sings a
melancholy aria:

> Why do you laugh, Vuval?
> Is it because I am helpless here?
> I cannot read and write myself.
> And we have no teachers to send to the villagers.
> Why do you laugh, Vuval? Why do you laugh?
> Is it because you know how ignorance
> Binds the hands of men who would be free?
> (156)

While Dessalines recognizes his vulnerability as an illiterate ruler, he is
powerless to stop the machinations of his mulatto courtiers. Vuval, who
has intentionally misrepresented Dessalines's wishes to the people through
his letters, helps turn public opinion against Dessalines without the emperor's knowledge.

The theme of class antagonism between light- and dark-skinned
Haitians is addressed again by Martel, Dessalines's loyal African-born
supporter. When Dessalines dreams of a land in which black men rule,
Martel imagines a better world in which racial and class prejudice is eliminated and where all people, black and white, are free:

> I dream a world where man
> No other man will scorn
> Where love will bless the earth,
> And peace its paths adorn.
> I dream a world where all
> Will know sweet freedom's way,
> Where greed no longer saps the soul
> Nor avarice blights our day.
> A world I dream where black or white,
> Whatever race you be,
> Will share the bounties of the earth
> And every man is free
> Where wretchedness will hang its head,
> And joy, like a pearl,

Attend the needs of all mankind.
Of this I dream, my world.
(164)

Martel's vision of a harmonious and egalitarian future is as optimistic as it is unrealistic. Immediately after Martel finishes his hopeful aria, Dessalines's mulatto courtier, Vuval, plots the emperor's downfall with Claire Heureuse. After the revolution, Dessalines rejected his common-law wife, Azelia (known in *Ouanga* as Defilée), and married Claire, a white French woman who despises Dessalines for his slave roots. Vuval and Claire plot Dessalines's assassination and plan their mutual escape to Paris, where Claire looks forward to joining French society.

Act 3 features the brewing class conflict within the imperial court and the collapse of Dessalines's rule. At a royal banquet, the new dark-skinned Haitian royalty are lampooned for their pomposity while Dessalines sings an aria that desperately asserts his importance:

I am the great Dessalines!
I have covered my scars with diamonds.
I have covered my head with plumes.
I have made myself Emperor of Haiti!
(233)

Dessalines's obsession with raising up the international reputation of Haiti make him focus exclusively on the trappings of royalty. He is unable to see that even during his formal banquet, in which musicians play French music, a group of dark-skinned dancers—whose "anklets are of beaten gold and whose bushy hair is adorned with the teeth of animals" (241)—gather in the back of the banquet hall. The "dark dancers" take the stage and "a tall male dancer enters, feathered and painted like a voodoo god" (243).

In this scene, the interruption of the Vodou dancers reminds Dessalines of his humble origins. Dessalines's shame—as a ruler of a "backward" nation who himself cannot read or write—causes him to side with his European-born wife Claire against the Haitian dancers. The dance gradually becomes "fierce, provocative and terrible" (245) prompting Empress Claire to cover her ears and shout "stop the drums!" (248). Dessalines sings an aria in which he condemns the "voodoo" drums as signs of Haitian unwillingness to join the ranks of civilized nations. He blames the bloated Haitian aristocracy for leaving their taxes unpaid and bringing the nation to the brink of ruin. As Dessalines threatens to institute forced labor practices reminiscent of slavery, the "voodoo" drums signal the beginning of the revolt against Dessalines.

In act 4, the peasants, who have supported Dessalines as their libera-
tor, carry on their lives unaware of the political events at the palace. In
Troubled Island, the peasants are portrayed as innocent and happy, their
sincerity reflected in their playful banter and heartfelt demeanor. Unlike
Ouanga, in which peasants actively contribute to Dessalines's downfall,
the peasants in *Troubled Island* are bystanders to the political plotting of
the light- and dark-skinned Haitian elite. Peasant earnestness contrasts
with the deviousness of the scheming mulatto courtiers and the pompous
black aristocracy who put their own personal desires ahead of the people.
The peasants describe their simple lives in a lilting chorus:

> A peasant folk are we
> A fisher folk are we
> Living by the earth
> Living from the sea
>
> . . . .
>
> A barefoot folk are we
> A water folk are we
> Plowing, planting, reaping
> Sailing on the sea.
> (269–76)

Later, vendors call out in hocket, advertising their wares of "salt sea fish,
mangoes, yams, cocoanuts, sugar cane, and thimbles" (277–79). The
mood is lightened further with a humorous exchange between a market
woman and a fisherman:

> Man.   You've got a good man on your mind.
> Woman.   A good man I don't need!
>   One more mouth for me to feed!
> Man.   Listen woman, understand, I'm an honest
>   fisherman!
> Woman.   Out of my way and let me pass!
>   All men's tongues are full of sass!
>   (280–84)[8]

The juxtaposition of peasant innocence with upper-class duplicity
reflects Hughes's interest in "giving voice to the 'low-down folk'" (Sanders
2002, 1).

Dessalines is eventually ambushed by his former mulatto soldiers and
shot in the back. Several "ragamuffins" try to steal the dying emperor's
clothes but Azelia, Dessalines's spurned first wife, drives the beggars
away to comfort her husband in his final moments. Viewed by the other

peasants as delusional—because she claims to have been Dessalines's wife—Azelia nonetheless proves her mettle in this scene. Dessalines reconciles with his wife by recognizing that his court was full of self-serving sycophants who forgot the true meaning of the slave revolution:

> Azalia. Jean-Jacques!
>
> Dessalines. Azalia! They've all gone!
>
> Azalia. They were never with you.
>
> Dessalines. Only you remain.
>
> Azalia. Yes, Jean-Jacques.
>
> Dessalines. And you forgive me?
>
> Azalia. I love you.
> (Dessalines gasps convulsively and sinks downward in death.)
> (344)

Azelia's love for Dessalines also reconciles him with his forsaken peasant roots and comports well with Dessalines's status as a tragic hero in Haitian history. Azelia declares that "our destiny is in the stars, I live to kiss your scars" (348). Through her physical gesture of kissing the scars of the murdered former slave, Azelia proclaims that Dessalines's importance to subsequent generations of Haitians will be as an eternal reminder of Haiti's struggle for independence.

While the drama for *Troubled Island* clearly reflected Langston Hughes's sympathy for the "people without shoes" and his antipathy for the upper-classes of Haitian society, the opera's music was less concerned with reinforcing the message of class conflict. According to Still's wife, Verna Arvey, only two musical moments were connected to Haitian cultural practice:

> During the creation of [*Troubled Island*], Mr. Still spent many hours in research, only to discover that at that time there was almost no authentic Haitian musical material to be found in the United States. Accordingly, with the exception of two native themes (a Meringue, used in the last act; and a Voodoo theme, greatly altered, in Act I), which were supplied by John Houston Craige, author and former U.S. Marine officer stationed in Haiti during the occupation, all the themes and their various treatments were original with Mr. Still. He devised his own musical idiom to fit the subject and the locale. (Arvey 1975, 96)

The méringue in act 4 resembles the popular Haitian tune "Angélique ô," an anti-American song that used *pwen*-style lyrics to tell U.S. troops to "ale kay manman w" (go to your mother's house). Haitian historian Jean Fouchard noted that "Angélique ô" "maliciously satirized and teased

Angelique Cole, the wife of the Marine Commandant, Colonel Cole" (Fouchard 1988b, 116; Averill 1997, 46). The Vodou theme in act 1, played on a trio of drums, loosely resembles the kita, "a fast version of the Petwo dance" (Wilcken 1992a, 107), but it has been modified too much to make an accurate comparison. In the context of a Vodou ceremony intended to incite rebellion in the slave population, the Petwo spirits "are hot tempered and volatile" (Brown 2001, 101) and are associated with the active resistance connected with the revolution.

Still's source for Haitian musical materials, John Houston Craige, was familiar with Haitian cultural practices. Yet, Craige's paternalistic views of Haitians and their culture call into question his reliability as an observer of Haitian musical style. Craige made a living from exploiting his experiences in Haiti, writing two sensationalistic books—*Black Baghdad* and *Cannibal Cousins*—that cast Haiti as a place where tropical heat, isolation, and sexually loose women posed a threat to American troops. Craige thought that his time in Haiti made him vulnerable to what he perceived to be the foreboding message of Haitian music. Craige wrote that "the drums were always throbbing. . . . It wore on my nerves" (Craige 1933, 231). While there is no evidence of Still's belief in Craige's assertions about Haitian culture, Still's singular reliance on Craige's musicological advice is in sharp contrast with Clarence Cameron White's desire to have musical materials in his opera that would accurately represent the varieties of music available in Haiti.

GENDER, VODOU, AND CLASS IN *OUANGA* AND *TROUBLED ISLAND*

While Dessalines is clearly the principal protagonist of the tragedy, the female characters in *Ouanga* and *Troubled Island* play equally important roles, not only in the unfolding of the plot but also in their capacity as intermediaries for the spiritual health of the Haitian nation. According to Partha Chatterjee, nationalist debates often identify culture as having material and spiritual spheres, with the spiritual side of culture being identified with the "inner" world of the feminine (Chatterjee 1993, 73). The Défilée/Azelia character is clearly associated with both, tending to Dessalines's defiled corpse and ensuring that his memory will continue; she sings "our destiny is in the stars" to the dying Dessalines.[9] Joan Dayan observes that "Défilée's actions also suggest a preoccupation with proper rituals of burial and fear of the unquiet dead" (1995, 45). As the custodian of Dessalines's corpse, Défilée takes responsibility for the nation, ensuring that the body will not be used against Haitians in the future:

> The figure of Défilée transcends the role of witness and devotee. More like the oungan or manbo who prevents the dead from returning to life

to harm the living, Défilée assembles Dessalines's remnants in order to make sure they are suitably buried, thus thwarting their resurrection by a sorcerer. Read in this way, the figure of Défilée transposes apparently contradictory traditions with fluent and convincing ease: the penitent devotee turns into the wise diviner, and the fear of stunted burial is joined to the promise of glorious resurrection. (Dayan 1995, 45)

In both operas, Défilée/Azelia represents women as caretakers of the visceral as well as the spiritual. According to several historical accounts, Défilée picks up the bloody pieces of Dessalines's fragmented corpse and takes them away for proper burial. Her act of caretaking is the physical manifestation of her spiritual duty to ensure the legacy of Dessalines and the slave revolution.

While *Ouanga* and *Troubled Island* both draw upon Vodou, in Hughes's words, "for scenery and atmosphere," each opera casts female characters as deeply implicated in either the promotion or suppression of Vodou. In *Ouanga,* lower-class females are representatives of the people's will through Vodou practice. Défilée is torn between her love for Dessalines and her devotion to the spirits of Vodou. In *Ouanga*'s plot synopsis, the production notes read:

Dessalines tells Défilée of his vision of L'Ouverture's warning to shun vain glory and ambition, to hold steadfast to the ancient heritage of the "Ouanga," to beware of the new order of things and the bloody strife which will surely follow. But he is convinced that his way is better. Swayed by her love for Dessalines she is on the point of consenting, when the echoes of the drums reverberate down the mountain side. Défilée draws back in fear and, shuddering, refuses. (White and Matheus 1955, ii)

Only the sound of the drums brings Défilée back from her dream of a life of freedom with Dessalines. Défilée's double devotion—to her religious beliefs and to her husband—are the driving force of the drama. When Dessalines turns his back on the Vodou-practicing masses, they turn against him. At the end of the drama, it is Défilée's love that redeems the deluded Dessalines.

While Défilée's double devotion is ultimately good for the nation, it is personally disastrous for her. In several historical accounts, the Défilée character is depicted as driven mad, either from the harsh experiences she suffered as a slave woman, from seeing Dessalines's defiled corpse, or, perhaps, from Dessalines's rejection of her affections. In *Troubled Island,* Azelia's delusions are a sign of her ability to see things that others cannot.

She is unable to revive the fallen emperor, but her unwavering vision of Dessalines as the founder of Haitian independence ensures that his legacy will live on the minds of future generations of Haitians.

If, however, *Ouanga* credits a woman (Défilée) with resuscitating Dessalines's memory, it also blames a woman (Mougali, the Vodou priestess) for precipitating his downfall. In the first scene of the opera, Mougali warns Dessalines by proclaiming "death to all who desert Legba." She tries to put a *ouanga* or magic curse on Dessalines for turning his back on Vodou. While Défilée dissuades her momentarily, Dessalines resents Mougali's defiance and her refusal to recognize his own power as superior to the practice of Vodou. The dramatic high point in the opera comes when Dessalines orders Mougali to be shot, for his attempt at self-preservation effectively severs his ties to the people.

In the character of Mougali, White and Matheus present the spiritual side of Haitian national culture, as associated with femaleness and with Vodou. Mougali's role is more than spiritual, however. Her anger at Dessalines reflects not only her frustration with Dessalines's anti-Vodou policies but also her resistance to Dessalines's tyrannical rule evidenced by his desire to reinstate the plantation system. While Mougali's dramatic function is to engage Dessalines in a struggle over Vodou practice, her political role as defender of the independent farmer is equally important. In *Ouanga*, Défilée and Mougali represent the people's will through their support of Vodou practice and their lower-class origins.

Troubled Island heightens the positive role of the Haitian lower classes by demonizing a female bourgeois character. Here, Dessalines's new white wife, Claire Heureuse, represents upper-class resistance to Vodou as both a religious practice and a class-specific activity. While Claire Heureuse plays a relatively minor role in *Ouanga*, she has a pivotal part in *Troubled Island*. Claire marries Dessalines for his power, yet she despises his slave origins. Claire is repulsed by the scars that Dessalines received as a slave, the same scars that Azelia kisses in the final scene of the opera. Claire is also revolted by Vodou, which she sees as an unpleasant reminder of all that is wrong with the new Haitian republic. In act 3, during a banquet scene at Dessalines's palace in which entertainment is provided by Haitian musicians, Claire "covers her ears with her jeweled hands and cries aloud to Dessalines, 'Ow, stop the drums!'" (Still and Hughes 1949, 248). Claire's disapproval of Vodou prompts Dessalines to sing an aria in which the presence of Vodou is blamed for Haiti's inability to create a civilization "equal to anywhere" (251). Claire's scheming with Dessalines's mulatto scribe, Vuval, emphasizes the Haitian elite's disdain for Vodou and their repudiation of Haitian culture.

Despite their differing depictions of Dessalines's story, *Ouanga* and *Troubled Island* both demonstrate the importance of class in the African American imagination. For White and Matheus, the downtrodden masses of Haiti are given voice through the "vast storehouse" of black folk culture in Vodou. Dessalines is punished for his hubris and his ignoring the will of the people. By turning toward Vodou as a powerful force of black agency and of lower-class black culture, White and Matheus distinguished their depiction of Vodou from most contemporaneous beliefs about Haitian traditional religion. For African American audiences, *Ouanga* proclaims the power of black folk culture in shaping the destiny of a nation. By incorporating a range of musical styles within Haitian culture—from the "Bomba hen!" chant to the parlor meringue—White and Matheus tried to infuse their drama with cultural meaning.

Ouanga's connection to Haitian culture was, however, received differently by white and black critics. Carter Harman's review in the *New York Times* of a 1950 Philadelphia performance of *Ouanga* praised White for his incorporation of a Vodou "flavor":

> The music matched [the sets] in attractiveness and evocativeness. Dr. White apparently made little effort to keep up with the Copelands but it might be said that he is happily in step with the Puccinis. His arias have considerable lyric quality and his choral writing is strong. For this work he drew on Haitian folk songs and rhythms, gathered during a visit there, and they added flavor. . . . Best of all was the scene in the third act, where the pagan ritual was aptly rendered in sound and the characters on stage achieved a sense of movement. (Harman 1950)

For Harman, White's decision to set his drama in a musical language that emulated nineteenth-century Italian opera rather than a more modernist sound confirmed White as someone who would give audiences what they expected. Part of that expectation was a depiction of Haitian "pagans" whose rituals were "aptly rendered in sound"; a sound that was authenticated in Harman's mind by White's sojourn to Haiti.

For African American critic Mary Church Terrell, it was White's winning the Bispham Medal for *Ouanga* in 1932 and his immersion in Haitian culture that made his contribution to the operatic stage noteworthy. She wrote:

> After steeping himself in the history of Haiti, seeing the people with his own eyes, learning their traditions and observing their customs, some of them very curious and quaint, Mr. White was more eager than ever

to weave all these new and interesting things into the musical score of an opera. (Terrell 1933)

Terrell's characterization of Haitian customs as "curious and quaint"—as opposed to Harman's description of "pagan ritual"—downplayed the exoticism so prevalent in the mainstream press of the time. Moreover, Terrell's chronicle of White's efforts to get his opera performed, including a protracted dispute with several potential backers of the project, showed African American audiences that bringing a powerful story of black struggle to the stage paralleled their own struggles for self-determination.

In *Troubled Island*, the conflicts between the black rich and poor in Haiti underscore a similar tension in African American society. Hughes, who spent much of his career criticizing class prejudice among African Americans, used *Troubled Island* to bring issues of class and color discrimination to African American audiences. For Hughes, Haiti's failures rested on the country's inability to manage its internal class and color divisions.

Both operas clearly demonstrate the connections between Haitians and African Americans as oppressed people. Eschewing the popular portrayals of Vodou as devil worship, the operas present Vodou as a black cultural activity that has the power to undermine a corrupt state. Yet, the commercial failure of both operas provides one example of how middle-class blacks throughout the African diaspora were caught between their notions of black nationalism and their connections to the capitalist system of their particular nation-state (Robinson 1994, 144). In the international market of the 1930s and 1940s, Vodou was already a commodity that exuded sensationalism and exoticism. Both operas were produced in the United States, where most white audiences expected stereotypical "voodoo" gore yet most black audiences hoped for nationalist inspiration. Black and white audiences alike, however, expected musical and cultural exuberance in a drama about "the black republic" that would confirm Haiti's sobriquet of "Africa in the Americas."

~ 5 ~
ETHNOGRAPHY
AND MUSIC IDEOLOGY
The Music of Werner A. Jaegerhuber

In his study of Haitian political history, Michel-Rolph Trouillot observes that the Haitian peasantry is not isolated in Haiti's mountainous countryside but has maintained an active and vital presence in the
country's urban centers. Trouillot suggests that the "physical to-and-fro
of the peasantry from the hinterland to the urban trenches means that it has
come to occupy part of the urban social and cultural terrain" (Trouillot
1990, 114). He adds:

> While the economic and political divisions [between elites and peas-
> ants] may be reminiscent of trench warfare, the cultural relations be-
> tween the classes are more reminiscent of a guerrilla war. The peasantry
> is not master of this space—or never for long—but it penetrates it
> deeply and harasses the enemy, while remaining ready to retreat at any
> point. It does not dictate the dominant cultural codes, but those who
> impose them must take its values into account. For example, there is no
> aspect of Haitian economic and political life that explains why the
> Jaegerhubers, a commercial family of German origin firmly ensconced
> within the bourgeoisie, should have invested a considerable amount of
> time at the beginning of this century in transcribing peasant songs.
> (Trouillot 1990, 114)

In this chapter, I argue that Haitian art music provides a fruitful locus
for investigating the political and economic relationships between Haiti's
rural peasant majority and its urban elite minority. In the period after the
U.S. occupation of Haiti, Haitian artists, ethnographers, and politicians
saw Haitian cultural life in general, and art music in particular, as a deeply
politicized space in which economic and social issues could be debated.
    I suggest that Haitian composer and amateur ethnographer Werner
Anton Jaegerhuber's (1900–1953) interest in the songs of the Haitian

peasantry was part of a larger debate about the utility of peasant culture to the Haitian nation. Through his transformations of Haitian peasant songs from ethnographic transcription to arrangements for voice and piano and finally to choral pieces in a "vodouesque" style, Jaegerhuber helped to realize Jean Price-Mars's dream of making the products of the Vodou ceremony a cultural commodity that could be shared with an international audience. Jaegerhuber viewed such transformations as socially progressive because they recognize the artistic production of the Haitian peasantry as having value—or "cultural capital" in the words of Pierre Bourdieu (1984). By transforming the roughhewn music of the Haitian rural underclass into a product suitable for the piano parlor, Jaegerhuber sought connections with the peasantry that would transform not only the peasants' social and economic relationships with Haitian elite classes but also Haiti's political relationships with foreign powers, especially the United States. As a cultural worker at the forefront of the tourism industry that burgeoned after the end of the Second World War, Jaegerhuber found an outlet for his compositions that could demonstrate the value of Haitian peasant culture to Haitian audiences and would pique the interest of foreign tourists during their brief visits to the "pearl of the Antilles."

Yet, Jaegerhuber's experience reflects some of the limits facing cultural workers as they attempted to share their materials with a wider audience. In his own way, Jaegerhuber challenged the tendency of foreign observers to cast Haitian traditional religion as a dangerous and destructive force; his sympathetic use of melodies and rhythms from Haitian traditional music was in sharp contrast to foreign commercial depictions of Haitian music that presented Vodou as evil. At the same time, Jaegerhuber's attempts to distance himself from the sensationalist accounts of Vodou music in foreign media went to the opposite extreme. His efforts to universalize Haitian traditional music, to trace its origins not only to the songs and dances of West and Central Africa but also to the Gregorian chants of the early Christian church in Europe and the songs of ancient Greece, downplayed the importance of African religious and linguistic influences on Haitian music.

The tension created by claiming Haitian art music as being both culturally unique and musically universal placed artists like Jaegerhuber in a creative bind. By working with cultural materials that became too volatile to control once they were transformed into musical compositions, Jaegerhuber invoked the ire of elite Haitians who were ashamed of their culture's Vodou antecedents as well as the disdain of Haitian classical musicians who felt that the music of the Vodou ceremony was not sufficiently sophisticated to warrant arrangements in European-style art compositions.

Figure 5.1. Werner Anton Jaegerhuber. Photo courtesy of Anna-Maria Jaegerhuber
Etienne and Anton Jaegerhuber.

Understanding the social and cultural tensions under which composers
work requires a concomitant examination of how artistic merit is identified
and evaluated. Like most of the other Haitian composers described in this
book, Jaegerhuber never enjoyed widespread fame or fortune for either his
musical compositions or his ethnographic work on Haitian music, in part
because of Haitians' ambivalence toward his music. Yet, it is precisely
because Jaegerhuber's work generated conflicting reactions for Haitian

audiences that his work should be seen as important to an understanding of Haitian culture.

A member of a German-Haitian family who was born in Haiti and spent his formative years in Germany, Jaegerhuber returned to Haiti as an adult and was immediately taken with the beauty and power of peasant song. His early forays into ethnographic research on peasant music led him to conclude that "this primitive music has a surprising splendor by the height of its expression and by the richness of its profound feeling. Its structure recalls the grandeur of a Handel" (Jaegerhuber 1948, 40). Despite the obvious Eurocentrism of his remarks, Jaegerhuber's self-consciously chosen role as a cultural translator put him in an advantageous position in relation to his bourgeois peers. Jaegerhuber was perhaps the first composer to systematically document his contact with Haitian peasants and use his ethnographic data for compositions that associated the melodies sung in the sugarcane fields and precipitous mountains with the "grandeur of a Handel."

Jaegerhuber's biography reflects the importance of transatlantic intellectual commerce in early twentieth-century Haiti. Like Occide Jeanty, Justin Elie, and Ludovic Lamothe, Jaegerhuber received his musical training in Europe. Compared to other Haitian composers of his day, however, Jaegerhuber had even stronger ties with his European ancestry. Born on 17 March 1900 in the Turgeau district of Port-au-Prince, Werner Anton Jaegerhuber was the son of Anton Jaegerhuber, a naturalized American citizen of German descent, and Anna Maria Tippenhauer, the daughter of an elite German-Haitian family. The marriage of Anton Jaegerhuber and Anna Maria Tippenhauer brought together two Haitian families with strong ties to Germany. German businessmen frequently married into elite Haitian families during the late nineteenth century, usually with the effect of consolidating their political influence and maintaining their economic power (Bellegarde-Smith 1990, 69; Trouillot 1990, 55). Like Jagerhuber himself, Jaegerhuber's mother, Anna Maria Tippenhauer, was also the product of such a marriage.

In 1915, one year after the outbreak of World War I, United States military forces invaded Haiti. Immediately after the invasion, Jaegerhuber's family sent him to Germany to be educated. During the U.S. occupation of Haiti, persons of German descent were perceived as a military and economic threat by the Americans, who feared German intervention in Haitian affairs. Anton Jaegerhuber, who worked in a Haitian bank, was in a particularly vulnerable position when the Americans invaded Haiti.

Upon his arrival in Germany, Jaegerhuber matriculated at the Voigt Conservatory in Hamburg, where he studied composition.[1] Jaegerhuber returned to Haiti briefly in 1921 and, according to Roger Savain (1950), became interested in Haitian folklore. Yet, after this brief visit to Haiti, Jaegerhuber did not return to the Caribbean until 1937 when the National Socialists were gaining power in Germany and persecuting persons of color.[2]

In 1937, with Hitler in power in Germany and the American occupation forces withdrawn from Haiti, Jaegerhuber returned to Haiti and immediately immersed himself in the study of Haitian folklore. He organized two conferences at the Société Scientifique in Port-au-Prince to make a plea for establishing a national music based on a study of the nation's folklore (Jaegerhuber 1943). Jaegerhuber believed that only through a careful collection and examination of the musical folklore of the country could composers use folk music as a part of their art. Jaegerhuber would lead the way by undertaking ethnographic research himself and using the transcribed melodies as the basis of his own works. In 1937, Jaegerhuber returned to a Haiti that was significantly different from the one he left. In 1915, Haiti was at the beginning of a nineteen-year occupation, and German-affiliated citizens were targeted by the U.S. military as dangerous to national security.

By the time Jaegerhuber returned to Haiti, German political influence had waned, but Haitians of German descent had regained some of the economic ground they had lost during the occupation. In addition, the U.S. occupation had encouraged an increased dependency on U.S. goods and services within the Haitian economy; the occupation thus had the effect of permanently eclipsing European economic power in Haiti. As tourism became an increasingly important part of Haiti's economy and Haitian culture assumed its place as an export commodity, artists found themselves in the unique position of having their work valued, especially if it reflected newly fashionable Haitian subjects.

POLITICS AND THE PEASANTRY IN EARLY TWENTIETH-CENTURY HAITI

Jaegerhuber's return to Haiti shortly after the end of the United States occupation in 1934 came at a time when Haitian intellectuals were fighting over who would assume control of the Haitian state. At least three groups vied for control in the wake of the withdrawal of occupation forces: the mulatto elites, the noiristes, and the socialists. The mulatto elite, whose numbers included Haitian diplomat Dantès Bellegarde and politician François Dalencour, had been kept in power throughout the occupation period by U.S. forces. The Haitian presidents who served full terms during the occupation—Louis Borno (1922–30) and Sténio Vincent (1930–41)—were both members of the lelit milat.

Bellegarde, who had been ambassador to France, the Vatican, and the United States, as well as the Haitian delegate to the League of Nations (Bellegarde 1938, v), was adamantly opposed to noiriste as well as socialist visions for the Haitian nation. For Bellegarde, the history of Haiti followed a "mulatto legend" that highlighted the glories and accomplishments of light-skinned political figures such as Jean-Pierre Boyer and Alexandre Pétion at the expense of dark-skinned figures like Toussaint Louverture and Jean-Jacques Dessalines (Nicholls 1979). Bellegarde saw the noiriste and socialist interest in anthropology as antithetical to his view of Haitian culture. According to one of Bellegarde's biographers, "Bellegarde abhorred anthropology and equated the interest of anthropologists with preconceived notions of savagery" (Bellegarde-Smith 1985, 94). While Bellegarde respected Jean Price-Mars personally, he was skeptical of Price-Mars's motives for emphasizing Haiti's anthropological connections with things African and viewed Price-Mars's "Black assertiveness as a leftist trend related to communism and 'reverse' racism" (Bellegarde-Smith 1985, 81).

Most mulatto ideologues' interest in the Haitian peasantry was confined to how best to insure lower-class compliance with Haitian elite policies. Indeed, peasants were not really part of the mulatto concept of the Haitian nation. Borrowing from W. E. B. Du Bois's notion of the "talented tenth," Bellegarde believed that Haitian elites had the responsibility to lead the nation; the unspoken part of this syllogism was that the duty of the peasantry was to follow that lead without question or interference.

Other mulatto leaders preferred to attack the noiriste position by denouncing dark-skinned Haitians as being "French under the skin." Haitian President Sténio Vincent derided noiriste claims of Haiti's African ancestry by accusing noiristes of disingenuousness: "Paris was their headquarters. But who among them had ever thought of making a small expedition in some area of the Sudan or the Congo in order to communicate a little with the souls of our distant ancestors" (Vincent 1931, 153–54; quoted in Dash 1981, 125).

While the lelit milat granted the peasantry a servile role in Haitian society, noiristes and communists granted peasants a more prominent place in their visions of the Haitian nation. Noiristes, who traced their provenance to the early nationalist writings of Jean-Price Mars as well as to nineteenth-century writers like Louis-Joseph Janvier and Anténor Firmin, argued for a political movement based on the idea of black political power.

In 1932, the noiriste "Griots" group was founded by Louis Diaquoi, Lorimer Denis, and François Duvalier, three black middle-class intellectuals who were frustrated by the limitations of black advancement in a political system that favored light-skinned, socially connected individuals. When Diaquoi died in 1932 at the age of twenty-five, Denis and Duvalier continued their political activities, eventually founding the journal *Les Griots* in 1938. Named for the French word for the West African praise-singer and oral historian, *Les Griots* featured political, sociological, and artistic articles intended to bolster the idea that Haitian culture owed its inspiration to African rather than European antecedents. Carl Brouard, a Haitian poet and early director of the journal, penned the following description of an African griot as an example of the mystical inspiration that African cultures provided Haitian intellectuals:

> Over there, in the mysterious countries of Africa, when passing the griots, men and women spit as a sign of contempt, for they are poets and sorcerers and men are afraid of their power. Wrists and neck-lines charged with ouangas, they have eyes full of nostalgia and they sink down into the underbrush of dreams. They sing of love, red like the flamboyant tree, and of the strange immobility of death. The spirits speak to them in dreams more true than reality, reality being no more than the shadow of a dream. When they resonate the war drums, warriors dream of an apotheosis; the griots form a separate caste. When they die, their wretched spirits do not go to a place in the gardens of paradise, and their distantly disposed cadavers become the prey of jackals. (Brouard 1950, 359)

Likening the Haitian griots to their African counterparts, Brouard claimed the poetic and dramaturgic talents of the griots as well as the their mystical, magical powers. Brouard asserted the authenticity of his own griot group because of its connection to the positive aspects of African griots (including their spiritual power and ability to inspire others), as well as the negative aspects (like the griot's "wretched" social position and their dangerous commerce with angry spirits). As a movement dedicated to giving dark-skinned Haitians more control over Haitian affairs, the noiristes self-consciously associated themselves with that part of Haitian society held in contempt by the light-skinned elite: the dark-skinned, poverty-stricken Haitian majority. According to this logic, critics of the noiristes were associated with those sectors of Haitian society that would deny dark-skinned Haitians agency in Haitian politics and society. While the noiristes did not involve themselves in any economic or political projects that would benefit poorer Haitians, their practice of speaking for lower classes allowed them to use the rhetoric of racial prejudice to assert their claims as spokespersons for all Haitians.

As J. Michael Dash has noted, although the noiriste journal *Les Griots* promoted itself as a "scientific and literary" journal, it was, properly speaking, neither literary nor scientific in any systematic way (Dash 1981, 113). Rather, the journal was a collection of writings that discussed the relationship of an unproblematized notion of African culture to Haitian politics and literature. Like Brouard's rhapsody on the African griot, other contributions to *Les Griots* tended to focus on the spectacular aspects of African-derived Haitian culture. Perhaps the most popular examples of Haitian culture featured in *Les Griots* were Vodou ceremonies. In his "La Danse sous la Tonnelle" (Dance under the Arbor), published in *Les Griots* in 1939, Franck Legendre describes an encounter with a group of Vodou practitioners on their way to a Vodou ceremony. Legendre's account includes descriptions of several pretty young women who lead him to the ceremony, the isolated location "about a kilometer from the village," where the ceremony was held, and finally, a frenetic dance in which all members of the Vodou entourage are possessed by spirits (Legendre 1939). In the next article in the issue, "Nuits d'Haiti" (Haitian Nights), Félix Morisseau-Leroy describes several Vodou ceremonies he attended. His account gives details about the drum rhythms—the *cata* [kata drum] combines with the other drums to give a feeling of "delivery"—and the body movement of participants including one dancer who "danced like a snake" (Morisseau-Leroy 1939, 365).

The Vodou ceremonies described in such detail and with such immediacy in *Les Griots* reveal much about the perspective of the events' observers. All of the descriptions of Vodou activity in *Les Griots* place a Haitian elite observer in the position of recounting personal experiences for a reading audience that presumably would have no access to the ceremony. Rarely do any of the descriptions delve into local perspectives on Vodou activities; the accounts in *Les Griots* feature neither interviews with nor personal statements from worshipers themselves. Rather, descriptions of Vodou ceremonies tend to focus on surface behaviors, onto which writers project their interpretations. For example, in "La Danse sous la Tonnelle," Legendre describes the climax of the ceremony this way:

> All were possessed by the demon of art, trembling, restless, rising up with its powerful voice. Their ardent eyes, which roll back in their heads, reflect the tempest of their anguished souls. The mask of their countenance, disfigured by emotion, becomes quasi-frightful. A nervous flow like the jet of a flame rises up to the head. One has the impression of a

person on fire. Their feet seem to lose contact with the ground and the guitar raves in a language almost human. (Legendre 1939, 359)

This preference for the more spectacular aspects of possession trance, including editorial comments on participants "burning" while engaged in religious observances or having "anguished souls," is typical of most accounts of Vodou ceremonies in *Les Griots*. Descriptions of the "fearful countenances" of the ceremony's participants bring the reading audience closer to a visceral experience of the ceremony while simultaneously repelling readers with a frightening and somewhat sinister interpretation of Vodou ceremonial behavior.

In addition to their interest in bringing the practices of the rural, Vodou-practicing majority to urban Haitian readers, noiristes were determined to promote the idea of a racial spirit or "geist" (Dash 1988, 55) that would scientifically prove the primacy of African influence on the culture and religion of Haiti. In their "Question d'anthropo-sociologie: Le determinisme racial," Denis and Duvalier argue that racial characteristics, including psychological dispositions, are inherited, not learned (Denis and Duvalier 1939, 307). Therefore, according to Denis and Duvalier, the psychology of a racial group is preserved despite historical and sociological circumstances; French cultural influence was no more than a patina on the Haitian racial mentality. The noiriste views of the Haitian Griots bore some resemblance to pan-African movements such as *négritude*, but Haitian noirisme eventually moved toward justifying totalitarian rule by a black elite. In the 1960s, François Duvalier was to draw upon biological arguments about racial characteristics to rationalize his own political goals of eliminating mulatto opposition to his "presidency for life."

Haitian communists shared the noiriste vision of the Haitian peasantry as the root of Haitian culture. However, communists objected to the noiriste claim that class was subsumed by issues of race. Jacques Roumain (1907–44), a Haitian poet and political activist who founded the Haitian Communist Party (P.C.H.) in 1934, was an outspoken critic of noiriste ideology, especially the idea that the black middle-classes were suitable representatives for the downtrodden Haitian masses. In his *Analyse schématique* (1934), Roumain sharply criticized the noiristes for exploiting class tensions for their own political gains. "The duty of the P.C.H. . . . is to alert the proletariat, the poor 'petit bourgeoisie' and intellectuals to the danger of black middle-class politicians who would like to exploit for their own ends the former's justified anger" (quoted in Dash 1981, 139).

For all of his political activism on behalf of the Communist Party, Roumain was not a doctrinaire Marxist. While he was jailed several times in the 1930s for his communist politics, his interpretation of Marxism was tempered with a strong sense of Haitian nationalism and anti-occupation sentiment. However, it was Roumain's views of Vodou as a Haitian cultural resource that put him most at odds with a Marxist interpretation of Haitian traditional religion. In his pamphlet *A propos de la campagne 'anti-superstitieuse'* (1942), Roumain echoed the Marxist critique of Haitian religion as "false consciousness" while acknowledging Vodou's unique place in Haitian society. Believing that the need for Vodou would disappear when the material conditions of the Haitian peasantry improved, Roumain, like Jean Price-Mars, argued for improved education and access to scientific advances to ameliorate peasant misery:

> Naturally, it is necessary to free the Haitian masses from these mystical shackles. But one does not triumph over these beliefs by violence or by the threat of hell. It is not the executioner's axe, the pyre's flame, nor the religious inquisition that destroys sorcery. It is the progress of science, the continuous development of human culture, a knowledge each day more profound of the structure of the Universe. (Roumain 1942, 11)

Roumain realized, however, that his hope for Haiti's future progress was dependent upon more than just education. In the early 1940s, Haiti's Vodou-practicing majority was under attack by the Haitian government as a threat to national security.

Roumain's pamphlet was a response to the "anti-superstition campaign" that began immediately upon the inauguration of Haitian president Elie Lescot in 1941. Lescot was a light-skinned Haitian elite who, like Louis Borno, was vehemently opposed to Vodou and vowed to rid the country of so-called superstitions through a vigorous employment of sporadically enforced anti-Vodou laws. Urged by Monsignor Paul Robert, the bishop of Gonaïves, to stamp out Vodou's alleged pernicious influence on Haitian morality, Lescot allowed Haitian military police to invade Vodou temples in order to confiscate and destroy ceremonial objects including drums and altar objects.

While the campaign was brief—violence against middle-class churches in Port-au-Prince brought the campaign to a halt—the damage done to Vodou communities was profound and long lasting.[3] The anti-superstition campaign was a direct attack on the heretofore marginalized and ignored practice of Vodou. Even after Lescot stopped the campaign, he continued to believe that Vodou was a bad influence on Haitians and maintained an active, albeit more surreptitious policing of overt Vodou activity. Still, despite Lescot's personal animosity toward Vodou, he recognized that Haitian traditional religion, if properly controlled and directed, was a potential source of information about the Haitian peasants' mentality.

In October 1941, Lescot asked Jacques Roumain, his political enemy and harsh critic, to found the Bureau d'Ethnologie d'Haïti. Lescot made a deft political move. By asking Roumain, a respected poet and political activist to head the Bureau, Lescot could better control his rival's criticism and be free of charges of nepotism. Roumain's interest in a more "scientific" approach to the study of Haitian folklore also allowed Lescot to exclude a more noiriste version of Haitian traditional religion from the bureau's mission. Lorimer Denis, who would assume the directorship of the bureau after Roumain's brief tenure, would steer the bureau on a noiriste course, but Roumain's charge "to inventory archeological and ethnological items, to investigate and preserve archeological sites, to organize a Museum of Haitian ethnology, and to publish a quarterly bulletin of the Bureau's research" (Statement of Purpose 1956, vii) continues to the present day under the reorganized Faculté d'Ethnologie at the Université d'Haïti.

During his year-long tenure as head of the bureau, Roumain actively participated in ethnographic research and later in teaching. Initially, the bureau was devoted exclusively to research; soon after its founding, Jean Price-Mars, at the invitation of the president, founded the Institut d'Ethnologie, a teaching institution staffed by members of the bureau. Roumain taught pre-Columbian archeology and anthropology (Fowler 1980, 216). In his capacity as anthropologist, Roumain conducted original fieldwork with the *ougan* or Vodou priest Abraham in preparation for his *Le sacrifice du tambour assoto(r)* (1943). *Le sacrifice* followed a model of close ethnographic description established by Melville Herskovits in his *Life in a Haitian Valley* (1937). Roumain's documenting the intricate details of making the large and ceremonially important *asotò* drum served to support Herskovits's thesis that African culture not only survived but shaped the mentality of persons of African descent, especially in Haiti.

If Roumain's research set an important precedent for the institutionalization of ethnographic work in Haiti, his fictional accounts of the Haitian peasantry have provided an enduring commentary on the worldview of the rural masses. Several of Roumain's works concern the peasantry, but two works in particular—*La montagne ensorcelée* (The Bewitched Mountain) and *Gouverneurs de la rosée* (Masters of the Dew)—explore what Roumain biographer Carolyn Fowler calls "the peasant mentality" that earlier Haitian authors tended to ignore. According to Fowler, other attempts to write about Haitian peasants, most notably Antoine Innocent's *Mimola* (1906/1970), tend to depict Vodou as "archetypal religious beliefs and [as] a stage through which all religions pass" (Fowler 1980, 128). Innocent's work, while sympathetic to peasants, still ascribes their motives to ignorance and superstition, thus conforming to the rhetoric of the anti-superstition campaign.

Roumain tried to combine his interest in ethnography with his literary goals. In *La montagne ensorcelée,* for example, Roumain used phrases in Haitian creole as well as "the Haitian divergences of morphology [and] syntax" (Fowler 1980, 121) to give readers a sense of immediacy and connection to characters that would otherwise be unfamiliar.

It was, however, Roumain's *Gouverneurs de la rosée* that brought him international acclaim and presented the Haitian masses to an international audience. Finished in 1943 and published posthumously, *Gouverneurs de la rosée* tells the story of Manuel, a Haitian sugarcane cutter who, upon returning to his natal village after working in Cuba, discovers that his town has been decimated by a drought and split by a feud. Realizing that the town must pull together in order to deal with its desperate plight, Manuel invokes the idea of the *konbit* or cooperative labor group as a model for remedying their situation. Despite Manuel's enlistment of a local woman, Annaïse, to help him, Manuel's dream of a verdant and prosperous future for his village is thwarted at every turn by suspicious and jealous neighbors. Manuel's ultimate demise at the hand of one of Annaïse's spurned suitors is redeemed by his dying gift: the discovery of water that will benefit the village. Annaïse, who carries Manuel's unborn child, oversees the irrigation of the peasant fields and hopes for a better future. Despite its proletarian leanings (i.e. its emphasis on class over race), *Gouverneurs de la rosée* bears a close resemblance to noiriste depictions of peasant life, specifically in its tendency to cast the Haitian peasant in a timeless, universal context.[4]

Just as noiriste writers in *Les Griots* were interested in shaping their descriptions of Vodou ceremonies to conform to an Africanist worldview, so Roumain used ethnographic techniques to cast Haitian traditional religion as a cultural artifact that expressed not just a connection to Africa but a universalist appeal to other cultures. While Roumain was not the first Haitian author to use Haitian Kreyòl in literature, his descriptions of peasant activities, complete with footnotes to explain Haitian customs, put rural life in terms more amenable to middle-class readers.

As Haitians sought to rebuild their country after the U.S. occupation, all three political groups—mulatto elites, noiristes, and socialists—had differing ideas about how best to put peasant culture to their own uses. Noiristes and communists, however, shared the conviction that the Haitian peasantry was essential in defining a unique Haitian culture and that ethnography would provide insight into that culture. As ethnography became a more accepted and expected element in presentations of Haitian culture in the late 1940s and early 1950s, the tourism industry incorporated the newly configured Haitian peasant into its own version of Haitian culture. Vodou, with its spectacular versions of possession trance, became a primary focus for tourist accounts. This touristic version of Haitian culture was intended to create a cultural commodity that would distinguish Haiti as unique while proving it worthy of comparison with other nations.

REPRESENTING HAITIAN CULTURE:
THE SIMULACRUM OF "VOODOO"

Haiti's relationship with the rest of the world, and especially with the United States, was transforming rapidly during the 1940s. Earlier, during the U.S. occupation of Haiti, Vodou was seen as little more than superstition that, in its more spectacular forms, made suitable entertainment for foreigners craving tropical excitement. Vodou shows, especially under the anti-Vodou regime of Louis Borno (president, 1922–30), flourished as a "contact zone" (Pratt 1992) between Haitians interested in making money through presentations of folkloric culture and foreigners who were eager for an "authentic" experience with a religious practice that, for them, represented the occult, albeit in a palatable and relatively safe form.

Not all Haitians were thrilled, however, with the increased exposure of Haitian culture through Vodou. Dantès Bellegarde, in his *Haiti et ses problems* (1941) issued a withering critique of tourism's promotion of Haiti's African culture, describing Haiti as "in the center of the Americas, a Dahomean island, with a Bantu culture and a Dahomean religion for the amusement of Yankee tourists" (quoted in Dash 1981, 125). Before the beginning of the tourist trade in the 1940s, other writers like Jean Price-Mars, in his *Une étape d'evolution haïtienne* (1929), accused William Seabrook of exaggerating his experiences in Haiti in *The Magic Island* (1929) as a way to sell his book to gullible foreigners. Price-Mars accused Seabrook of inventing what he had hoped to find: "Thus, when foreign writers arrive in our country . . . they do nothing but draw out absurd beliefs, the most abracadabraish remarks and put them into the mouths of authentic personalities to give their stories a veneer of truth" (Price-Mars 1929, 155). Price-Mars's critique of Seabrook centers on the author's efforts to create a narrative of credibility based upon first-hand testimony. Seabrook describes many different "spiritual" contexts, from the making of a magic charm or *ouanga* to stories about magic spells driving Haitians insane. While many of Seabrook's so-called eyewitness accounts in *The Magic Island* are no more than twice-told tales he picked up from Haitian friends, Seabrook's book did make an effort to distinguish Vodou from magic, terms most earlier accounts of Haitian life tended to conflate.

As Laënnec Hurbon has shown, foreigners became active in the business of representing Haitian culture, especially from the 1920s onward (Hurbon 1995). After the publication of Seabrook's *The Magic Island*, there were several books published by white non-Haitian authors that featured the most objectionable stereotypes about Haitians. While such works were not based on ethnographic research per se, their first-person accounts, complete with eyewitness-style language and prurient detail, purported to place readers on site as witnesses to a virtual event.

Some of the more objectionable representations of Haitian culture in the 1930s included Faustin Wirkus and Taney Dudley's *The White King of La Gonave* (1931) and John Houston Craige's *Black Baghdad* (1933) and *Cannibal Cousins* (1934). Wirkus's book recounts his experiences as a U.S. Marine during the occupation of Haiti; he is "crowned king" by the destitute inhabitants of La Gonave, a poor and desiccated island in the Gulf of La Gonave, about thirty kilometers off the coast from Port-au-Prince. Wirkus sees himself as a civilizing force in this Haitian backwater; his persecution of Vodou practitioners and his hunting down of Kako resistance fighters is presented as unambiguously beneficial for his "subjects." John H. Craige's *Black Baghdad* and *Cannibal Cousins* cast Haitians as magic-practicing cannibals who would, for the right price, turn their unfortunate enemies into zombies.

The zombie (or *zonbi* in Haitian Kreyòl) has fascinated foreign audiences since the nineteenth century. While the concept of *zonbi* is internationally widespread, it has a very different meaning in Haiti than in the rest of the world. In Haitian folklore, the zonbi is a person whose soul has been stolen and who is forced to work against his or her will. The zonbi is a metaphor for the slave experience, the memory of which was very current in the minds of Haitians, especially the minds of those forced to work on labor gangs during the U.S. occupation. While the concept of zonbi implied a loss of freedom for Haitians in the 1920s, it conveyed a simultaneously dramatic and dreadful image for foreigners. Perhaps that is why the first "horror film" created in Hollywood was based on Seabrook's *The Magic Island* and titled *White Zombie* (1932) (Hurbon 1995, 192). As Hurbon points out, zombies in particular and Vodou in general "inspire in the outside observer a sense of 'disquieting strangeness' and ambivalent feelings of attraction and revulsion, onto which diverse fantasies can be projected" (Hurbon 1995, 181).

Foreigners' propensity to project their anxieties upon Haitian subjects has become a staple of U.S.-Haitian relations and continues to shape Haiti's international reputation as a dismal and dangerous place. Elsewhere, I have argued that Haiti has been engulfed by a "manufactured simulacrum" in which the word Vodou "conjures images of dolls pierced with pins, zombies that torment the living, and black magic in which malevolent sorcerers inflict pain and punishment on recalcitrant worshippers and hapless foreigners" (Largey 1998, 28). As the only republic ever founded on a slave revolt, Haiti was, during the nineteenth century, a grim reminder to U.S. slaveholders of the price that would be paid if slave-holders were to lose control. Thus, white American anxiety about Haitian (read black) agency in resisting slavery produced a literature of projection in which evil, subhuman behavior was attributed to Haitians. U.S. journalists were complicit in negative descriptions of Haiti. In 1895, the *New York Herald* ran a lengthy story claiming first-hand accounts of cannibalism and human sacrifice in Haiti. Such stories, which have continued through the twentieth century, consistently portray Haiti as a dangerous place. As late as 1994, when U.S. troops prepared to land in Haiti for the "intervasion" designed to reinstall ousted Haitian president Jean-Bertrand Aristide to power, CBS news anchor Dan Rather referred to Haiti as the land of "voodoo and mangoes." [5]

Simulacra, or models of reality in which facts are reordered to conform to a new "hyperreality," are often connected to commerce. The French cultural theorist Jean Baudrillard, who coined the term, has written about places like Disneyland as "alternative realities" that have their own conventions, behaviors, and rules. In the case of Haiti, simulated Voodoo and its attendant behaviors (zombies, human sacrifice, and evil magic) take on an existence separate from actual Vodou practice in Haitian communities. In the absence of evidence to the contrary, such simulacra can replace reality with a coherent, if exaggerated, "hyperreality" that becomes increasingly difficult to dislodge from the collective consciousness of a population. Thus, while foreigners have continued to explore the practices of Vodou in Haiti, Seabrook's accounts of Haitian "zombies" dominate the imaginations of foreign readers. As audiences in the United States watch such films as *The Serpent and the Rainbow* (1987) or *Voodoo Moon* (1990) on HBO, Vodou's continued success as commercial entertainment is a testament to the enduring power of the manufactured simulacrum known as Voodoo.

While the popular presentation of Haitian culture by foreign observers in the 1930s was misleading, such depictions were partially responsible for bringing Haiti to audiences in the United States and Europe. As foreign audiences' appetites for information about the "black republic" increased, they demanded materials that confirmed rather than challenged their impressions of Haiti as a hotbed of Vodou activity.

TOURISM IN HAITI: SELLING COMMODITIES, SELLING CULTURE

As foreigners clamored for Haitian cultural products, Haitians were actively developing different cultural programming that would capitalize upon the new international interest in Haitiana. The arts, especially painting, dance, and folkloric music, became growth areas for the Haitian tourism industry. Non-Haitians residing in Haiti were also active in the promotion of Haitian culture through tourism.

In 1944, DeWitt Peters, a conscientious objector from the United States, opened the Centre d'Art in Port-au-Prince. The center was both a teaching institute and a commercial art space, providing local Haitian artists with a unique opportunity to have their paintings displayed for Haitian elite and foreign tourist audiences. Many Haitian artists who would go on to become internationally known painters received their start at the center. Among them were Louverture Poisson (1914–84), Castera Bazile (1923–65), Rigaud Benoît (1911–86), Gerard Valcin (1923–88), Hector Hyppolite (1894–1948), and Philomé Obin (1892–1986). Hyppolite, a house painter from St. Marc, was brought to the Centre d'Art by Haitian novelist Philippe Thoby-Marcelin; his subsequent "discovery" by visiting French surrealist André Breton in 1945 brought Hyppolite to the attention of the international art world (Stebich 1992, 140). Philomé Obin was perhaps the most commercially successful artist to come from Cap Haïtien, the major port city in northern Haiti.

Vodou became an increasingly popular and profitable subject for Haitian painters, especially at the height of the Haitian tourism industry in the 1950s. The work of these Haitian artists has most often been labeled "primitivist," thus linking the style of Obin and Hyppolite with the exoticism of such European artists as Paul Gaughin (1848–1903). Hyppolite's taste in artistic subjects also included subjects from Vodou religious life. His *La Surene* (1947) and *La Maîtresse Sirène* (1947) feature the Vodou spirit Lasiren, the aquatic cousin of Ezili. By aligning Vodou with the "primitivist" vogue in European artistic circles, Haitian artists made Vodou presentable for European audiences eager for exotica.

Dance, especially dance associated with Vodou ceremonies, was also fostered by the growth of Haitian tourism and, like painting, was influenced early on by foreigners. Katherine Dunham, an African American dancer trained in anthropology at the University of Chicago, is perhaps the best-known proponent of folkloric dance based on the rhythms and movements of Vodou ceremonies. While Dunham herself was not initially involved with Haitian tourism, her efforts to bring the *yanvalou, kongo* and *mayi* dances to Haitian dance stages had the indirect effect of cultivating a taste for Haitian dance among Haitian and foreign audiences.

Dunham's interest in dance went beyond the promotion of Haitian movement as a viable alternative to modernist dance in the United States. As a protegé of Melville Herskovits and Robert Redfield, Dunham was interested in direct observation of Vodou ceremonies. Much to Herskovits's dismay, however, Dunham chose to become an active participant-observer. In a letter dated 6 January 1936, Herskovits warned Dunham to be cautious about going through the *ousi kanzo* initiation ceremony; his fear for her safety was mitigated, however, by his belief that Dunham had "probably inherited *loa* [*lwa* or spirits] that makes this possible" (quoted in Clark 1994, 193). Dunham eventually became a *manbo* or initiated female Vodou priest.

Dunham's forays into the world of Vodou strained her relationships with members of the Haitian elite. Dumarsais Estimé, president of Haiti from 1946 to 1950, was, in the 1930s, a rising political figure and a friend of Dunham's. Dunham claimed that Estimé disapproved of her involvement in Vodou, staying "unfriendly for some time after my initiation" (Dunham 1969/1994, 144). As a manbo, Dunham dedicated her life to presenting Haitian dance as a part of a larger Haitian culture, a culture that included the practice of Vodou.

Another foreigner who brought Haitian dance to foreign audiences was Maya Deren, a dancer, filmmaker, and amateur ethnographer who came to Haiti in September 1947 on a Guggenheim fellowship for "creative work in the field of motion pictures" (Deren 1953/1983, 5). Deren eventually abandoned her film project and devoted herself to the documentation of Vodou religious ritual, especially the dances associated with spirit possession. In 1953, Deren published a book titled *Divine Horsemen* in which she provides a sympathetic portrait of Vodou religious participants and outlines the structure of the sacred rituals.

In 1949, the Haitian government actively promoted Haitian dance and theater, constructing the Théâtre de Verdure and hiring Jean Léon Destiné to lead a national dance company there (Wilcken 1992b, 8). The construction of the theater was part of a larger public works campaign by the Estimé administration to capitalize on the increase in foreign tourism. The Cité de l'Exposition, known to Haitians as the Bisantnè—or "Bicentennial Square" in honor of the bicentennial of Port-au-Prince—was a large public square flanked by the central post office and the customs house. It was a two-minute walk from the wharf where large, tourist-filled cruise ships docked and vendors hawked souvenirs ranging from mass-produced Haitian paintings and ebony sculptures to postcards and bottles of inexpensive rum. The Bisantnè was intended to infuse the Haitian economy with foreign exchange and, according to Gage Averill, to "build an infrastructure for tourism, showcase Haiti (and especially Haitian indigenous arts), further the modernization of Haiti, and create a lasting monument to Estimé's *noiriste* revolution" (Averill 1997, 64).

In addition to foreign interest in Vodou, a few bourgeois Haitians became interested in performing Haitian music with connections to the Vodou ceremony. In 1937, Lina Fussman Mathon Blanchet founded the Choeur Folklorique National, an amateur group of Haitian singers who interpreted "folkloric" repertoire, that is, harmonized choral works set to Haitian themes (Dauphin 1983, 5). In 1941, Mme. Blanchet took a group of amateur Haitian singers to the Pan American conference in Washington, D.C. Calling themselves the "Legba Singers," Blanchet's choir was the first musical group to feature both Haitian music and dance on stage. Mme. Blanchet told me in 1988 that her group performed a "danse Congo" at the 1941 conference, but that the group's unfamiliarity with the rhythms of the Vodou ceremony meant that they didn't know if their Congo dance was done to Congo rhythms or to Ibo rhythms.[6]

Whether viewing a theatrical production while vacationing in Haiti or attending a dance performance by Haitians visiting the United States, foreign audiences valued Haiti for its exoticism. Haiti was believed to be a mystical place where the spirit and human worlds intersected. Haiti also provided an imaginary antidote to the rational, materialistic world of the foreign tourist. For the majority of Haitian elites in postwar Haiti, however, depictions of rural life continued to be repellent because of their discomfiting associations with the practice of Vodou. Haitian art music composers brought the music and culture of the Vodou ceremony to a Haitian elite audience that was predisposed to reject it. Musical compositions based on the music of Vodou were still regarded as potentially threatening to the social status quo in Haiti.

MAKING AN ETHNOGRAPHIC METHOD OF MUSICAL COMPOSITION IN HAITI

Moving the music of the Vodou ceremony to the concert stage during the late 1930s and 1940s required not only a concerted collection effort on the part of amateur musicologists, but also an ethnographic method that would suit the needs of both professional ethnographers and Haitian composers interested in using Vodou music in their own work. Upon his return to Haiti in 1937, Jaegerhuber began a multi-year folksong collection project in which he listened to the songs and rhythms of the Haitian peasantry and made transcriptions of Haitian music. He developed his own idiosyncratic ethnographic method to transform the songs he collected in his scrapbooks from monophonic tunes into concert pieces. His ethnographic approach borrowed from contemporaneous trends in German *Volkskunde* research, French studies of the urban poor, and long-term ethnographic studies conducted by U.S. researchers including Melville Herskovits and Harold Courlander.

Jaegerhuber was probably first exposed to the idea of folksong collection during his formative years in Germany. The study of folklore was pioneered by the German theologian Johann Gottfried Herder during the late eighteenth century; Herder's scholarship on the poetry of the "unlettered German masses" led the German literati "to an appreciation of folk poetry as a genuine locus of folkness" (Bendix 1997, 35). By focusing on the artistic production of the "folk" as an artistic and national treasure, Herder prepared the way for nineteenth-century German "folklore associations" in which "educated amateur scholars such as teachers, pastors, and lawyers often aided 'real' scholars in their collection efforts" (Bendix 1997, 101). Students from disciplines in the arts were encouraged to participate in the collection of Volkskunde as a way to connect their own subjects with that of the folk poetry movement started by Herder.[7]

While it is likely that Jaegerhuber was familiar with the German Volkskunde movement, his methods for extracting the folksong of the Haitian masses for use in his own compositions borrowed directly from a nineteenth-century French composer, Georges Kastner. In 1857, Kastner published *Les Voix de Paris*, a peculiar work that provided documentation of Parisian street song cries in the form of musical transcriptions. Like many people interested in the songs of the poor, Kastner believed that street songs were in danger of disappearing. By notating the songs of the street people of Paris, Kastner thought that he could not only preserve this allegedly disappearing art but also produce materials for French composers interested in connecting their work to "the people." Kastner's work contains the transcriptions of various street songs as well as a fully scored concert work, *Les cris de Paris,* which contains musical quotations from the ethnographic portion of the text.

Kastner's artistic sensibility combined an interest in preserving musical materials from the lower classes with a desire to create elite musical compositions that connected different strata of French society. Like Kastner, Jaegerhuber collected Haitian folk songs and used the melodies, rhythms, and lyrics of the songs to create a new art song style in his *Complaintes Haïtiennes* (1950). Jaegerhuber added harmony to these monophonic songs in hopes of transforming them into a work that could be shared with audiences outside Haiti as well.

Jaegerhuber also actively encouraged other Haitian researchers to follow Kastner's research example. At Jaegerhuber's urging, René Victor, a Haitian sociologist, wrote a study of Haitian street songs that used Kastner's model. Like Kastner, Victor supervised the collection of street people's songs in order to document the cultural practices of what he believed to be a rapidly disappearing segment of the population. Since members of the bourgeoisie were not thought to be carriers of this folkloric heritage, it was up to the sociologist to collect the songs of the street and interpret them for an upper-class audience. In *Les Voix de nos rues* (The voices of our streets) (1943), Victor compiled Haitian song texts and melodies that were collected by several well-known Haitian composers, including Jude Villard of Port-de-Paix, Othello Bayard of Les Cayes, and Georges Clérié of Jérémie. Victor thanked Jaegerhuber for his help in assembling the collection, noting that Jaegerhuber "has great fondness for the airs of our streets and has helped me understand the language of this music" (Victor 1943, 9).

While Jaegerhuber's interest in ethnographic work originated in Germany and was influenced by French sociological trends, his subsequent exploration of Haitian folklife was shaped as much by contemporaneous trends in Caribbean ethnography, specifically the work of Melville Herskovits and Harold Courlander. Melville Herskovits and his wife and fellow researcher, Frances, conducted fieldwork in the Mirebalais valley in Haiti in 1934–35. In 1937, Herskovits wrote *Life in a Haitian Valley* (1937), which was the first English-language ethnographic account of rural life in Haiti. The Herskovits' fieldwork came directly at the end of the U.S. occupation of the country; it was sanctioned by Haitian President Sténio Vincent, whom Herskovits thanked profusely in the preface of his book (Herkovits 1937, xxi).

The Herskovits' approach to fieldwork in Haiti signaled a significant departure from earlier treatments of life in the Haitian hinterlands and challenged the ways in which culture had been viewed in Haiti until that time. With its historical link to French-influenced ideas of refinement, breeding, and taste, "culture" had been considered something possessed only by Europeans. Herskovits's anthropologically oriented notion of culture as a dynamic system that underwent steady change over time challenged the idea that culture was the sole province of the ruling elite. As in his and his wife's earlier ethnography, *Suriname Folklore* (1936), *Life in a*

Haitian Valley began with a consideration of the historical and cultural background of the majority of the country's population: black people brought to the Americas from Africa in bondage. *Life in a Haitian Valley* assumed the primacy of African culture and described the cultural "amalgam" (1937, 48) of African, Indian, and European cultures in terms of "what the slaves found in Haiti" (33–47). Haitian culture, in Herskovits's eyes, began in Africa and was influenced but not completely determined by European culture. Herskovits's views of culture also reinforced the cultural critique voiced by Jean Price-Mars in the early 1920s; culture, in this case the African-derived culture of the Haitian peasant, was believed to reside more in the daub and wattle huts of the countryside than in the gingerbread houses of the Haitian elite.

Following the Herskovits's lead by locating the origins of Haitian culture in Africa rather than Europe, Harold Courlander, a folklorist and novelist from the United States, collected hundreds of Haitian songs between 1932 and 1938. Published in 1939, Courlander's *Haiti Singing* was the first book-length monograph devoted entirely to music of the Haitian countryside. Courlander collected hundreds of song texts and melodies with the help of Libera Bordereaux, André Jean, and Télisman Charles, rural Haitians who were hired by Courlander as fieldwork assistants; together they attended Vodou ceremonies on the plain of Léogâne, in the Cul-de-Sac region, and in Kenscoff, all places within driving distance of Port-au-Prince. For help transcribing the melodies of Haitian songs, Courlander enlisted Arthur Lyncée Duroseau, a Haitian violinist and member of a well-known elite musical family in Port-au-Prince.

Courlander was interested in making a ritual taxonomy of Haitian music by collecting and classifying as many songs as possible associated with the Vodou ceremony since Vodou, in Courlander's and Herskovits's views, was one of the richest repositories of African culture in the Americas. He was less interested in musical genres that he believed were not associated with Haiti's African past:

> If it seems that the Catholic element in Haitian religious life has been neglected somewhat in this book, I can only say that I was especially interested in African survivals. Some of the songs I gathered, for example, were so obviously Catholic and Catholic-Haitian that they failed to interest me. The more archaic they appeared in form, content, and spirit, the better I liked them. (Courlander 1939, 234)

As a result, the Catholic prayers and *cantiques* (hymns) that are part of the opening of Vodou ceremonies are absent from Courlander's account. By ignoring the Catholic elements in the ceremony and relying on his intuition about what sounded most "archaic" and thus what he thought to be most authentically connected to African culture, Courlander wrote a description of Haitian music that focused on a narrow portion of a much larger repertoire.

Courlander's *Haiti Singing* included 126 song melodies with text as well as transcriptions of the drum parts for two Haitian dances (Courlander 1939, 177–226). Courlander and Arthur Duroseau spent countless hours listening to singers brought in from the area surrounding Port-au-Prince, with Duroseau transcribing the melodies and Courlander scribbling song texts as quickly as he could. Courlander describes the conflict between researchers and performers this way:

> We [Courlander and Duroseau] sometimes spent as long as an hour and a half on one short song, the singer or singers going on and on, everybody perspiring and determined. Sometimes to break the monotony the singers improvised with new words or variations on the melodies. We had to force them to 'be good.' We naturally recognized that what we took for improvisations might have been the proper form. We would argue about it, and sometimes they would admit that they were just encouraging themselves through the tedium; then we would begin again. (Courlander 1939, 231)

Courlander's distinction between "improvisations" and the "proper form" for each song underscored a common theme in the collection of Haitian music. While Courlander attended many different types of Haitian cultural performances during his time there, all of the transcriptions in *Haiti Singing* were made from the "studio sessions" Courlander described above. This somewhat artificial setting, as well as the belief that songs and texts could be reduced to a transcription "shorthand," in which salient characteristics of the song could be notated and then subjected to analysis, ignored the social, cultural, and political contexts in which these songs were used.

Of course, the inclusion of data about the cultural and social context of musical performance would have made the type of musical analysis Courlander wanted to do nearly impossible. By isolating songs and their texts and removing their cultural contexts, Courlander was only trying to create a manageable musical data bank that could be used by other researchers in their work on Haitian culture. His melodic transcriptions, with their standardized tempi, diatonically "corrected" pitch levels, and singular versions of repeated melodic patterns, were intended to provide grist for future study. Courlander didn't analyze the musical content of his transcriptions himself; that task was left to professionally trained music

scholars. For some of the more complicated multi-part drumming examples, Courlander asked George Herzog, an anthropologist and ethnomusicologist at Columbia University, to redo the transcriptions that Courlander and Duroseau made initially (Courlander 1939, 177–81; 234). For
Courlander, making a musically "clean" transcription, free from the va-
garies of inadvertent musical variation, was the best way to preserve and
accurately describe the essence of a particular song.

What such regularized transcriptions sacrificed, however, was the improvisatory nature of the music, the very quality that Courlander and
Duroseau attempted to suppress in their bored performers. Despite
Courlander's many visits to Vodou temples in Haiti, he never recorded or
made transcriptions of ceremonies in progress. When I met Courlander
in 1985, he told me that doing fieldwork in the 1930s was a very challenging task. With much of the Haitian countryside without electricity
and the roads poorly maintained throughout the country, it was nearly
impossible to use his cumbersome acetate disk recording equipment outside Port-au-Prince. Consequently, Courlander relied on Bordereaux and
Jean to find singers and bring them to the favorite destination of foreign
tourists, the Hotel Oloffson, where Courlander had set up his recording
equipment on the hotel's veranda.[8]

To be fair, Courlander did not present his research as fieldwork collected entirely in the mountains of the Haitian countryside. Courlander's
decision to do much of his song collecting on the veranda of the Hotel
Oloffson was due not only to the hotel's convenient location in Port-au-
Prince but also to Courlander's own goals for his song collection. Courlander's song collection was a distillation of melodic materials from a
larger Haitian repertoire; where he collected his musical examples was
less important to him than how many songs he collected. While Courlander hoped eventually to create a complete taxonomy of Haitian ritual music, he also realized that, in order for other researchers to make use of his
materials, he would have to reduce his song collection to easily comparable samples.[9]

Courlander's decision to focus his musical taxonomy on intervallic relationships within the songs reflected his belief that melodies could be
classified by the intervals they used; this focus caused him to ignore or gloss
over their salient differences but enabled his thesis that the melodies were
representative of a Haitian cultural essence. Perhaps this is why most of
the songs in Courlander's collection have the same key and meter signatures; all of the 126 transcriptions in the appendix of *Haiti Singing* are in
duple meter with a 2/4 time signature while nearly 60 percent of the songs
are in the keys of C major or A minor. By keeping the time signatures and

tonalities of the various melodies uniform, the transcriptions were easier to compare with each other.

Werner Jaegerhuber's method for transcribing Haitian folk songs followed Courlander's model closely. Just as Arthur Duroseau provided musical transcriptions for Courlander, Jaegerhuber worked with Haitian anthropologist Louis Maximilien, whose *Le Vodou Haïtien: Rites radas canzo* (1945) provided a detailed account of ritual practices in the Rada *nanchon* (or denomination) of Vodou. Chapter 16 of *Le Vodou Haïtien*, "Erzulie Freda Dahomey," was a collaboration between Maximilien and Jaegerhuber; Maximilien wrote the text of the chapter and Jaegerhuber provided several transcriptions of songs associated with Vodou religious practice.

Jaegerhuber's analyses of Vodou songs in *Le Vodou Haïtien* focused on three musical features: intervallic relationships, melodic phrase structure, and melodic modes. In his transcription of a song titled "Herzulie," Jaegerhuber noted that the opening phrase of songs to this Vodou spirit often begins with the same pattern: "The invocation of the spirit is a stable phrase that returns in all the melodies in which Erzulie is invoked in the form: do-mi-sol" (Maximilien 1945/1982, 205). Jaegerhuber isolated the different phrases of the melodies and assigned them numbers; his analyses of songs for Erzulie and Agouet (Agwe) refer to his enumerated phrases and their intervallic components (205–9).

While Courlander and Duroseau traced Haitian culture to Africa exclusively, Jaegerhuber and Maximilien's inclusion of Greek modes located the wellspring of Haitian song in both Africa and Europe. Jaegerhuber's use of modal language did not stop with the modes themselves; Jaegerhuber saw a more fundamental relationship between the Greek musical modes and Haitian religious music that implied a direct connection between Haitian culture and the culture of ancient Greece: "The music that accompanies Erzulie, and vodouesque rhythm more generally," wrote Maximilien, "is in the Lydian mode. These melodies are confirmed in the Lydian mode with the pentatonic ascension maintained by the rhythms of Demeter" (Maximilien 1945/1982, 200).

In a manuscript titled "Considerations sur le folklore: À propos de la musique de Werner Jaegerhuber" (1952), Louis Maximilien approvingly outlined Jaegerhuber's philosophy of musical composition, a philosophy that drew upon not only the European art music tradition but also the classical world of ancient Greece:

Mediterranean classicism, accepted as a paragon by the Atlantic civilization, has been formed by the contributions of numerous peoples. Its apex was reached—strangely and brusquely in a cryoscopical way—by the Greek miracle in an atmosphere saturated with cultural elements flowing in from their continents at the propitious moment of the twilight of the gods, at the time when Aeschulus, projecting on the scene the solemnity of religion, unable to sustain a religious trance of the past, restored . . . the tragic mask. That was a time of [nascent consciousness] of classicism, of unity, of clarity, of simplicity, and of measure with the help of the transformation of art under the pressure of philosophical values. That time has come for Haiti. (Maximilien 1954, 8–9)

In this passage, Maximilien equates Haiti's cultural condition with that of Ancient Greece just prior to the birth of tragedy. Just as Greek civilization transformed its pantheon of gods into a cultural resource for future generations, Haitian culture was, in Maximilien's opinion, poised to make the spirits of Vodou a legacy for artists, musicians, and writers. Maximilien compared the Vodou myths associated with the sea spirit Agouet [Agwe] with the myth of Osiris, "the drowned god whose limbs are devoured by fish except the membrum virile by which the resurrection is performed." Maximilien asked rhetorically, "is this not classical art?" (Maximilien 1954, 14).

For Jaegerhuber and Maximilien, Haitians would develop a new, vibrant form of culture akin to Greek drama when they learned to treat Vodou myths in the same way that Greek dramatists treated Greek myths—as material for art. Maximilien asserted that the classical synthesis of ancient Greece was played out in the relationship between art and folklore. He claimed that "art rests on folklore, and takes its roots from it, since both contain existential solutions and eschatological tendencies which hardly have varied notwithstanding modern intellectuality and refinements" (Maximilien 1954, 4). According to Maximilien, the successful combination of art and folklore brought out the "spirit of the people," while "extracting it from the gangue of superstition and sorcery weighing it down in a wholly unjustified way" (6).

Jaegerhuber certainly extracted Vodou from the "gangue of superstition"; his transformation of Vodou repertoire into art songs removed the music from its ceremonial context. However, stripping Vodou songs of their religious associations was not his primary goal. His motives for using Vodou-inspired melodies came more from his understanding of the composer's role in bringing art and folklore together. For Jaegerhuber, it was the example of the "great composers" in the European art music tradition that most successfully expressed the fusion of popular sentiment with classical sensibility. Maximilien noted:

As paradigms he sets before us nothing less than Bach, Mozart, Mahler, and Brahms. . . . According to Jaegerhuber the secret of classical music is the expression of a pure sentiment, centered in God or man withou any egocentric influence, which heightens the value of the human being and his deeds. (Maximilien 1954, 7)

Maximilien went on to claim that the classical fusion of art and folklore—symbolized by the architectural form of the arch, or *voute*—was most perfectly realized by Jaegerhuber in his treatment of Haitian traditional music:

> [Jaegerhuber] has endowed the Voodoo melody with all the requirements for visibility and universality by having it rendered accessible to occidental ears, and by having it opened to the inspiration of the artists of the planet. He has succeeded in his attempt because of his solid musical training, because of his capacity [for] applying the laws of harmonization and of counterpoint, also because of his ethnological knowledge. It is due to him that a classical production has taken birth from the Haitian folksong. (Maximilien 1954, 15–16)

ORTHOGRAPHY, TRANSCRIPTION, AND MUSIC IDEOLOGY

Jaegerhuber's and Maximilien's philosophical impulse to link Haitian culture to Europe was common among elite Haitians, especially when dealing with Haitian myths. When they came to transcribe the music of the Vodou ceremony, however, they entered into a politically charged debate about musical notation that echoed debates about the proper orthography for the Haitian Kreyòl language.

While ethnomusicologists have argued throughout the last century about the problems of using Western notation for musics outside the European art music canon (List 1974, Nettl 1983), and about the subjectivity of musical transcription (Jairazbhoy 1977), few researchers have focused on how the process of fixing sound in written form occurs within particular historical and political contexts. In the following section, I turn to arguments about the politics of orthography, the representation of the Haitian Kreyòl language in written form, to demonstrate that Jaegerhuber's musical transcriptions of peasant songs can be understood as politicized statements about Haitian peasant life.

In their study of orthographic debates about the proper written form of Haitian Kreyòl, sociolinguists Bambi Schieffelin and Rachel Doucet claim that written language cannot be distilled to an "authentic" form that accurately conveys the "essence" of a particular language. Rather, orthography, or the way in which a language is written, is the result of choices made as competing ideologies of power vie for control in a particular historical moment. In the case of Haitian Kreyòl, debates about how to write the language are part of a larger discourse of control in which different political views are expressed through different representations of language:

> Language ideology often determines which linguistic features get se-
> lected for cultural attention and for social marking, that is, which ones
> are important and which ones are not. In countries where "nation-ness"
> is being negotiated, every aspect of language—from its phonological
> features to lexical items to stylistic alternatives to multilingualism—can
> be contested, and often is. Similarly, in such situations, there is rarely a
> single ideology of language. Rather, one finds multiple, competing, and
> contradictory ideologies of language that are offered as the "logic" for
> which features may be contested. Such logics are often claimed to be
> strictly scientific, when, in fact, they are culturally constructed and rep-
> resent particular political and social interests. (Schieffelin and Doucet
> 1998, 286)

Similarly, the transcription of musical sound into a visual format is a potent venue for debates about Haitian "nation-ness" and reflects different
political positions of competitive ideological groups within Haitian society.

In the 1940s, the symbolic representation of both Haitian Kreyòl language and music were hotly contested. The first scholarly study of Haitian was published by Suzanne Sylvain; her *Le Créole Haïtien, morphologie et syntaxe* (1936) posited a grammatical link between Haitian and Ewe,
a West African language. While Sylvain did not propose a specific orthography in her work, her support of an African provenance for the contemporary Haitian Kreyòl language did underscore a belief that Haitian
peasant classes were culturally close to their African ancestors. In 1940,
Ormonde McConnell, a Northern Irish Methodist missionary, developed
an orthographic system that was drawn primarily from a phonetic alphabet; the American Frank Laubach helped revise McConnell's original system (Schieffelin and Doucet 1998, 295). The McConnell-Laubach orthography was different from most earlier, ad hoc orthographic systems
that derived their spellings from French. McConnell's system was criticized by Haitian linguist Charles Fernand Pressoir, whose *Débats sur le
créole et le folklore* (1947) posited a more French-looking orthographic system that criticized the use of such "Anglo Saxon looking" letters such as
w and *y* (Schieffelin and Doucet 1998, 297). The relative success of Pressoir's orthographic system was due in no small part to the degree of anti-
American—here equated with Anglo-Saxonism—sentiment still present
after the U.S. occupation.[10]

As Schieffelin and Doucet demonstrate, the debates in the 1940s about
how to notate Haitian Kreyòl were less about the orthography (or spell-

ing) and orthoepy (or pronunciation) of the language than they were about the political positions that such systems imply and reinforce. Whether or not McConnell-Laubach's or Pressoir's systems were phonemically "correct" was less important than whether their representation of the sound of Haitian Kreyòl in written form emphasized an acceptable etymological basis for the language. As linguistic notations, both systems were constrained by the social and political circumstances of their time. Despite its orientation toward a more international phonetic alphabet, the McConnell-Laubach orthography was perceived as catering to "foreign" (i.e. American) tastes—that is, away from Haitian elite views that favored a more French-derived image of the Haitian Kreyòl language. The debate about how best to represent the sounds of Haitian Kreyòl was more than an academic conflict over writing systems. It was "about the conception of [Haitian] kreyòl itself as a language and as an element of Haitian national identity, about how Haitians situate themselves through languages at the national and international levels, and about the notions of Haitianness, authenticity, nationalism and legitimacy" (Schieffelin and Doucet 1998, 300).

Similarly, debates about the representation of Haitian musical genres are more than just conflicts over stylistic preferences for how to notate musical phenomena. Musical transcriptions become transformative, politicized acts that imbue the process of producing ethnographic musical notation with meaning and power. In the case of ethnographic musical transcriptions of Haitian peasant music, the selection of specific rhythms, modes, and meters takes on a political dimension that links Haitian musical practices to specific historical and cultural contexts. When ethnographic musical transcription is then put to use as the basis for a concert music tradition, art music becomes a representation of local culture through its notational depictions of peasant music, as well as an expression of a cosmopolitan ethos through its use of universally readable Western notation.

For Jaegerhuber, the process of musical composition was shaped, in part, by what may be termed a "music ideology" in which contested notions of identity and representation that are found in language ideology are replicated and played out in musical notation. Such a music ideology postulates a particular way of doing things, or as Schieffelin and Doucet describe it, which features "are important and which ones are not" (1998, 286). Both Courlander and Jaegerhuber focused on the proper collection and notation of their respective folksong repertoires in order to reinforce their own assumptions about the social and political importance of Haitian song.

For Werner Jaegerhuber, transcribing Haitian folk songs and translating them into art music compositions involved following a carefully outlined method that would demonstrate the music's unique Haitian sensibility. Jaegerhuber's song collecting and transcription techniques followed Courlander's precedent in important ways, most notably in their shared concern for capturing the melodic and lyric "essence" of a song in order to make easily comparable melodic transcriptions.

Jaegerhuber and Courlander differed, however, in how they imagined the music of the Vodou ceremony to be connected to the experience of bourgeois Haitians. For Courlander, Vodou represented what was African about Haiti; the melodies and rhythms of Vodou ceremonial songs served as confirmation of the uniqueness of Haitian culture as an African-derived entity. Bourgeois Haitians were irrelevant to the musical practices of the Haitian peasant; Vodou songs stood as a testament to the enduring power of African culture. For Jaegerhuber, however, the music of the Haitian peasant was the point at which elite and peasant culture met. Haitian art music could only realize its potential with the enlivening infusion of Vodou musical materials. Conversely, the music of the Vodou ceremony could only be claimed by all Haitians once composers separated it from what Maximilien termed the "gangue of superstition."

In his article about Jaegerhuber's compositional philosophy, Louis Maximilien claimed that Jaegerhuber treated the music of the Vodou ceremony as the most inspirational source for his own work: "How often, upon hearing a Voodoo melody, has he exclaimed: 'What material for a powerful symphony for a giant like Beethoven!'" (Maximilien 1954, 17). If only there were repertoire that was symbolically linked to Haitian culture as Beethoven's works were tied to German culture, Haitian art music might, in this view, assume its place among the great musical traditions of the world. It might also help to redeem Haitian culture in the eyes of the Haitian elite, an elite that looked more toward Paris than Port-au-Prince for its musical inspiration.

The paradoxical duty of the nationalist composer, in Jaegerhuber's view, was to create a music tradition that simultaneously celebrated the uniqueness of the home culture and demonstrated that culture's universal aesthetic appeal. In this situation, ethnographic transcription provided the link between local and cosmopolitan cultures, between rural and urban musical styles, and between elite and peasant communities. Jaegerhuber believed that the collector/composer was the conduit for such a national music since he or she was knowledgeable about both worlds and drew upon that knowledge to create a new, traditionally infused art music.

In Jaegerhuber's mind, one step toward fashioning a Haitian art music that combined African and European ideas was to choose suitable rhythmic and metrical notations for his work. According to Jaegerhuber, careless use of indiscriminate rhythmic meters could result in a gross distortion of the original musical source. He bemoaned the practice of reducing folk songs to mere outlines of their melodies, preferring instead to set the melody in a rhythmic framework that communicated the original feeling of the song. He said "it is quite evident that if we exclude irregular and varied rhythms and imprison them in a rigid 2/4 measure, it will result in a false syncopation, invariably deceptive in modern usage, having no affinity with the ancient music of African folklore" (Jaegerhuber 1943, 53).

For Jaegerhuber, maintaining a musical link with Haiti's African cultural past was best realized through the use of a unique metrical and rhythmic notation that maintained a connection to African antecedents and reflected the artistic sensibility of the nationalist composer. According to Maximilien:

> Jaegerhuber insists on the rhythm of 5/8. He considers it as the only typical basis of the African music in Haiti. He has noticed that the melodies are short when circumscribed by this rhythm; they do not exceed an octave. The rhythm of 5/8 and the melody of an octave are the fundamental characteristics. (Maximilien 1954, 34)

Jaegerhuber thought that 5/8 meter captured the aesthetic sensibility of Haitian music and that it also reflected a deeper Haitian mentality, one that allowed the elite composer to tap into the exuberant ethos of Haitian ceremonial music:

> [Jaegerhuber] proposes that the isolated 5/8 be used instinctively in moments of psychological tension: anxiety, apprehension, joy, nostalgia, agony, or death, and the moment of incantation, of evocation "when the Negro with hands injured by work and disdain strikes the earth intent on thus entering in contact with the gods, and there from drawing solace." All the great songs of Haiti, of a religious nature, have the rhythm of 5/8. It contains the Negro's highest emotional expressions. The Haitian rediscovers in this rhythm his spontaneity, his grandeur, and his liberty. The Haitian composer has confined himself to the valse and the méringue solely because he did not understand the majesty, the magnificence, and the depth of those melodies in 5/8 which would have given him the inspiration for dramatic music in the grand style. (Maximilien 1954, 35–36)

Thus, in this view, meter provides not only a representation of a particular song's rhythmic organization but also a bridge between the inspirational potential of folk music and the transformative power of classical music. In this case, meter also allows "the Negro" to "rediscover . . . his

Example 5.1. O. Jeanty, père et fils, *Petite grammaire musicale*, p. 14

spontaneity, his grandeur, and his liberty," thus linking black people in the Americas to an ancestral rhythmic memory.

Other Haitian composers shared Jaegerhuber's interest in accurate meter for transcriptions of Haitian music, but their rationales for choosing particular meters—and their music ideologies—differed considerably from Jaegerhuber's. For most Haitian composers, 5/8 meter was one option among several for the proper notation of the Haitian méringue, a pan-Caribbean popular music and dance genre.

Debates about the proper rhythmic notation of the Haitian méringue reflected the "music ideology" of different elite factions during the late nineteenth and early twentieth centuries. As early as 1882, Occilius Jeanty, père et fils, Haiti's premier band composers, authored a music theory textbook titled *Petite grammaire musicale* (1882). The Jeanty's argued that the proper notation of the five-pulse méringue rhythm should be expressed as a quintolet, that is, five pulses over a duple meter (see ex. 5.1).

According to the Jeantys, "the quintolet, which one finds only in the méringue, is executed exactly like a triplet, observing the same value for five eighth-notes for two beats, with three eighth-notes of the triplet for one beat" (Jeanty 1882, 14). However, the Jeantys also mentioned that it was common for people to interpret the méringue rhythm differently. They observed that "the five eighth-notes of the measure may be replaced, depending on one's taste, by a group of three eighth-notes and two sixteenth-notes, written in the following manner" (see ex. 5.2).

The Jeantys were trying to establish a unique rhythmic notation for a dance genre that existed in different versions throughout the Caribbean,

Example 5.2. O. Jeanty, père et fils, *Petite grammaire musicale*, p. 15

including the Dominican Republic, Puerto Rico, and Venezuela (Austerlitz 1995, 17).

The Jeantys suggested notation for the quintolet was challenged in the 1910s by Théramène Ménès, a music professor at the Lycée Pétion in Pétionville. Ménès argued that the proper notation of the quintolet should only be a five-note rhythm over a duple meter:

> We . . . have sacrificed the quintolet; but since the importation of the American two-step, we have recognized our error and we have thus tried to adopt—for the notation of our meringue—the American method which is good. We say that the American method is good because the two-step, in sum, is nothing but the méringue written correctly and danced in an English style. (Ménès in Vincent 1910, 276)

Ménès's description of the proper notation of the Haitian méringue referred to one of his own compositions, "Magistrat Vincent," a political promotion song composed for Sténio Vincent, a rising Haitian legislator who would eventually become Haiti's president during the U.S. occupation. For Ménès to write music that captured the Haitian méringue rhythm in a notation accessible to and easily interpreted by American musicians underscored Vincent's political aspirations to open Haitian markets to U.S. investors. Ménès's claim that the American two-step was nothing but the "méringue written correctly and danced in an English style" aligned Haitian and American culture in ways that stressed their similarities and downplayed their differences.

When Werner Jaegerhuber introduced his 5/8 meter for the "proper" notation of Haitian folk music, he entered an ongoing debate about how Haitian culture should be represented to Haitian and foreign audiences. For Haitian musicians in the early twentieth century, meters and rhythms based on patterns of five connoted a nationalistic position on the notation of the méringue and evoked the memory of Occilius and Occide Jeanty, two of Haiti's most revered musicians. Conversely, duple meter renditions of the dance rhythm were associated with the encroachment of American political influence. It was no wonder that the amateur Haitian musicologist and composer Constintin Dumervé challenged Jaegerhuber's assertion that contemporary méringues should be notated in 5/8 meter. Dumervé claimed that "when using the 5/8 meter, the axis of the méringue is completely displaced [and] the structure is weakened to the point of leading Haitian and foreign performers of the rhythm astray" (Dumervé 1968, 309). For Dumervé, the issue was clear; the rhythm of a Haitian piece of music should be made accessible for all interpreters, Haitians as well as foreigners, through "correctly" notated phrases. Dumervé's view was that Haitian musicians' performance practices were irrelevant to the proper execution of the méringue; unless musical notation could graphically link Haitian and foreign interpreters to the méringue, such interpreters would inevitably be led "astray" rhythmically. For Jaegerhuber, the issue was more complex. Jaegerhuber agreed that the notation of Haitian rhythms should be accessible to both Haitians and foreigners, but he realized that achieving such accessibility was not easy to do. He believed that Haitian musicians should not sacrifice their "rhythmic" connections to their African ancestry—especially the use of 5/8 meter—in order to make folk music-based Haitian classical music legible to foreign audiences.

COMPLAINTES HAÏTIENNES AND THE
PRESENTATION OF HAITIAN CULTURE

It was Jaegerhuber's turn toward the ethnographic documentation of Haitian folk song that most clearly demonstrated his desire to link the music of the Haitian countryside with the concert hall and afforded a partial answer to the question of how a Haitian composer could preserve cultural connections between Haitian folk songs and art songs. From 1937 until 1948, Jaegerhuber collected folk songs that he kept in several music notebooks. Two of his notebooks, published by the Haitian Bureau of Ethnology in 1985, contained transcriptions of Vodou songs along with the composer's musical analyses of the pieces (see Grohs-Paul 1985; Jaegerhuber 1985).[11]

As Waltraud Grohs-Paul observes in her description of the Jaegerhuber collection, "Jaegerhuber's analyses refer primarily to [the transcriptions'] musical aspects. The socio-cultural context is minimal" (Grohs-Paul 1985, 73). For example, in the notes to his fourth song in the collection, "Agoue," Jaegerhuber gives the following impressionistic analysis of the piece: "Like with the Greeks where the minor tonality signifies the masculine principle, [the song "Agoue"] similarly speaks to us of the master of the oceans and of his personality, his grandeur and his powers" (Jaegerhuber 1985, 80).

Although he had an expressed interest in preserving the music of the Haitian peasant, Jaegerhuber did not initially interview many non-elite performers of Haitian song. One of his principal informants was Libera Bordereaux, the singer who provided many of the songs for Harold Courlander's books on Haitian folklore (Courlander 1939 and 1960/1985). The most frequently cited performers in his folksong notebooks were, however, members of the Haitian elite who were active participants in the Haitian art music movement that Jaegerhuber was promoting. Among

Jaegerhuber's principal performers were Rose Brierre (related to the poet Jean Brierre), Anna Nau (descendant of historian Émile Nau), Valerio Canez (amateur musician and member of the Pro Arte chorus), Lina Fussmann Blanchet (composer and director of the Choeur Folklorique National), René Victor (sociologist and author of *Les Voix de nos rues*), and Doctor Louis Mars (psychiatrist and son of Jean Price-Mars).

It would be easy to dismiss Jaegerhuber's folksong collections as misrepresentations of a Haitian cultural legacy since they were drawn from elite rather than peasant sources. In his study of the Grimm brothers, John Ellis criticizes the Grimms' similar reliance on elite sources for their editions of fairy tales. For Ellis, the Grimms' use of middle-class consultants "undermined the folk origin of the tales, and . . . the untutored, natural quality of their transmission by word of mouth, without benefit of literacy and education" (Ellis 1983, 26). It also brought their collection methods into question since most of the consultants they relied upon lived in bourgeois neighborhoods. Rather than inconvenience themselves to go among the rural folk and collect their tales, the Grimm brothers likely conducted fieldwork in their own homes. Finally, the elites who acted as raconteurs for the Grimms were probably French Huguenots and did not even speak German, the language of the folk tales, at home (Ellis 1983, 27).

Although Jaegerhuber did not engage in misleading rhetoric like the Grimms by claiming that his folk sources were "authentic" and taken from the mouths of the folk, his use of middle-class informants does call into question some of his own theories about the importance of the preservation of the Vodou heritage in Haiti. First, Jaegerhuber believed that there was a difference between the orally transmitted music of the Haitian peasant and the classical music of the Haitian elite. His theoretical claims about the melodic structure of Vodou melodies indicated that Jaegerhuber saw the music of the rural Vodou practitioner as determined by his/her location in the rural sphere. He believed that singers of these rural songs who made their way to the city were simply out of their natural context, unable to absorb the "higher" forms of musical composition championed by elite composers.

Also, Jaegerhuber's direct exposure to music of the countryside came relatively late in his life. After suffering a debilitating illness in the 1940s, Jaegerhuber spent much of his time in the mountains above Kenscoff, in a village called Obléon, near Furcy. He spent the last few years of his life working in a modest cottage, composing when he had the energy and interacting with local singers. It is unlikely, however, that Jaegerhuber ever made any excursions into the countryside during that period of his life, considering his weakened physical condition and the difficulty of navigating the mountainous terrain.

Finally, since most of the sources for Jaegerhuber's folksong collection were members of the elite, the songs were sung by persons who were bilingual in French and Haitian Kreyòl and probably spoke a great deal of French at home. Although he was interested in the preservation of the folkloric heritage of Haitian song, Jaegerhuber drew his material from people who performed these songs in contexts that little resembled the Vodou ceremony or the cooperative labor team of the konbit. Many of the elites Jaegerhuber interviewed either participated in or were familiar with the peasant songs through folkloric presentations of music, not from direct exposure to the music in a rural performance. In most folkloric presentations of music, Haitian Kreyòl and French texts were both considered appropriate if the subject of the song related to a folkloric theme.[12]

Despite these concerns about the ethnographic reliability of Jaegerhuber's song collections, it would be a mistake to dismiss his research as unimportant and brand his song transcriptions as "unauthentic." The idea of authenticity, especially in reference to materials drawn from the traditions of the poor, has, until recently, been considered the most important attribute of an oral tradition. However, as the focus of authenticity debates has shifted from the identification of an authoritative version of a particular practice to a valuative attitude that historians and folklorists project onto their research subjects, the notion of authenticity has

> become a nonissue, not simply because authenticity is itself an evanescent value, but because folklorists no longer believe that folk tradition derives wholly from, or reflects a "pure" society, or that traditions are necessarily "unchanging" or "inviolable." Appeals to the authority of tradition are likewise suspect in light of the popular need to create, innovate, renew, and see the past and the present with a fresh vision. (Porter 2001, 400)

Jaegerhuber's use of peasant sources as the basis of a new, synthetic musical tradition—a tradition that brought together Haitian elites and peasants in heretofore unimaginable ways—can thus be seen as a demonstration of Haitian cultural vitality that reflects the changing relationship between Haitian elites and peasants in the early to mid-twentieth century.

As I have argued elsewhere, the preoccupation with the authenticity of Haitian rituals and traditions has tended to erase the historical and political contexts in which such practices were used (Largey 2000, 242). During Jaegerhuber's career, a nineteen-year military occupation ended in Haiti, Haitian peasant resistance movements were effectively controlled by a newly established military force, ethnographic research on Haitian peasants began, the Haitian tourism industry flourished, and a new generation of Haitian intellectuals turned to the culture of Haitian peasants for artistic inspiration. In addition, Jaegerhuber personally found himself negotiating his own cultural connections to the music of the Haitian countryside. As a German-Haitian who came of age outside Haiti, Jaegerhuber turned his European-honed musical skills to a repertoire that connected him to that part of his ancestry that had become a liability in Nazi-controlled Germany. Jaegerhuber was, like so many other researchers who used folklore and culture to make "classical" art forms, liminal in relation to the Haitian culture that he presented to the larger artistic public.[3]

While Jaegerhuber himself did not leave a narrative chronicle of his fieldwork practices, his music transcription notebooks reveal a gradual shift away from sole reliance on Haitian elite singers to a more socioeconomically diverse group of musical consultants. In the Jaegerhuber song collection held by Micheline Laudun Denis, for example, several of the songs collected in 1948 were from local singers who came to visit the ailing Jaegerhuber. Unlike the Haitian elite singers who were listed by their full names, the singers Jaegerhuber worked with in the mountains were identified by their first names (or nicknames) and the location of the encounter, usually the mountain town of Obléon or nearby Furcy. Of the thirty-five surviving transcriptions Jaegerhuber made of Haitian songs, six were made in 1948 by rural singers, including two songs by "St. Elois," two songs by "Ti Notable" (Little Dignitary), and one song each by "Se Alma" (Sister Alma), and "Banboch" (Party).

While Jaegerhuber did work with some rural singers during his time in the Haitian mountains above Port-au-Prince, his first published song collection, *Chansons folkloriques d'Haiti* (1945), and a second edition of the same songs, titled *Complaintes Haïtiennes* (1950), were drawn primarily from his work with his elite friends and the professional consultant, Libera Bordereaux. These songs took the melodies he transcribed and set them to diatonic harmonies with piano accompaniment.

Complaintes Haïtiennes, taken together with the ethnographic notebooks that Jaegerhuber compiled in the 1930s and 1940s, illustrate Jaegerhuber's "music ideology." His choices about what to include in his transcriptions and his published song collection conform to his social and political goals of bringing together Haitian elites and peasants in an artistic form. Even more important, however, Jaegerhuber's transcription process traces the transformation of a participatory type of performance to a more presentational one. In his study of music, nationalism, and cosmopolitanism in Zimbabwe, Thomas Turino outlines a model for looking at musical genres that goes beyond a piece of music's form and style. For Turino, the categories of "participatory" and "presentational" music "contrast musical arts along a series of continua involving distinct ideologies and goals of creation; a process-product continuum in relation to the conception of music; types of settings for production and reception; different degrees of mediation; and the types of role interaction involved. These, in turn, influence sound style in critical ways" (Turino 2000, 47–48). Jaegerhuber's transformation of peasant song into art music compositions moves a particular musical product through a process that leaves aspects of the original version intact—the melodies are altered little from their transcription source—while modifying the musical context of performance to emphasize "presentational" values. At the same time, Jaegerhuber's presentational art songs selectively emphasized "participatory" qualities that appealed to Haitian audiences.

In the context of the Vodou ceremony, songs are deeply participatory. While the song leader or *sanba* may provide musical leadership during a ceremony, worshipers are expected to participate in frequent call and response refrains as they call the spirits from their home in ancestral Africa or Ginen. Turino suggests that "participatory music is defined and shaped stylistically by the fundamental goal of inviting the fullest participation possible, and the success of an occasion is judged primarily by the amount of participation realized" (Turino 2000, 48). Vodou songs collected in an actual ceremony would have been performed as part of a much larger ritual that included dancing, praying, foodways, and social interactions.

As Jaegerhuber's transcription notebooks indicate, none of his song transcriptions were made in a ceremonial context; they were likely dictated to Jaegerhuber by their respective singers either at his home in Pétionville or in his mountain cottage near Furcy. In addition, while the names of the Vodou spirits were retained in the song titles for *Complaintes Haïtiennes*, the collection itself was named for the *complainte* or "plaintive song" of the Haitian peasant; a far cry from the religiously efficacious *chan lwa* or spirit song. Even the English and Spanish glosses of the title—"Haitian Folklore Songs" and "Canciones del Folklore Haitiano" respectively—deemphasized the religious connotations of the songs. The title of the first edition of *Complaintes Haïtiennes*, titled *Chansons folkloriques d'Haiti* (1945), also underscored the songs' folkloric rather than religious connotations.

In order to make *Complaintes Haïtiennes* sound both culturally unique and musically universal, Jaegerhuber blended contrasting musical ideas to emphasize both the participatory and presentational aspects of the songs. For example, in the fourth song of *Complaintes Haïtiennes*, "Gros Loa Moin" (My Great Spirit), Jaegerhuber harmonizes a monophonic song from his fieldwork collection in the key of G minor. In measures 8 and 25 of the song, Jaegerhuber introduces an E major chord, disrupting the minor tonality and drawing attention to his transformation of the monophonic song (see ex. 5.3). The remainder of the song stays squarely in G minor, giving the two moments of E major—one in the piano introduction and one in the vocal melody—more "presentational" weight.

At the same time, Jaegerhuber's use of 5/8 meter for the duration of the song confirms his commitment to using what he believed was a uniquely Haitian rhythmic organization. By using 5/8 rather than a duple meter with a syncopated melody, Jaegerhuber echoed Maximilien's assertion that "all the great songs of Haiti, of a religious nature, have the rhythm of 5/8" (Maximilien 1954, 35). As discussed earlier, the use of 5/8 meter was part of a larger political debate conceptualized as Haitian vs. foreign musical notation. By claiming 5/8 as a representation of a unique Haitian rhythmic sensibility, Jaegerhuber could graphically demonstrate his song's cultural and musical distinctiveness.

As Turino indicates, participatory and presentational musics are ideal types, not strict classifications; they provide points of comparison between musical genres that are put to use in different contexts. As an example of a "presentational" music form, *Complaintes Haïtiennes* selectively suppressed the songs' specific Vodou connotations while infusing the art song format with Haitian cultural ideas. However, participatory and presentational types of music are not confined by the artistic choices of the composer; audiences may also engage presentational forms of music in participatory ways. For example, in the collection of thirty-five ethnographic transcriptions I have labeled "Jaegerhuber Notecards," Jaegerhuber included *tambour* (drum) parts for nineteen of the transcriptions. While the transcribed drum parts were not transferred to the piano versions in *Complaintes,* their presence in Jaegerhuber's fieldnotes raises questions about his musical intentions. For several of the Haitian musicians I interviewed in 1988, Jaegerhuber's music made the listener "tande tanbou" (hear the drum) whether or not such a drum part appeared in the score.[14] The Haitian poet Jean Brierre, in his introductory "hommage" to Jaegerhuber in *Complaintes Haïtiennes,* claimed that "one hears distinctively the soliloquy of the drum in the silences of [his] music" (Brierre 1950). For those Haitian listeners who understood Jaegerhuber's commitment to preserving the legacy of Haitian peasant song, his "hidden" drum part was a confirmation that Haitian musical elements would survive the transformation of peasant songs into art music compositions. The *tanbou kache* (hidden drum part) also demonstrated that the Haitian composer and audience asserted their own forms of agency in the production and consumption of Haitian art music.

"Gros Loa Moin" also illustrates Jaegerhuber's presentational goal of making Haitian music "universal" by linking Haitian art song and the

Example 5.3. Werner A. Jaegerhuber, "Gros Loa Moin," mm. 1–25

African American concert spiritual. Rather than translate the title of the song as "My Great Spirit," Jaegerhuber opted for a transcription more in keeping with African American vernacular, calling the song "Great Spir't O' Mine."

> Great spir't o' mine (repeat)
> O God Zimbi

225 ~ ETHNOGRAPHY AND MUSIC IDEOLOGY

Great spir't o' mine (repeat)
Papa Zimbi
My li'l boat
Is now standing still
And, can't cross the bay
O, I wonder Great spir't o' mine
What can it be (repeat)
Oh!
(Jaegerhuber 1950)

Jaegerhuber's translation gestures toward a cosmopolitan audience, but it does so using a transcription that follows a dialect model associated more with the African American concert spiritual—"my li'l boat," and "great spir't o' mine"—than the French chanson, another genre that Jaegerhuber used effectively.[15] By evoking the concert spiritual, Jaegerhuber was making a case that Haitian art music's universal appeal may be specifically tied to Afrodiasporic concert practices rather than to a generic cosmopolitan audience associated with white, Euro-American culture and values. Jaegerhuber's "cosmopolitans" were fellow African-descended people, black audiences that shared an affective response to specific musical genres while participating in an elite, presentational form of music. This phenomenon, whereby black elites are attracted to Western artistic forms but use these forms to convey values associated with other African, African American, or Caribbean cultures, is an instance of the "diasporic cosmopolitanism" discussed in chapter 4.

At the same time it reached out to non-Haitian black audiences, *Complaintes Haïtiennes* participated deeply in the presentational practice of promoting European and white American tourism to Haiti. *Complaintes Haïtiennes* contained six Haitian songs "collected and harmonized" by Werner Jaegerhuber with English translations for foreign audiences. In addition, the back cover of the song collection contained a photograph of Haitian performers standing in a circle, hands linked in the air while engaged in a folkloric dance (see fig. 5.2). Underneath the photograph, a French language caption read: "Haiti, 'Rendez-vous' of Peace, invites you to the 'Fraternal Circle of Enlaced People' near the Bay of Port-au-Prince." The English language caption for the photo read:

Visit Haiti!
The 'Rendez-vous' of Song
The 'Rendez-vous' of Dance
The 'Rendez-vous' of Love
(Jaegerhuber 1950)

Visit **HAITI !**

The " Rendez-vous " of Song
The " Rendez-vous " of Dance
The " Rendez-vous " of Love

HAITI, " Rendez-vous " de la Paix,
vous convie à la " Ronde Fraternelle des
Peuples enlacés " autour de la Baie de
Port-au-Prince.

Figure 5.2. Photograph of folkloric dancers. Werner A. Jaegerhuber, *Complaintes Haïtiennes* (1950), back cover.

Apart from the pen and ink drawing of a ceremonial drum from the Rada nanchon on the inside back cover of the booklet, *Complaintes Haïtiennes'* only other references to the practice of Vodou were in the lyrics to the songs themselves. Even the cover photograph—a sinuous pool of water nestled in a grove of palm trees—evoked the languid atmosphere of the tourist hotel (see fig. 5.3).

Complaintes Haitiennes

(Haitian Folklore Songs)

(Canciones del Folklore Haitiano)

Recueillies et Harmonisées

par le

Professeur WERNER A. JAEGERHUBER

2e Edition
Juin 1950

Figure 5.3. Werner A. Jaegerhuber, *Complaintes Haïtiennes* (1950), front cover.

While the elements of Jaegerhuber's work aimed at tourist audiences negotiated participatory and presentational ideas, the pieces written for specifically Haitian audiences—such as his mass on Vodou themes—were too volatile for Haitian audiences even when they played down the sounds of Vodou. Jaegerhuber had difficulty presenting his Vodou-inflected musical compositions to Haitian elite listeners. The Roman Catholic church in Haiti was especially vigilant against what they perceived to be Vodou influences infiltrating the celebration of the mass. A year after his death, Jaegerhuber's *Messe tirée de Thèmes Vodouesques* was scheduled to be performed at a celebration of the 150th anniversary of Haitian independence at the Roman Catholic cathedral of Gonaïves. Monsignor Paul Robert, a Catholic cleric who was instrumental in the "anti-superstition campaign" of the 1940s and was also an ardent opponent of any rapprochement between Vodou and the Catholic church, cancelled the performance when he heard that the mass was based on "Vodou themes." The mass was eventually performed in a theater constructed at the Casernes Dessalines, the army barracks directly behind the National Palace in Port-au-Prince.

In fact, Jaegerhuber could not have done more to take Vodou out of the work; the text of the mass was in Latin, and the melodies Jaegerhuber employed were not direct quotations of music from Vodou ceremonies. Still, the performance of Vodou-sounding music in a religious setting was a difficult idea for elites to reconcile with their views of Haitian traditional religion. Even the performers of the mass—members of the Haitian bourgeoisie—were conflicted about whether they should be participating in such a controversial piece of music. According to Micheline Dalencour, one rumor that circulated after the performance was that the parts that were distributed to the elite choristers were labeled *Messe Folklorique Haïtienne* while the conductor's score was labeled *Messe Voudouesque* as a way to disguise the mass's associations with Vodou.[16] From what I can deduce, Dalencour's account is accurate; in the music collection at Ecole Ste. Trinité, the choral parts for the mass are labeled "folklorique" while the conductor's score is titled "voudouesque."

In addition to his folkloric songs and "voudouesque" mass, Jaegerhuber penned at least two operas, both of which illustrate his commitment to bringing Haitian elite and peasant protagonists together in an artistic fusion. In *Gouverneurs de la rosée*, Jaegerhuber set Jacques Roumain's proletarian novel to music. Although there is no evidence that Jaegerhuber finished the opera, his interest in Roumain's story, in which a Haitian peasant rouses his community to action despite danger, demonstrates Jaegerhuber's concern for bringing Haitian peasant perspectives to a wider audience.

In Jaegerhuber's other opera, *Naïssa*, a young Vodou-practicing peasant woman named Naïssa has a love tryst with a young member of the Haitian bourgeoisie, called L'Amant (The Lover).[17] Naïssa has been betrothed since birth to a fellow peasant called L'Ami (The Friend). The Vodou community expects Naïssa to consummate her marriage to L'Ami while Naïssa longs for a relationship with L'Amant. An intervention by the spirit Shango indicates that while Naïssa must fulfill her ritual obligations to L'Ami through a "spiritual marriage," she may pursue her relationship with L'Amant. But Shango also makes clear that L'Amant must allow Naïssa to maintain her relationship with her community—a community that includes her African ancestral spirits.

Not only the plot but also the music of *Naïssa* put Haitian elite and peasant protagonists in relationship with each other, demonstrating a cultural link between upper and lower classes. While most of the arias are sung in French, the opera features both L'Amant and Naïssa singing Vodou songs drawn from Jaegerhuber's ethnographic transcriptions, including "Erzulie oh, Erzulie sa!," "Gros Loa Moin," and "Bouclé nouè." At one point, both the peasant Naïssa and the bourgeois L'Amant sing Vodou songs while possessed by African ancestral spirits:

Naïssa (in trance).
> *Erzili oh Erzili é ça oh*
Chorus of Male Vodou initiates.

Gros Loa moin, gros Loa moin	My great spirit, my great spirit
Papa Simbi	Father Simbi

The Lover (in trance).

Erzulie coté ou yé?	Erzulie, where are you?
Ou pa ouè moin nan d'leau	You don't see me in the water
Coté ou yé Grann' Erzulie?	Where are you, Great Erzulie?
Ouap maché nan caill' oh	You are walking in the house, oh
(Dauphin 2000)	

The theme of class division in both musical dramas is not surprising. *Gouverneurs de la rosée* was based on a libretto by Jacques Roumain—who was deeply concerned with class—while *Naïssa*'s libretto was penned by Jaegerhuber's friend and colleague, Louis Maximilien. However, it is *Naïssa*'s idea of class reconciliation through the transgression of Haitian elite social norms that dramatically captures Jaegerhuber's ideal of bringing together Haitian elites and peasants as cultural agents in the promotion of a new, synthetic Haitian society, a society that would eventually transcend social hierarchy. While Jaegerhuber's vision of a new Haitian society that could compete with more powerful nations on an artistic level was unrealistic, it did capture the sentiment held by many progressive Haitian elites that Haiti's woes could be transcended, if only temporarily, by forging connections between Haitian elites and peasants.

Jaegerhuber's effort to establish an empirical link between elites and peasants through his documentation of Haitian folksong is important not only for its hopeful view of Haitian society but also for the way it presents Haitian music as being part of a larger, "universal" repertoire. In addition, Jaegerhuber's gestures toward other Afrodiasporic musical forms shows that he was not only interested in being accepted by foreign white audiences but also by black audiences abroad who shared his vision of diasporic cosmopolitanism. If, as Michel Rolph-Trouillot claims is true, "the peasantry cannot be said to be victorious in the [Haitian] cultural sphere, but it has an implicitly acknowledged presence there, to a degree as yet unmatched in the political and economic arenas" (Trouillot 1990, 114), then Werner Anton Jaegerhuber's work to bring the music of the Vodou ceremony to a wider audience demonstrates Haitian peasants' reciprocal relationship with Haitian elites and points to the importance of artistic production to Haitian cultural nationalism.

EPILOGUE

Roots Music and Cultural Memory

On 9 July 1988, I traveled with ethnomusicologist Gage Averill and several friends from the Haitian *mizik rasin* or "roots music" groups Boukman Eksperyans and Sanba Yo to a Vodou ceremony a few miles north of Gonaïves, Haiti (Averill 1997, 140). The ceremony was a Priyè Ginen (African Prayer) intended to rejuvenate the village compound of Mystique Souvenance, one of the largest sites of Vodou activity in Haiti. The senior priest at Souvenance told us that Priyè Ginen ceremonies were usually held once every seven years, but that it had been fourteen years since the last ceremony and that participants were eagerly awaiting the festivities. Priyè Ginen celebrates the spirits of the Rada denomination who are associated with agricultural productivity and coolness, so we expected a ceremony that would feature the graceful steps of the yanvalou dance along with songs that would praise such spirits as Danbala and Azaka.

Averill and I were interested in how Haitian "roots music" groups used their experiences at Vodou ceremonies as the inspirational basis of their own new brand of Haitian music. Theodore "Lolo" Beaubrun, the leader of Boukman Eksperyans, had already accompanied Averill and me on another trip to Souvenance, where we documented a yearly Easter celebration. Beaubrun had told me in an earlier conversation that many of the rhythms his group used were based on ideas they had gathered at Souvenance ceremonies, so the infrequent Priyè Ginen was sure to provide ample inspiration for Boukman's future repertoire. Prior to our trip, Averill and I had negotiated with Mèt Bien-Aimé, the ougan or head priest of the temple, to document the Priyè Ginen with videocameras, and Beaubrun received permission to have the members of his band perform on the temple grounds during the ceremony. While our research and participation were sanctioned by the religious officials, we were aware that

Boukman's musical participation could be a potential distraction to the ceremonial aspects of the festival. The members of Boukman were especially concerned that their musical entertainment not be seen as disrespectful to the potent spiritual event. Yet, all of us were excited to be participating in this important ceremony.

At 5:00 P.M. the ceremony began with prayers of intercession taken from the Catholic liturgy. Several chickens and goats were sacrificed over a large hole cut in the floor of the peristil while other smaller ceremonies took place outside the temple. Meanwhile, a group of musicians gathered under a *tonnèl* or arbor, playing *kontradans,* a formal couple dance that was brought to colonial Haiti in the eighteenth century. As one of the couples deviated from the strict formality of the kontradans by engaging in a close embrace, the dance caller shouted "nou pap danse konpa isit!" (we don't do popular music dances here), reminding participants that their revelry was taking place in a sacred site. Later, members of a Kongo society held a dance outside the temple. The atmosphere was charged with the sounds of many different styles of ceremonial and rural music on display.

Around 10:00 P.M., Beaubrun and the rest of Boukman Eksperyans set up their instruments and amplifiers under a tree within sight of the ceremony. Since Souvenance did not have electricity, Boukman's musicians brought their own gasoline-driven generator to power their instruments and provide light for their evening performance. The lighting consisted of a single incandescent bulb hung from the branch of the tree overhead, so performers' faces were obscured in shadows. Boukman's drum battery was audible above the roar of the generator and the sound of the amplifiers. Onlookers crowded around the members of Boukman, making it difficult for the musicians to move while they played their instruments. The atmosphere was tense as the musicians struggled to perform under these challenging conditions. Meanwhile, inside the peristil or temple, Bien-Aimé officiated at the opening ceremony of the Priyè Ginen as the *ousi* or Vodou initiates danced to the steady beat of the temple's own ceremonial musicians.

Outside the temple, Boukman began performing "Se Kreyòl Nou Ye" (We're Creole), a song based on a rhythmic pattern collected at La Souvenance during an earlier visit. The first line of the song describes an encounter with a Vodou spirit who tells Haitian listeners to be proud of their African ancestry and their Haitian Kreyòl language. The rhythm of the music caught the attention of several of the ousi who were participating in the religious ceremony in the temple. Clothed in white dresses and headwraps and dancing barefoot, a half-dozen ousi emerged from the ongoing ceremony. The members of Boukman were visibly excited and a little nervous, fearful that the dancers would scold them for interrupting their sacred ceremony. Instead, the women recognized the underlying rhythmic pattern of "Se Kreyòl Nou Ye" and began dancing to the beat. The musicians beamed as they watched the ousi connect Boukman's "roots music" with its actual roots in the movements of Vodou dance.

Boukman Eksperyans's Priyè Ginen experience at La Souvenance is an example of a larger phenomenon in the late twentieth- and early twenty-first centuries to revivify the connection between rural and urban Haitians through musical performance. Like Haitian art composers, mizik rasin musicians draw upon the musical resources of the Haitian countryside at a time when Haitian national sovereignty has been under threat. Mizik rasin's turn toward Haitian rural culture began as the Duvalier dictatorship was at its most repressive and has continued through the tumultuous presidency of Jean-Bertrand Aristide. For example, Boukman Eksperyans's 1992 song "Jou Nou Revolte" (The Day We Revolt), includes a line "the day has come for us to make a revolution," which many listeners interpreted as a call to arms against the military junta who ousted President Aristide in 1991. The song's chorus—"jou nou revolte, jou n a revolte" (the day we revolted, the day we will revolt)—makes an explicit connection between the contemporary political struggle in Haiti and the historical struggle for independence in the eighteenth century.

Mizik rasin musicians also draw upon the Lenten processional music called Rara to connect with urban Haitian audiences. Combining a Carnival-like road march style with a religious sensibility rooted in Vodou practice, Rara is often used by Haitians to voice political sentiments that might otherwise be squelched by Haitian authorities. During the turbulent period between the downfall of the Jean-Claude Duvalier regime and the removal of Jean-Bertrand Aristide, Rara-based mizik rasin became a popular vehicle for voicing politically charged rhetoric. In 1990, Boukman Eksperyans used a Rara-influenced sound in their Carnival hit, "Ké-M Pa Sote" (My Heart Doesn't Leap or I am Not Afraid). As Gage Averill has observed, the lyrics to the song invoked the warrior spirit, Ogou Balendjo, and criticized the military junta in power with a series of encoded insults in the form of point songs (Averill 1997, 181). Another example is RAM's 1993 hit, "Ambago" (RAM 1993), which lamented the effects of the United States' embargo on Haiti during the military dictatorship after the removal of President Jean-Bertrand Aristide in 1991. Invoking the *vaksin* or bamboo trumpet of the Rara band and featuring an enthusiastic retinue of revelers in the background, "Ambago" laments the suffering of the Haitian people while providing a danceable beat.

Since the 1980s, mizik rasin groups have been increasingly active recording and documenting Haitian traditional music. Not only have mizik rasin groups tried to connect the music of the Vodou ceremony to upper- and middle-class Haitians, they have also bridged the gap between Haitian and foreign audiences, bringing the sounds of the Vodou drum battery into the homes of North American and European listeners. Mizik rasin has been recognized in the international music market as a success-ful export of Haiti's stalled economy. Boukman Eksperyans's *Vodou Adjae* was nominated for a Grammy award, while Haitian band RAM's "Ibo Lele (Dreams Come True)" was on the soundtrack of Jonathan Demme's 1993 Oscar-winning film *Philadelphia* (RAM 1993). Other mizik rasin groups like Rara Machine, Koudyay, and Boukan Ginen travel between Haiti, the United States, and Europe, playing concerts and music festivals and spreading the sounds of Haitian ceremonial drumming to new audi-ences. Mizik rasin has even inspired non-Haitians to form their own groups. Sweden's Haitian roots group Simbi—named for a Haitian water spirit—performs covers of Haitian traditional songs and contemporary politically engaged Haitian artists in addition to their own songs written in Haitian Kreyòl.

Like their counterparts in the *mouvement folklorique* of the early twen-tieth century, roots musicians draw upon Haitian traditional repertoire to further their social and political goals of resisting oppression. Even the gentle genre known as *konplent* (lament) that Werner Jaegerhuber transcribed for voice and piano in the 1950s has been included in sev-eral mizik rasin recordings, the best known example being Boukman Eksperyans's "Fèy" (Leaf) in which a Haitian parent weeps over a sick child:

Mwen ale nan konbit isit	I go out with this work group
Tout moun manje nan asyèt	Everyone eats from a plate
Mwen se nan fèy yo ban mwen	I eat from a leaf they gave me
Oh, oh, oh	Oh, oh, oh
Fèy o	Leaf, oh
Sove lavi mwen	Save my life
Nan mizè mwen ye o	I'm in such misery
Pitit mwen malad	My child is sick
Mwen kouri kay gangan	I ran to the house of the healer/priest
Si li bon gangan	If he is a good priest
La sove lavi mwen	He'll save my life
Nan mizè mwen ye o	I'm in such misery
(Boukman Eksperyans 1992)	

By adding one stanza to this well-known Haitian lament, Boukman turns Fèy into a point song that criticizes those in power who deny the poor their due. In the first stanza, a konbit or cooperative labor worker complains that he is forced to eat from a leaf while others, presumably those paying him to harvest their crops, eat off plates. As the worker moves on to the lament proper—the stanza about the konbit worker was added by Boukman—listeners identify with the worker and, ideally, criticize those who abuse their authority as they sing along with this well-known folk song.

In the wake of the United States' "intervasion" of Haiti in 1994 to reinstall President Jean-Bertrand Aristide, roots musicians have continued the construction of a "Vodou Nation" which seeks to educate Haitian audiences about their culture by developing new ways to integrate traditional culture into popular music performance. Like the Haitian art composers examined in this book, roots musicians have laid claim to ceremonial music as a form of cultural inheritance while giving listeners a visceral connection to Vodou practice, albeit from a safe remove.

Both Haitian roots musicians and art composers have used Haitian traditional music as a means to educate Haitian audiences about the value of their culture. Three years before his death, Werner Jaegerhuber was working on bringing Haitian folkloric songs to the Haitian public school system. In the introduction to Jaegerhuber's *Complaintes Haïtiennes,* Roger Savain, the director of the Haitian government's music agency, reported that Jaegerhuber was preparing a book of folkloric songs in three voices for use in the Haitian school system (Savain 1950).[1] He was also responsible for helping other musicians who were active in the mouvement folklorique gather materials for their public presentations, including Lina Fussman-Mathon Blanchet, the leader of a folkloric troupe that performed at the 1941 National Folk Festival in Washington, D.C.

Jaegerhuber's work also influenced other folksong collectors to employ their materials as the basis of a folkloric repertoire that could be performed on the Haitian stage. As Kate Ramsey has shown in her study of the mouvement folklorique in the 1940s, the Haitian government was deeply interested in using Haitian folklore as the basis of a new, national culture at the same time that it suppressed the practice of Haitian traditional religion (Ramsey 2002). By making folkloric performance a "national" art that could represent Haitian culture, the Haitian government institutionalized a practice that would eventually turn Haitian culture into an internationally marketable commodity.

As a result of Jaegerhuber's advocacy for ethnographic research on Haitian music, several folkloric choirs formed in Port-au-Prince in the 1960s and 1970s, including the Choeur Simidor. One of Lina Fussman-Mathon

Blanchet's protégés was her godson, Férère Laguerre, a dentist by training who was also a composer and director of the Choeur Simidor, a group of students from the Université d'Etat d'Haïti. Unlike Blanchet, who relied on the ethnographic research of musicians like Jaegerhuber, Laguerre did his own research on Haitian music, turning his attention to codifying the different rhythmic patterns of Vodou music and creating a typology of Haitian musical instruments, which he published in *Conjonction*, a journal sponsored by the Institute Français d'Haïti (Laguerre 1975).

Laguerre's work as a composer and ethnographer presaged the musicological "research" of mizik rasin musicians; his efforts constitute a bridge between the mouvement folklorique of the 1940s and 1950s and the roots music successes of the late 1980s. Laguerre was, for example, an early advocate of recognizing the sacred origins of the Lenten processional music known as Rara. While some Haitian elites dismissed Rara as a "poor person's Carnival," Laguerre stressed that Rara and Carnival should be seen as aspects of Haiti's sacred music traditions (Laguerre 1981). The Choeur Simidor also foreshadowed the mizik rasin movement in its programming of a variety of Haitian traditional music for the concert stage and in its use of folk-based choreography.

Contemporary Haitian folkloric choirs continue the tradition of the Choeur Simidor with their incorporation of gestures and other performance practices that connect them with traditional music. Emile Desamours (b. 1941), a civil engineer and choral composer, has written several pieces based on traditional themes for his folkloric choir, Voix et Harmonie. His "Noël Ayisyen (A Haitian Noël)" (Desamours 1996) is an a capella work for four-part choir that imitates the sounds of the bamboo trumpets used for Rara, the manibula (a wooden box with metal strips, similar to the mbira) used in rural dance music, and the tanbou or drum which is featured in most Haitian music genres.

The sonic texture of "Noèl Ayisyen" not only cues Haitian audiences to listen for cultural references that link them with the familiar sounds of Haitian folklore, it also prompts the choir members themselves to participate in the music in ways that go beyond their normal stage behavior. I have performed this piece twice; once in 1981 as a member of the bass section of the Schola Cantorum, the adult choir associated with the music school of Ecole Sainte Trinité in Port-au-Prince, and once in 1988 as the choral director of the Grande Chorale Sainte Trinité, a later incarnation of the Schola Cantorum. In the 1988 performance, "Noèl Ayisyen" was the final choral presentation. Both the audience and chorus responded to the Haitian music in ways that differed sharply from their behavior following the European-derived music during the rest of the concert. Audience enthusiasm was at its highest point for this final piece, bringing to mind Averill's observation of a similar response during popular music performances in which audience members were *chofe* or "heated up" by the music (Averill 1997). Also, the choir's performance behavior changed dramatically during "Noèl Ayisyen." Unlike most of the musical presentations of European origin in which choir members stood motionless before the audience, "Noèl Ayisyen" elicited unprompted behaviors from choir members, including turning to face other members of the group, smiling at the audience and one another, as well as a more relaxed body attitude. Since I was directing the work in the 1988 performance, I am certain that the choir never discussed using a particular stage behavior for "Noèl Ayisyen" in rehearsal. Rather, the members of the choir behaved spontaneously during the performance itself. Like the ousi who responded positively to the sounds of Vodou ceremonial music coming from Boukman Eksperyans during the Priyè Ginen, art music audiences were moved to click their tongues along with the banda rhythm of "Noèl Ayisyen."

Such a visceral and immediate reaction by a Haitian audience does not mean, however, that the ambivalence that many Haitian elites feel about Vodou has been erased. As Ramsey's work on the mouvement folklorique has shown, interest in folkloric presentations of Haitian music were encouraged at a time when the Haitian state was mounting its most aggressive campaign against traditional religion. Desamours, himself an observant Baptist, was not interested in the religious connotations of the ceremonial music that inspired his own work. Desamours never conducted ethnographic research of his own, but he did tell me that once he was walking home after attending a church service led by Pasteur Nerée, a famous Haitian evangelist, and he heard the music of a tanbou playing somewhere in the distance. Desamours said that at that moment, he felt "neither Protestant, nor Catholic, nor Baptist." As he put it, he listened to the music "san konpleks" (without a complex), preferring to hear the commonality of the Haitian experience through the sound of the drum. Despite the antagonism between his Protestant upbringing and his interest in Vodou-influenced Haitian music, Desamours was able to find a way to reconcile these two powerful influences on his composition.

Given the historical tension between organized Christianity and Vodou practice, it is somewhat ironic that the Episcopal Church in Haiti has been the most consistent supporter of Vodou-influenced music in recent years. The Ecole Sainte Trinité (Holy Trinity School) in Port-au-Prince has sponsored a music program since 1971 when Sister Anne-Marie Bickerstaff founded the Orchestre Philharmonique Sainte Trinité (OPST). Intended as a student orchestra to provide opportunities for Haitian children to play classical music, the OPST quickly developed several feeder orchestras and, eventually, a wind band program. Eventually, the school added choral music to their curriculum with the Schola Cantorum, led by James Smith, which changed its name to the Grande Chorale Sainte Trinité in the mid 1980s.

John Jost, a Mennonite student from the United States who worked as a music volunteer at Ecole Sainte Trinité during the 1970s, transcribed several Haitian classical music pieces for the orchestra, including Ludovic Lamothe's piano arrangements "Danzas No. 3 and 4," Justin Elie's "Dance de l'Homme des Grottes," Werner Jaegerhuber's folksong arrangement of "Erzulie Malade," Lina Mathon Blanchet's folksong arrangement of "Soufle Vent," and Férère Laguerre's "Un Sèl Badjo." Jost's arrangements for the OPST are an important component of the orchestra's Haitian classical repertoire.

The OPST's former musical director and conductor, Julio Racine, has also written several art music compositions including his "Tangente au Yanvalou" (1975) for flute and piano, and arrangements of Haitian traditional music, including his *Chansons folkloriques d'Haïti* (2004). While Racine's music is not based on ethnographic research, he brings a deeply felt awareness to the performance practice of Haitian art music. For example, in 1988, Racine was conducting an OPST rehearsal of Lina Mathon Blanchet's folksong arrangement of "Soufle Vent." I was playing in the percussion section of the orchestra on an instrument called "ogan"—a struck piece of metal that provides the organizing rhythmic pulse in many Haitian Vodou songs. Despite our accurate realization of the notated percussion parts, the orchestra was having difficulty coordinating the rhythmic pulse for the piece. We could see Racine's frustration growing; he finally shouted at the percussion section: "bat kata!" (play the kata rhythm). Most of the players in the percussion section had experience playing folkloric music in other groups; one of our members was well known as a ceremonial drummer. We knew that Racine was asking us to ignore what was written in the score and to play a rhythmic pulse that was drawn from the Vodou ceremony. As I played the short, staccato rhythms of the kata on my instrument and my colleagues found an appropriate beat, the violins found the appropriate rhythm and Racine gave us in the percussion section an approving nod.

Racine's instinctive response to a poorly notated Haitian rhythm focused us on those culturally unique aspects of Haitian classical music that only a knowledgeable performer would understand. Every performance of mizik savant ayisyen underscores the relationship between the shared heritage that Haitian musicians draw from in their art music and the proper performance practice of Vodou-derived music. While each musician's relationship to traditional religious practice may be unique, Vodou continues to serve as a guide for Haitian musicians from a variety of traditions, from art composers to roots musicians. Through their use of musical materials from the Vodou ceremony, Haitian art composers and roots musicians renegotiate their relationships with Haitian traditional religion and present alternative representations of their oft-maligned culture to an international audience.

GLOSSARY

Alfò straw bag (or "halefor")

Ason sacred rattle used by Vodou priests

Asotò large drum used in special Vodou ceremonies; subject of an ethnographic study by Jacques Roumain

Abitan Haitian peasant

Ayibobo exclamation made at the beginning or end of Vodou songs; a form of praise for the spirits

Banda fast rhythm associated with Gede spirits in Vodou

Bondyè name for God in Vodou religion

Boula smallest drum in Rada drum battery

Cantiques French for "hymns" in Christian traditions

Complainte (Kreyòl, *konplent*), "complaint" or lament; Haitian song genre

Corvée conscription labor practice during the U.S. occupation of Haiti

Fresco shaved ice sold from a pushcart vendor

Fèt chanpèt countryside celebration

Kachimbo clay pipe (or "cachimbo")

Kata smallest drum in Petwo drum battery (also spelled "cata"); derived from Kikongo, meaning "to cut"

Kase literally, "to break"; refers to the break in a rhythmic pattern during a Vodou ceremony

Kreyòl Creole; refers to language spoken in Haiti (kreyòl ayisyen) and Haitian culture as an amalgamation of different cultural influences, most notably French, Native American, and various West and Central African cultures

Koupe tèt, boule kay "cut heads, burn houses"; motto of Haitian general Jean-Jacques Dessalines during the Haitian Revolution

Lakou yard or compound; refers to area inhabited by a person's extended family

Lanbi conch shell; used during Vodou ceremonies; associated with the mawonaj (runaway slave) phenomenon in colonial times

Lwa Vodou spirit

Manbo female Vodou priest

Méringue (Kreyòl, *mereng*), Haitian dance music that is associated with five-note rhythmic pattern known as quintolet

Milat light-skinned person

Mizik savant ayisyen Haitian art or "learned" music

Moun andeyò literally, "people outside"; elite term for rural people in Haiti

Nanchon "nation" or denomination in Vodou

Nwa from "black" or dark-skinned person

Ogou Vodou spirit associated with fire, iron, and war

Ouanga magic charm or talisman; title of opera about Haiti by Clarence Cameron White and John Matheus

Ougan male Vodou priest

Ousi Vodou initiate

Peristil covered dancing area associated with a Vodou temple

Petwo a principal nanchon or denomination in Vodou; associated with heat and action

Pwen "point" or message; associated with Vodou songs

Peyi san chapo the land of the dead; literally, "the country without hats"

Rada a principal nanchon or denomination in Vodou; associated with coolness and productivity

Rechèch "research" conducted by Haitian elites on rural Haitian culture

Tonnèl a thatched-roof structure with no walls

Vodou a dance associated with the Rada denomination; also used to describe the entirety of African-derived Haitian traditional religion

NOTES

INTRODUCTION

1. In Haitian Kreyòl, the Haitian elite class is usually referred to as *lelit,* or "the elite." I have used this term throughout the book, despite its conflict with standard English usage.

2. In Haiti, the word Vodou is most often used to refer to a specific rite in the Rada denomination of spirits (Ramsey 2002, 33). Recently, some writers have used the term to refer to all religious rituals in the Rada denomination of spirits (Brown 2001; McAlister 2002). Despite the fact that Haitians do not have a single term to refer to all religious rituals associated with African ancestral spirits, I use the term Vodou to refer to spiritual practices in general. My purpose is both to draw attention to the constructed nature of Vodou for Haitian elites and to contrast the practice of Vodou with the stereotypical depiction of Haitian spirituality known as "voodoo." Since the standardization of Haitian Kreyòl orthography in the early 1980s, Haitian traditional religion has been spelled "Vodou." During the 1920s, however, Vodou was spelled in a variety of ways, either as vaudou or vaudoux (in French), or voodoo (in English). Since North American depictions of Haitian traditional religion have been so overwhelmingly negative, the spelling "voodoo" has come to symbolize evil magical practices in both Haiti and Louisiana. I use the spelling "voodoo" only when it occurs in a direct quotation.

3. In a chapter on the music of Haiti and the French Caribbean in Peter Manuel's *Caribbean Currents: Caribbean Music from Rumba to Reggae* (1995), I have described some of the general characteristics of Vodou ceremonial music: "*Lwa* are organized according to *nanchon* or 'nations' which take their names from geographic locations or ethnic groups in West and Central Africa. Lois Wilcken has called Vodou *nanchon* 'confederations,' recognizing the coalescence of different African spiritual practices into a single worship service. Ceremonies often salute the *lwa* of Rada, Petwo, Nago, Ibo, and Kongo with their songs and dances. Each *nanchon* probably had its own musical ensemble at one time, but today the major *nanchon* use either Rada or Petwo instruments.

The Rada *nanchon* uses an ensemble of three *tanbou* (drums) called *manman* (mother), *segon* (second or middle), and *boula* (or *kata*). The ensemble is similar in function to the *tumba francesa* and *batá* ensembles of Cuba, since in each of these it is the largest, lowest pitched drums that lead the group. The *manman* is the largest drum and is played with a single stick and one hand. The master drummer plays the *manman;* he (most drummers are male) directs the ensemble and determines when the musicians will move to another rhythm or song. The *segon,* slightly smaller than the *manman,* plays rhythmic patterns and can vary the pattern slightly, but not to the extent permitted by the lead drummer. The *boula* plays a steady rhythmic pattern and helps keep the other drummers coordinated. The drums used in the Rada ensemble are made from hard woods and are covered with cow skin and tuned with pegs that are driven into the body of the instrument. The Petwo *nanchon* uses two drums made of softer wood than Rada drums; the heads are covered in goatskin, are fastened to the body of the instrument with cords rather than pegs, and are always played with the hands" (Largey 1995, 124).

4. Haitian culture has been the subject of several recent works, including Karen McCarthy Brown's *Mama Lola* (2001), which examines the life of a female Vodou priest or *manbo* in Brooklyn, and Joan Dayan's *Haiti, History, and the Gods* (1995), which, among other things, analyzes Vodou rituals as sources of historical importance. J. Michael Dash's two books—*Literature and Ideology in Haiti* (1981) and *Haiti and the United States* (1988)—investigate the class conflicts in Haitian society through close readings of Haitian literature.

Gage Averill's *A Day for the Hunter, A Day for the Prey: Music and Power in Haiti* (1997) is the first scholarly monograph devoted to the study of Haitian music. Averill's work looks at music as an important locus of power relations in Haiti and argues that political and social conflicts are addressed, but rarely resolved, through musical performance.

5. Cultural nationalism has been the focus of several recent ethnomusicological studies. In addition to Turino's study of nationalism and cosmopolitanism in Zimbabwe, Sue Tuohy's (2001) work explores the sonic dimensions of musical nationalism in China and Kelly Askew's (2002) book examines music and cultural politics in Tanzania. In Latin America, scholarship has studied how music, class, and national identity work together in the cross-class transformation of musical style. Robin Moore's *Nationalizing Blackness* (1997) examines how race is used in the construction of Cuban national identity. Peter Wade's study of *música tropical* in Columbia, *Music, Race, and Nation* (2000), also examines race but is more generally about "how multiple and unequal representations of national identity relate to each other through contestation, appropriation, and transformation in a society stratified by class and race" (2). Musicians have taken the music of the steel band in Trinidad (Stuempfle 1995), *merengue* and *bachata* in the Dominican Republic (Austerlitz 1995; Pacini-Hernandez 1995), and *zouk* in the French Caribbean (Guilbault 1993) and have transformed their local popular musics into nationally identified styles. Averill's (1997) study of music and power in Haiti examines similar class dynamics in Haiti, but only as manifest in contemporary popular music genres.

6. Book-length studies about art music in Latin America and the Caribbean have been few. Gerard Béhague's study of musical nationalism in Brazil (1971) was among the early theoretical treatments of nationalism and art music in Latin America. Béhague's *Music in Latin America* (1979) updated Slonimsky's art music survey, but his attention to ethnomusicolgical issues in the production of art music make his work more useful than Slonimsky's. Béhague's *Music in Latin America* provides analyses of Cuban art music; however, it does not include Haitian art compositions. Béhague's study of Brazilian composer Heitor Villa-Lobos is an important contribution not only to the literature on Latin American composers but also for its treatment of Villa-Lobos's music

in the context of musical nationalism (Béhague 1994, 145–57). Nicholas Slonimsky's *Music in Latin America* (1945) was an early survey of the Latin American art music repertoire that lacked any systematic treatment of cultural or national issues as they related to music. Slonimsky's work was, however, the first scholarly study in English to mention Haitian composers Occide Jeanty, Ludovic Lamothe, and Justin Elie.

7. Haitian composers' efforts to create unique yet universal musical works are not without precedent. Richard Crawford has described a similar tension in nineteenth-century music in the United States and has described a dialectic between "authenticity and accessibility." According to Crawford, "authenticity arose as an ideal countering the marketplaces's devotion to accessibility" (Crawford 1986, 87).

8. J. Michael Dash, for example, explores Haitian elite discourse about peasant culture through an examination of elite Haitian literature (Dash 1981; 1988).

9. During my fieldwork among Haitian elites, I interviewed two elite Haitian women and asked them to speak to me in Kreyòl since my speaking skills were much stronger in Kreyòl than in French. Both women said that they would try to speak Kreyòl, but they would have difficulty doing so since French was their native language. At the end of a two-hour interview in which they spoke only French, one of the women said, in Kreyòl, that the reason she could not conduct an interview in Kreyòl was because it was not a real language; it did not possess a grammar. (Kreyòl se pa youn lang bon vre. Li pa gen gramè.) The other woman reminded me, in French, that Kreyòl was "une diffamation de la langue française" (a defamation of the French language).

10. Current scholarship on nationalism has moved toward a more inclusive position, acknowledging the rise of state institutions in the formation of contemporary nationalism (Gellner 1983), the importance of print-capitalism in the development of "imagined" national communities (Anderson 1991), and the primacy of gender in the formation of nationalist consciousness (McClintock 1996; Sommer 1991).

11. Manuel Peña describes a similar tension in the music of the Mexican-American *orquesta* (Peña 1999, 15–21).

12. Cultural memory in the African diaspora is the subject of two recent works: Geneviève Fabre's and Robert O'Meally's edited collection of essays on *History and Memory in African-American Culture* (1994) and Samuel A. Floyd Jr's *The Power of Black Music: Interpreting Its History from Africa to the United States* (1995). Reworking Pierra Nora's concept of "lieux de memoire," or sites of memory, O'Meally and Fabre suggest that African American cultural practices that fall outside the archival record—for example, "dances, paintings, buildings, journals, and oral forms of expression" (O'Meally and Fabre 1994, 9)—may "taken together, create a collective communal memory" (9). Floyd investigates the relationship between African and African American musical "tendencies" and claims that "these tendencies and beliefs continue to exist as African cultural memory" (Floyd 1995). *Vodou Nation* looks at such African "tendencies" as not only aesthetic preferences that make connections between Africa and the rest of the African diaspora but also as social and political choices that composers make to negotiate their relationship with the nation.

Elizabeth Rauh Bethel (1992, 828) was the first to identify Haiti as a "lieu de memoire" for African Americans, claiming that "Afro-Americans incorporated the Haytian *lieu de memoire* into a consciously constructed history which revised and challenged the assumptions of inherent racial inferiority and the moral rightness of racial subordination implicit in the Euro-American cultural tradition."

CHAPTER ONE

1. Toussaint Louverture spelled his name without an apostrophe, yet many writers insist on inserting one to make his name conform to the conventional French spelling, i.e., L'Ouverture. While I refer to him by his last name, Haitians tend to refer to Toussaint Louverture simply as Toussaint.

CHAPTER TWO

1. Edmond Roumain (1856–1931) was trained in Germany as a pharmacist and also worked as a geologist, but was well known in Haiti as an improviser on the piano; Toureau Lechaud (1845–1919) was a graduate of the Ecole Nationale de Musique under Geffrard and traveled briefly to Paris to study piano; Louis Astrée père (1844–1928) was the director of the Musique du Palais National (Dumervé 1968, 80–82; 102–5; 74).

2. Ciceron Desmangles, interview with the author, Port-au-Prince, 1 August 1988.

3. Jean Brierre, interview with the author, Port-au-Prince, Haiti, 28 July 1988.

4. Ibid.

5. Frantz-Gerard Verret. Interview with the author, Port-au-Prince, Haiti, 15 June 1988.

6. Micheline Dalencour, interview with the author, Pétionville, Haiti, 23 July 1996.

CHAPTER THREE

1. In 1955, two years after Lamothe's death, his brother Jean and cousins Antoine and Fernand Lamothe published a collection of his music entitled *Musique de Ludovic Lamothe* (Lamothe 1955). The collection contained thirty-three pieces including nine Danses Espagnoles, four Danzas, and several Scènes de Carnaval.

2. Jean-Claude Desmangles, conversation with the author, Port-au-Prince, 1988.

3. According to Averill (1997, 220, n. 41), "*Mereng koudyay*, essentially indistinguishable from *mereng kanaval*, evolved out of fast, celebratory songs of the early Haitian military sung on the occasion of a military victory, which were later adopted at carnival-like festivities."

4. "Ayibobo" is an exclamation frequently used to open and close Vodou ceremonial phrases. It is used in conjunction with names of spirits in order to praise them.

5. Elie's concerts in Jamaica were chronicled extensively in the Jamaican press. Justin Elie's daughter, Simone Stecher Elie, has a collection of newspaper clippings from her father's recitals. They include "M. Elie's Recital: Successful Entertainment," 1909; "Cine Recital: M. Elie's Bow to a Kingston Audience," 1909; "Pianoforte Recital in Kingston," 1909; and "Pianoforte Recital: M. Elie's Farewell Concert," 1909.

6. An "experiential program" is a personal interpretive statement made by an audience member upon listening to a piece of music. Experiential programs may take the form of newspaper articles, poems, or incidental writings inspired by the performance of a musical composition.

7. "Soirée Musicale." Program from the Alliance Français de New-York, 22 November 1923. Private collection of Simone Elie Stecher. Pétionville, Haiti.

8. "Gala Concert." Program for the Music and Art Lovers' Club, 12 March 1923. Private collection of Simone Elie Stecher. Pétionville, Haiti.

9. Letter, QRS Piano Roll Company to Justin Elie, 1921. Private collection of Simone Elie Stecher. Pétionville, Haiti.

10. Music historian Dumervé (1968) erroneously lists five movements for the *Ancient Mountain Legends:* 1. "Milida" [*sic*]; 2. "Isamao" [*sic*]; 3. "Prière du soir";

4. "Nostalgie"; and 5. "Nocturne." The Carl Fischer Company published "Melida" in 1927 as a "Creole Tropical Dance" for chamber orchestra and "Prière du soir" as a piece for chamber orchestra (with an additional arrangement for solo piano).

11. The *Ancient Mountain Legends* were eventually arranged for chamber orchestra in 1927 by Charles Roberts and published by Carl Fischer Music, Inc.

12. It is possible that Ratner's essay and the article by Lee Somers cited later in this chapter were written for Carl Fischer Music, Inc. as a promotion of Elie's compositions and not as a scholarly evaluation of Elie's work. Certainly, the rhapsodic prose and the unsubstantiated claims of ethnographic work make it difficult to take Ratner's and Somers's accounts seriously. Whether or not either writer was hired by Carl Fischer Music to create an exotic identity for Elie, or Elie himself supplied these writers with inflated claims of his own research exploits, their descriptions cast Elie as a representative of an exotic Caribbean culture who was able to draw upon his ethnic heritage and putative ethnographic experience.

13. Simone Elie Stecher, interview with the author, Pétionville, Haiti, 4 May 1988.

14. Ibid.

CHAPTER FOUR

1. The term "ouanga" is a Haitian Kreyòl term for magic charm or amulet. Normally, it is used to provide someone protection from unseen spiritual forces, but in the case of the opera *Ouanga*, the magic charm is used against the opera's protagonist, Jean-Jacques Dessalines.

2. White and Matheus were both mobile African American academics with access to travel funds even if their personal finances did not allow for exorbitant spending. White was the recipient of several grants for his work, including a scholarship of $500 from Mrs. Azalia Hackley for study in England, a prize from the Harmon foundation of $400 that paid in part for his and Matheus's trip to Haiti, and a grant of $3,000 from the Julius Rosenwald Fund to support his finishing the opera *Ouanga!* in Paris. White eventually extended his scholarship and was given an additional $1,800 from the Rosenwald Fund. White's lengthy stay in England from 1908 until 1911 was funded not only by Mrs. Hackley but also from personal donations by individual African Americans and from various church groups (Edwards and Mark 1981, 55–56).

3. Harriet Gibbs Marshall also drew praise for her 1930 work of Haitian history entitled *The Story of Haiti*, which was written for young people "to give them more vision and a higher appreciation of justice, brotherhood, and life itself" (Marshall 1930, 7).

4. White eventually published a méringue titled "Tambour" for piano with Carl Fisher Music, Inc. in 1931.

5. "Cocomacaque" is a Haitian Kreyòl word for baton or cudgel. I have been unable to find any indication of why White and Matheus selected this title for the first draft of the libretto. Haitian ethnomusicologist and *ougan* (Vodou priest) Gerdès Fleurant suggested that the popularity of the cocomacaque as a weapon of control during the United States occupation of Haiti would explain Matheus's familiarity with the term (Fleurant, conversation with the author, New York City, 3 November 1995). David Geggus suggests that a heavy cudgel was a symbol associated with the Kongo Bankimba society, a religious organization present in Saint-Domingue that used sorcery as part of its defensive arsenal (Geggus 1991, 34). If Geggus is correct, both opera titles, *Cocomacaque* and *Ouanga*, evoke magic as they describe potential weapons employed by the Haitian peasant.

6. John Janzen, an anthropologist working in modern Zaire on the origins of Lemba societies, translated this chant for Carolyn Fick in her study of the slave contributions to the Haitian Revolution (Fick 1990, 266; 290 n. 58). The chant is in Kikongo and is translated "Eh, eh! Rainbow spirit, eh! eh! / Tie up the BaFioti / Tie up the whites (or witches)."

7. For a history of the performance and reception history of *Troubled Island*, see Kernodle 1993.

8. The exchange between the fisherman and market women is crossed out in the full score to the opera. The scene is included, however, in the recording of *Troubled Island* which was made from the March 31, April 10, and May 1, 1949 performances of the opera (Still 1990). Although the recording was not made for commercial release, it is available through William Grant Still Music in Flagstaff, Arizona.

9. This image has permeated most dramas and historical accounts of the Haitian Revolution; the figure of Défilée has been represented both as a heroic figure, inspiring troops to march (hence her sobriquet *defile:* to march or parade) and as a woman who follows the insurrectionary troops providing sex (Dayan 1995, 44–46).

CHAPTER FIVE

1. Jaegerhuber's professors at the Conservatory included Anita Von Hillern, Brun Eisner, Carl Muck, Carl Merckens, Paul Graener, and Egon Pollad. During Jaegerhuber's time in Germany, he was very active in musical circles. He taught counterpoint at the Conservatory of Von Bernuth and was director of the music section of the Spetzgart Conservatory (Savain 1950). He was also active as a conductor, working with the Hamburger Gesangsverien, and as a pianist, accompanying singers and instrumentalists in recitals throughout Germany. In 1928, he married Anne Burkhart.

2. Personal communication with the author. Montréal, Québec, 12 November 1989.

3. Vodou practitioners in Léogâne, Haiti spoke to me about the effects of the anti-superstition campaign when I conducted fieldwork in the 1990s on Haitian Rara, a Lenten processional tradition closely associated with Vodou religious activity. Normally, military activities outside Port-au-Prince are limited to public areas such as highways or streets in town; rarely do soldiers enter the private space of the *lakou* or village compound. Several people told me that the anti-superstition campaign was particularly pernicious since the Haitian military ignored their own long-standing practice of staying out of Vodou temples when on patrol in Léogâne (Largey 2000, 248).

4. Peasants have standardized roles to play in discussions of the nation. Peasants, especially in mid-twentieth-century depictions of Haitian rural life, are most often cast as ahistorical subjects locked in a cycle of misery that offers little hope for change and as apolitical entities whose homogeneous collective identity precludes direct political action (Weinstein and Segal 1984, 5–6). According to Florencia E. Mallon (1995, 11), rural communities in both Mexico and Peru have suffered similar fates: "Many analysts of rural history and peasant politics have shared an undifferentiated view of the rural community. Identities were stable and given, and communities were endowed with primordial fixity and collective legitimacy that did not need to be explained. In this context, political action was simply the representation, in the political sphere, of this unproblematic collective identity." Other research (including Lundhal 1979; Mintz 1985; Moral 1961) identifies the Haitian peasantry as having several strata that are demarcated by wealth, status, and property. This "differentiated" view of Haitian

peasant life is at odds with the homogenized view in which peasants are in a state of self-imposed exile, fearful of the "contamination" of urban life and of modernity in general. In reality, the Haitian peasantry may be one of the most fully integrated working classes in the Western hemisphere (Mintz 1974; Trouillot 1990).

5. For a comprehensive look at the treatment that Haiti, and especially Vodou, has received in the foreign press, see Lawless 1992, 72–92.

6. Lina Mathon Blanchet, interview with the author, Pétionville, Haiti, 20 January 1988.

7. While Jaegerhuber spent the bulk of his later career on Haitian music, German music was a significant focus of his before 1937. Most of Jaegerhuber's vocal work composed before 1937 was set in German. Jaegerhuber's vocal works set in German included "Meine Lieber Mutter" (1935) for voice and piano and large-scale choral works, such as the *Oster Kantate* (1932) and *Die Auferstehung* (1934).

8. Harold Courlander, personal communication with the author, July 1985. I met Courlander with fellow ethnomusicologist David Yih during the summer of 1985. We spent a pleasant afternoon with Courlander who told us of his deep admiration of the work of Melville and Frances Herskovits. The Hotel Oloffson, where Courlander conducted his recording sessions, continues to be an attraction for foreign visitors. During the 1990s, the hotel regularly featured folkloric performances of Haitian dance. The owner of the Oloffson, Richard A. Morse, is the founder of the Haitian popular music group RAM.

9. In an appendix to *Haiti Singing* titled "Notes on Method," Courlander provided a detailed explanation of how he collected his texts and what problems he encountered (Courlander 1939, 229–38). Courlander himself wrote many books about folklore and culture, including *The Drum and the Hoe: The Life and Lore of the Haitian People* (1960/1985).

10. After some minor changes, Pressoir's orthography became the principal orthographic system for the next thirty years. Although it was never officially adopted by the Haitian government, the McConnell-Laubach orthography was used primarily by American Protestant missionaries in their translations of the Bible.

11. Jaegerhuber collected at least 47 songs between 1937 and 1953. The only published version of Jaegerhuber's folksong transcriptions are 24 songs that are held in the Bureau National d'Ethnologie in Port-au-Prince and that appeared in the *Bulletin of the Bureau National d'Ethnologie* as "Chants vaudouesques" (Jaegerhuber 1985). Three other collections of Jaegerhuber's folksong transcriptions are in private hands; two are held by Micheline Laudun Denis, a friend of Jaegerhuber's and a Haitian concert pianist. The first set of Jaegerhuber songs in the Denis collection, identified here as "Jaegerhuber Notecards," is a series of 35 melodies transcribed on a set of 4" x 6" music manuscript cards. The melodies appear on one side of the card and are enumerated, titled, and list the performer of the song; on the reverse side, Jaegerhuber included musical analyses of the melodic intervals of each song. The second set of songs held by Mme. Denis is titled "Folklore d'Haïti"; it is a set of 23 songs in a spiral-bound music manuscript notebook. Finally, the Société de Recherche et de Diffusion de la Musique Haïtienne (SRDMH) in Montréal, Québec holds an unpublished set of Jaegerhuber's transcriptions (Dauphin 1983, 16–17). Robert Grenier (2001) has analyzed the songs in the SRDMH collection.

12. In a rehearsal of the Choeur Voix et Harmonie I attended in June 1988, the program included standard Haitian repertoire such as "Haïti Cherie," "Angélique ô,"

and "Choucoune" as well as French songs set in a méringue rhythm like "Mademoiselle, je vous aime." When used in conjunction with the rhythmic inspiration of Haitian music, French was considered to be an appropriate vehicle for folksong expression among elites participating in the folkloric choirs.

13. While the concept of "liminality" is associated with Victor Turner's (1977) work on African initiation rituals, other researchers have applied the idea to a variety of contexts, including the practice of ethnography (Jackson 1990) and the eighteenth-century collection of the controversial Ossian poems by James Macpherson (Porter 2001).

14. Julio Racine, personal communication with the author, June 1988.

15. Jaegerhuber's French songs include "Mon Bras Prenait ta Taille Frète" (text by Victor Hugo, 1951a), "Pour Ma Rose" (1951b), and "Trois Chansons sur Poemes de Ida Faubert" (1951c).

16. Michelene Dalencour, interview with the author, Port-au-Prince, Haiti, 4 March 1988.

17. *Naïssa* has never been fully staged, but the Société de Recherche et Diffusion de la Musique Haïtienne in Montréal, Québec, performed an abridged concert version of the opera that was recorded on CD (Dauphin 2000).

EPILOGUE

1. Alzire Rocourt, interview with the author, Port-au-Prince, Haiti, 18 March 1988.

BIBLIOGRAPHY

Anderson, Benedict. 1991. *Imagined Communities: Reflections on the Origin and Spread of Nationalism*. London: Verso.

Anderson, Paul Allen. 2001. *Deep River: Music and Memory in Harlem Renaissance Thought*. Durham: Duke University Press.

Anonymous. 1923a. Untitled article. Clipping from the *Evening Telegram*. Private collection of Simone Elie Stecher. Pétionville, Haiti.

———. 1923b. Untitled description of Mlle. Hasoutra. Clipping from the *New York Musical Advance*. Private collection of Simone Elie Stecher. Pétionville, Haiti.

Antoine, Jacques. 1981. *Jean Price-Mars and Haiti*. Washington, D.C.: Three Continents Press.

Aptheker, Herbert. 1974. "Introduction." In W. E. B. Du Bois, *The Negro* (1915). Reprint, Millwood, N.Y.: Kraus-Thomson Organization, Ltd.

Arvey, Verna. 1975. "Still Opera Points the Way." In *William Grant Still and the Fusion of Cultures in American Music*, edited by Robert Bartlett Haas et al., 94–98. Los Angeles: Black Sparrow Press.

Askew, Kelly M. 2002. *Performing the Nation: Swahili Music and Cultural Politics in Tanzania*. Chicago: University of Chicago Press.

Austerlitz, Paul. 1995. *Merengue: Dominican Music and Dominican Identity*. Philadelphia: Temple University Press.

Averill, Gage. 1989. "Haitian dance bands, 1915–1970: Class, Race, and Authenticity." *Latin American Music Review* 10, no. 2: 203–35.

———. 1994. "*Anraje* to *Angaje:* Carnival Politics and Music in Haiti." *Ethnomusicology* 38, no. 2: 217–48.

———. 1997. *A Day for the Hunter, A Day for the Prey: Music and Power in Haiti*. Chicago: University of Chicago Press.

Baker, David N., Lida Belt, and Herman Hudson, eds. 1978. *The Black Composer Speaks*. Metuchen, N.J.: Scarecrow Press.

Barnes, Sandra. 1989. *Africa's Ogun: Old World and New*. Bloomington: Indiana University Press.

Bauman, Richard. 1992. "Contextualization, Tradition and the Dialogue of Genres: Icelandic Legends of the Kraftasklád." In *Rethinking Context*, edited by Charles Goodwin and Alessandro Duranti, 125–45. Cambridge: Cambridge University Press.

Béhague, Gerard. 1971. *The Beginnings of Musical Nationalism in Brazil.* Detroit: Information Coordinators.

———. 1979. *Music in Latin America: An Introduction.* Englewood Cliffs, N.J.: Prentice-Hall.

———. 1994. *Heitor Villa-Lobos: The Search for Brazil's Musical Soul.* Austin: Institute of Latin American Studies/University of Texas Press.

Bellegarde, Dantès. 1938. *La Nation Haïtienne.* Paris: J. de Gigord.

———. 1941. *Haiti et ses problems.* Montréal: Valiquette.

Bellegarde-Smith, Patrick. 1985. *In the Shadow of Powers: Dantès Bellegarde in Haitian Social Thought.* Atlantic Highlands, N.J.: Humanities Press International, Inc.

———. 1990. *Haiti: The Breached Citadel.* Boulder, Colo.: Westview Press.

Bendix, Regina. 1997. *In Search of Authenticity: The Formation of Folklore Studies.* Madison: University of Wisconsin Press.

Bervin, Antoine. 1969. *Benito Sylvain: Apôtre du relèvement social des Noirs.* Port-au-Prince: Imprimerie La Phalange.

Bethel, Elizabeth Rauh. 1992. "Images of Hayti: The Construction of An Afro-American *Lieu de Mémoire.*" *Callaloo* 15, no. 3: 827–41.

Bhabha, Homi. 1994. *The Location of Culture.* London: Routledge.

Blanchet, Jules. 1932. "Cadences Créoles." *La Releve* 3 (1 Septembre): 15.

Bontemps, Arna, and Langston Hughes. 1932/1993. *Popo and Fifina.* New York: Macmillan. Reprint, New York: Oxford University Press.

Boukman Eksperyans. 1992. *Kalfou Danjere: Dangerous Crossroads.* Mango Records 162-539 927-2.

Bourdieu, Pierre. 1984. *Distinction: A Social Critique of the Judgement of Taste.* Translated by Richard Nice. Cambridge, Mass.: Harvard University Press.

Brierre, Jean. 1950. "Hommage à Jaegerhuber." In *Complaintes Haïtiennes—Haitian Folklore Songs—Canciones del Folklore Haitiano: Recueillies et harmonisées par le Professeur Werner A. Jaegerhuber,* 2d ed., 6–7. Port-au-Prince: Compagnie Lithographique.

———. 1960. *Aux champs pour Occide sur un clavier Bleu et Rouge.* Collection Librairie Indigène. Port-au-Prince: Imprimerie N.A. Théodore.

Brouard, Carl. 1950. "Afrique" and "Les Griots." In *Panorama de la poesie haitienne,* edited by Carlos Saint-Louis and Maurice A. Lubin, 357–58. Port-au-Prince: Editions Henri Deschamps.

Brown, Karen McCarthy. 1987. "Alourdes: A Case Study of Moral Leadership in Haitian Vodou." In *Saints and Virtues,* edited by John Stratton Hawley, 144–67. Berkeley and Los Angeles: University of California Press.

———. 1989. "Systematic Remembering, Systematic Forgetting: Ogou in Haiti." In *Africa's Ogun: Old World and New,* edited by Sandra T. Barnes, 65–89. Bloomington: Indiana University Press.

———. 2001. *Mama Lola: A Vodou Priestess in Brooklyn.* Berkeley and Los Angeles: University of California Press.

Browner, Tara. 1997. "'Breathing the Indianist Spirit': Thoughts on Musical Borrowing and the 'Indianist' Movement in American Music." *American Music* 13, no. 3: 265–84.

Brutus, Timoléon C. 1947. *L'homme d'airain: Étude monographique sur Jean-Jacques Dessalines, fondateur de la nation haïtienne.* Vol. 2. Port-au-Prince: Imprimerie de l'Etat.

Burr-Réynaud, Frédéric. 1933. "Hommage à Occide Jeanty: 1804." *Le Temps* 2, no. 88 (30 Dec): 8.

Chatterjee, Partha. 1993. *The Nation and Its Fragments: Colonial and Postcolonial Histories*. Princeton: Princeton University Press.

"Cine Recital: M. Elie's Bow to a Kingston Audience." 1909. Clipping from unidentified Jamaican newspaper. Private collection of Simone Elie Stecher. Pétionville, Haiti.

"Clarence Cameron White returns from Haiti with Material for Opera." 1928. Newspaper clipping from *New York Age*. Scrapbook: Haiti. Schomburg Center for Research in Black Culture. New York Public Library.

Clark, VèVè. 1994. "Performing the Memory of Difference in Afro-Caribbean Dance: Katherine Dunham's Choreography, 1938–87." In *History and Memory in African-American Culture*, edited by Geneviève Fabre and Robert O'Meally, 188–204. New York: Oxford University Press.

Clifford, James. 1997. *Routes: Travel and Translation in the Late Twentieth Century*. Cambridge: Harvard University Press.

Cohen, William B. 1980. *The French Encounter with Africans: White Responses to Blacks, 1530–1880*. Bloomington: Indiana University Press.

"Le concert de M. Cameron White." 1928. Newspaper clipping from *Le Matin*. In Scrapbook: Haiti. Clarence Cameron White Collection. Schomburg Center for Research in Black Culture. New York Public Library.

Connerton, Paul. 1989. *How Societies Remember*. Cambridge: Cambridge University Press.

Corvington, Georges. 1987. *Port-au-Prince au cours des ans: La capitale d'Haïti sous l'occupation, 1922–1934*. Port-au-Prince: Imprimerie Henri Deschamps.

———. 1993. *Port-au-Prince au cours des ans: La métropole Haïtienne du XIXe siècle, 1804–1888*. Port-au-Prince: Imprimerie Henri Deschamps.

Cosentino, Donald. 1987. "Who is that Fellow in the Many-colored Cap? Transformations of Eshu in Old and New World Mythologies." *Journal of American Folklore* 100, no. 307: 261–75.

Courlander, Harold. 1939. *Haiti Singing*. New York: Cooper Square Publishers.

———. 1960/1985. *The Drum and the Hoe: The Life and Lore of the Haitian People*. Berkeley and Los Angeles: University of California Press.

Craige, John Houston. 1933. *Black Bagdad: The Arabian Nights Adventures of a Marine Captain in Haiti*. New York: Minton, Balch.

———. 1934. *Cannibal Cousins*. New York: Minton, Balch.

Crawford, Richard. 1986. *The American Musical Landscape*. Berkeley and Los Angeles: University of California Press.

Dahlhaus, Carl. 1989. *Nineteenth-Century Music*. Translated by J. Bradford Robinson. Berkeley and Los Angeles: University of California Press.

Dalencour, Micheline. 1983. Conférence presentée par Micheline Dalencour. Section Musicale, L'Ecole Sainte Trinité. Port-au-Prince, Haiti. 14–18 December.

Dash, J. Michael. 1981. *Literature and Ideology in Haiti, 1915–1961*. Totowa, N.J.: Barnes and Noble.

———. 1988. *Haiti and the United States: National Stereotypes and the Literary Imagination*. New York: St. Martin's Press.

Dauphin, Claude. 1980. "La méringue entre l'oralité et l'écriture: Histoire d'un genre musical haïtien." *Canadian University Music Review* 1: 49–65.

————. 1981. *Brit kolobrit: Introduction méthodologique suivie de 30 chansons enfantines haïtiennes recueillies et classées progressivement en vue d'une pédagogie musicale aux antilles.* Sherbrooke, Québec: Éditions Naaman.

————. 1983. *La Chanson haïtienne folklorique et classique.* Montréal: Société de Recherche et de Diffusion de la Musique Haïtienne.

————. 2000. Liner notes to recording of *Naïssa, opéra (abrigée).* Montréal: Société de Recherche et de Diffusion de la Musique Haïtienne.

David, Placide. 1934. "Cléopâtre: Musique de Justin Elie." *Le Temps* 3, no. 131 (5 December): 2–6.

Dayan, Joan. 1995. *Haiti, History, and the Gods.* Berkeley and Los Angeles: University of California Press.

Denis, Lorimer, and François Duvalier. 1939. "Question d'anthropo-sociologie: Le determinisme racial." *Les Griots* 3, no. 3: 303–309.

Deren, Maya. 1953/1983. *Divine Horsemen: The Living Gods of Haiti.* London: Thames and Hudson. Reprint, Kingston, N.Y.: Documentext.

Desamours, Emile. 1996. "Noèl Ayisyen (A Haitian Noël)." Champaign, Ill.: Mark Foster Music Company, MF 582.

Desmangles, Leslie. 1992. *The Faces of the Gods: Vodou and Roman Catholicism in Haiti.* Chapel Hill: University of North Carolina Press.

"Dessalines and Toussaint L'Ouverture: An Episode in the History of Haiti." 1848. *Daguerreotype* 2:369–75.

Dévot, Justin. 1901. *Le Centenaire de l'Indépendance nationale d'Haïti.* Paris: Librarie Cotillon.

Dixon, Chris. 2000. *African America and Haiti: Emigration and Black Nationalism in the Nineteenth Century.* Westport, Conn.: Greenwood Publishing.

Duara, Prasenjit. 1995. *Rescuing History from the Nation: Questioning Narratives of Modern China.* Chicago: University of Chicago Press.

Du Bois, William Edward Burghardt. 1903/1989. *The Souls of Black Folk.* Chicago: A. C. McClurg. Reprint, New York: Penguin Books.

————. 1915/1974. *The Negro.* New York: Holt. Reprint, Millwood, N.Y.: Kraus-Thomson Organization, Ltd.

————. 1973. *The Correspondence of W. E. B. Du Bois,* vol. 1: *Selections, 1877–1944.* Edited by Herbert Aptheker. Amherst: University of Massachusetts Press.

Dupuy, Alex. 1989. *Haiti in the World Economy.* Boulder, Colo.: Westview Press.

Dumervé, Etienne Constintin Eugène Moïse. 1968. *Histoire de la musique haïtienne.* Port-au-Prince: Imprimerie des Antilles.

Dunham, Katherine. 1969/1994. *Island Possessed.* New York: Doubleday. Reprint, Chicago: University of Chicago Press.

Durand, Oswald. n.d./1896. *Rires et Pleurs.* vol. 1. Port-au-Prince: Editions Panorama, n.d. Reprint, Sein-et-Oise: Corbeil, 1896.

Durand, Robert. 1983. "Justin Elie, pianiste et compositeur haïtien." Private collection of Micheline Dalencour.

Edwards, Vernon H., and Michael L. Mark. 1981. "In Retrospect: Clarence Cameron White." *The Black Perspective in Music* 9, no. 1: 51–72.

Elie, Justin. 1920. *Méringues populaires: Arrangées et harmonisées pour piano.* New York: R. de la Rosière.

————. 1928a. *Babylon: A Suite of Four Orientalist Sketches.* New York: Carl Fischer Music, Inc.

————. 1928b. *Kiskaya: An Aboriginal Suite for Orchestra (in Four Parts)*. New York: Carl Fischer Music, Inc.

Elie, Louis Emile. 1944. *Histoire d'Haïti*. Port-au-Prince: n.p.

Ellis, John M. 1983. *One Fairy Story Too Many: The Brothers Grimm and Their Tales*. Chicago: University of Chicago Press.

Fauset, Arthur Huff. 1925/1992. "American Negro Folk Literature." In *The New Negro*, edited by Alain Locke. New York: Albert and Charles Boni, Inc. Reprint, New York: Simon and Schuster.

Favor, J. Martin. 1999. *Authentic Blackness: The Folk in the New Negro Renaissance*. Durham: Duke University Press.

Ferguson, Charles A. 1959. "Diglossia." *Word* 15: 325–40.

Fick, Carolyn E. 1990. *The Making of Haiti: The Saint Domingue Revolution from Below*. Knoxville: University of Tennessee Press.

Firmin, Anténor. 1885. *De l'égalité des races humaines*. Paris: F. Pichon.

Floyd, Samuel A. 1995. *The Power of Black Music: Interpreting Its History from Africa to the United States*. New York: Oxford University Press.

Fouchard, Jean. 1955/1988a. *Plaisirs de Saint-Domingue*. Reprint, Port-au-Prince: Editions Henri Dechamps.

————. 1973/1988b. *La méringue: Danse nationale d'Haïti*. Reprint, Port-au-Prince: Editions Henri Deschamps.

Fowler, Carolyn. 1980. *A Knot in the Thread: The Life and Work of Jacques Roumain*. Washington, D.C.: Howard University Press.

Frangeul, Fernand, arranger. 1910. "Antoine Simon dit ça: Méringue chantée." Port-au-Prince: Fernand Frangeul.

Gaines, Kevin K. 1996. *Uplifting the Race: Black Leadership, Politics, and Culture in the Twentieth Century*. Chapel Hill: University of North Carolina Press.

García Canclini, Néstor. 1995. *Hybrid Cultures: Strategies for Entering and Leaving Modernity*. Translated by Christopher L. Chiappari and Silvia L. López. Minneapolis: University of Minnesota Press.

Geggus, David. 1983. *Slave Resistance Studies and the Saint Domingue Slave Revolt: Some Preliminary Considerations*. Occasional Papers Series, 4. Latin American and Caribbean Center of Florida International University.

————. 1991. "The Bois Caïman Ceremony." *Journal of Caribbean History* 25, nos. 1–2: 41–57.

Gellner, Ernest. 1983. *Nations and Nationalism*. Oxford: Basil Blackwell.

"Générosité de Mr White." 1928. Clipping from unidentified newspaper. Scrapbook: Haiti. Schomburg Center for Research in Black Culture. New York Public Library.

"Gilda Gray at the Rendez-Vous." 1923. Clipping from unidentified newspaper. Private collection of Simone Elie Stecher. Pétionville, Haiti.

Gilroy, Paul. 1993. *The Black Atlantic: Modernity and Double Consciousness*. Cambridge: Harvard University Press.

Glissant, Edouard. 1989. *Caribbean Discourse: Selected Essays*. Translated by J. Michael Dash. Charlottesville: University of Virginia Press.

Gobineau, J. A. 1853–55. *Essai sur l'inégalité des races humaines*. Paris: Firmin-Didot et cie.

Gorbman, Claudia. 2000. "Scoring the Indian: Music in the Liberal Western." In *Western Music and Its Others: Difference, Representation, and Appropriation in Music*, edited by Georgina Born and David Hesmondhalgh, 234–53. Berkeley and Los Angeles: University of California Press.

Gourgouris, Stathis. 1998. *Dream Nation: Enlightenment, Colonization, and the Institution of Modern Greece.* Stanford: Stanford University Press.

Gregory, Derek. 1999. "Scripting Egypt." In *Writes of Passage: Reading Travel Writing,* edited by James Duncan and James Gregory, 114–50. London and New York: Routledge.

Grenier, Robert. 2001. "La Mélodie Vaudoo—Voodoo Art Songs: The Genesis of a Nationalist Music in the Republic of Haiti." *Black Music Research Journal* 21, no. 1: 29–74.

Grohs-Paul, Waltraud. 1985. "Notes sur les chants vodouesques de Werner A. Jaegerhuber." *Bulletin du Bureau National d'Ethnologie* 2:73–75.

Guha, Ranajit. 1988. "On Some Aspects of the Historiography of Colonial India." In *Selected Subaltern Studies,* edited by Ranajit Guha and Gayatri Chakravorty Spivak, 37–43. New York: Oxford University Press.

———. 1997. *Dominance without Hegemony: History and Power in Colonial India.* Cambridge, Mass.: Harvard University Press.

Guilbault, Jocelyne. 1993. *Zouk: World Music in the West Indies.* with Gage Averill, Édouart Benoit, and Gregory Rabess. Chicago: University of Chicago Press.

Handler, Richard. 1988. *Nationalism and the Politics of Culture in Quebec.* Madison: University of Wisconsin Press.

Harman, Carter. 1950. "'Ouanga' Offered in Philadelphia: Dra-Mu Opera Troupe Gives Clarence Cameron White Work which won Bispham Medal in '32." *New York Times.* October 28.

Heinl, Robert Debs, and Nancy Gordon Heinl. 1978. *Written in Blood: The Story of the Haitian People.* Boston: Houghton Mifflin Company.

Herissé, Félix. n.d. "Les Etoiles haitiennes." L'Ecole Sainte Trinité Collection, Port-au-Prince, Haiti.

Herskovits, Melville J. 1937. *Life in a Haitian Valley.* New York: Alfred A. Knopf.

Herskovits, Melville J., and Frances S. Herskovits. 1936. *Suriname Folklore.* New York: Alfred A. Knopf.

Herzfeld, Michael. 1997. *Cultural Intimacy: Social Poetics in the Nation-State.* New York: Routledge.

Holly, James Theodore. 1857. *A Vindication of the Capacity of the Negro Race for Self-Government, and Civilized Progress, as Demonstrated by Historical Events of the Haytian Revolution; and the Subsequent Acts of that People Since Their National Independence.* New Haven: Published for the Afric-American Printing Co., 1857. Reprinted in *Black Separatism and the Caribbean 1860,* edited, with an introduction, by Howard H. Bell, 17–66. Ann Arbor: University of Michigan Press, 1970.

Hughes, Langston. 1931. "People Without Shoes." *New Masses* 12 (October): 12.

———. 1932. "White Shadows in a Black Land." *The Crisis* 41 (May): 157.

———. 1949. "Troubled Island: The Story of How an Opera was Created." *Chicago Defender,* 26 March.

———. 1956. *I Wonder As I Wander: An Autobiographical Journey.* New York: Hill and Wang.

———. 1936/2002. *Emperor of Haiti (Troubled Island).* In *The Collected Works of Langston Hughes,* vol. 6, ed. Leslie Catherine Saunders, 278–332. Columbia: University of Missouri Press.

Hughes, Langston, and Carl Van Vechten. 2001. *Remember Me to Harlem: The Letters of Langston Hughes and Carl Van Vechten, 1925–1964.* Edited by Emily Bernard. New York: Alfred A. Knopf.

Hunt, Alfred N. 1988. *Haiti's Influence on Antebellum America: Slumbering Volcano in the Caribbean.* Baton Rouge: Louisiana State University Press.

Hurbon, Laënnec. 1995. "American Fantasy and Haitian Vodou." In *Sacred Arts of Haitian Vodou*, ed. Donald Cosentino, 181–197. Los Angeles: UCLA Fowler Museum of Cultural History.

Hurston, Zora Neale. 1935. *Mules and Men.* New York: J. B. Lippencott Company.

———. 1937. *Their Eyes Were Watching God.* New York: J. B. Lippencott Company.

———. 1938. *Tell My Horse: Voodoo and Life in Haiti and Jamaica.* New York: J. B. Lippencott Company.

Innocent, Antoine. 1906/1970. *Mimola, ou L'histoire d'une cassete. Petit tableau de moeurs locales.* Port-au-Prince: V. Valcin. Reprint, Nendeln, Lichtenstein: Kraus Reprints.

Ivy, Marilyn. 1995. *Discourses of the Vanishing: Modernity, Phantasm, Japan.* Chicago: University of Chicago Press.

Jackson, Jean. 1990. "*Deja Entendu:* The Liminal Quality of Ethnographic Fieldnotes." *Journal of Contemporary Ethnography* 19, no. 1: 8–43.

Jaegerhuber, Werner A. 1943. "Les origines de la musique folklorique haïtienne." *Cahiers d'Haïti* (December), 53, 55.

———. 1945. *Chansons folkloriques d'Haïti.* Port-au-Prince: Valerio Canez.

———. 1948. "Contribution à la musique voudouesque." *Conjonction* 10–11:39–40.

———. 1950. *Complaintes Haïtiennes—Haitian Folklore Songs—Canciones del Folklore Haitiano: Recueillies et harmonisées par le Professeur Werner A. Jaegerhuber.* 2d ed. Port-au-Prince: Compagnie Lithographique.

———. 1951a. "Mon Bras Prenait ta Taille Frète" (text by Victor Hugo). Unpublished manuscript. L'Ecole Sainte Trinité Collection, Port-au-Prince, Haiti.

———. 1951b. "Pour Ma Rose." Unpublished manuscript. L'Ecole Sainte Trinité Collection, Port-au-Prince, Haiti.

———. 1951c. "Trois Chansons sur Poemes de Ida Faubert." Unpublished manuscript. L'Ecole Sainte Trinité Collection, Port-au-Prince, Haiti.

———. 1985. "Chants voudouesques." *Bulletin du Bureau National d'Ethnologie* 2: 88–101.

Jairazbhoy, Nazir. 1977. "The 'Objective' and Subjective View in Music Transcription." *Ethnomusicology* 21, no. 2: 263–74.

James, C. L. R. 1963. *The Black Jacobins: Toussaint L'Ouverture and the San Domingo Revolution.* New York: Vintage Books.

Janvier, Louis. 1884. *L'Egalite des races.* Paris: G. Rougier.

Jeanty, Lydia. n.d. "Biographie d'Occide Jeanty." Typescript. Personal collection of Lydia Jeanty. Port-au-Prince, Haiti.

Jeanty, Occilius, père et fils. 1882. *Petite grammaire musicale.* Paris: Librarie Évangelique.

Johnson, James Weldon. 1927. *The Autobiography of an Ex-Colored Man.* New York: Alfred A. Knopf. Reprint, In *Three Negro Classics.* New York: Avon Books, 1965.

———. 1914/1995a. "Once More Haiti." *New York Age*, October 29. Reprinted in *The Selected Writings of James Weldon Johnson*, vol. 1: *The New York Age Editorials (1914–1923)*, edited by Sondra Kathryn Wilson, 230. New York: Oxford University Press.

———. 1920/1995b. "Self-Determining Haiti." The Nation 111:236–38, 265–67, 295–97, 345–47. Reprinted in *The Selected Writings of James Weldon Johnson*, vol. 2:

Social, Political, and Literary Essays, edited by Sondra Kathryn Wilson, 207–43. New York: Oxford University Press.

———. 1920/1995c. "The Truth About Haiti." *Crisis* 20 (1920): 217–24. Reprinted in *The Selected Writings of James Weldon Johnson,* vol. 2: *Social, Political, and Literary Essays,* edited by Sondra Kathryn Wilson, 244–52. New York: Oxford University Press.

———. 1927/1995d. *Native African Races and Cultures.* Pamphlet, John F. Slater Fund, Occasional Papers, no. 25. Charlottesville, Virginia. Reprinted in *The Selected Writings of James Weldon Johnson,* vol. 2: *Social, Political, and Literary Essays,* edited by Sondra Kathryn Wilson, 253–72. New York: Oxford University Press.

Kastner, Georges. 1857. *Les Voix de Paris: Essai d'une histoire littéraire et musicale des cris populaires de la capitale depuis le moyen âge jusqu'à nos jours; précédé de considérations sur l'origine et la caractère du cri en général, et suivi de Les cris de Paris, grande symphonie humoristique vocale et instrumentale.* Paris: G. Brandus, Dufor, et cie.

Kernodle, Tammy Lynn. 1993. "Still's *Troubled Island,* a Troubled Opera: Its Creation, Performance, and Reception." M.A. thesis, The Ohio State University.

Knight, Franklin W. 1978. *The Caribbean: The Genesis of a Fragmented Nationalism.* New York: Oxford University Press.

Laguerre, Férère. 1975. "De la Musique folklorique d'Haiti." *Conjonction* 126 (June): 9–32.

———. 1981. Recording of Vodou Rhythms and Traditional Music Conference. Unidentified Location. 21 July. Private collection of Férère Laguerre, fils.

Laguerre, Michel. 1993. *The Military and Society in Haiti.* Knoxville: University of Tennessee Press.

Largey, Michael. 1994. "Composing a Haitian Cultural Identity: Haitian Elites, African Ancestry, and Musical Composition." *Black Music Research Journal* 14, no. 2: 99–117.

———. 1995. "Haiti and the French Caribbean." In *Caribbean Currents: Caribbean Music from Rumba to Reggae,* edited by Peter Manuel, with Kenneth Bilby and Michael Largey, 117–42. Philadelphia: Temple University Press.

———. 1998. "How to Watch a Voodoo Movie: Rules for a Postmodern Age." *The Ryder* (October): 28–31.

———. 2000. "Politics on the Pavement: Haitian Rara as a Traditionalizing Process." *Journal of American Folklore* 113 (449): 239–54.

Lamothe, Ludovic. 1935. "Pouvons-nous avoir une musique nationale?" *Le Temps* 9:11–12.

———. 1936. "Musique Haïtienne." *La Releve* 6 (December): 4–6.

———. 1937. "Le Folklore." *La Releve* 6 (July): 33–36.

———. 1955. *Musique de Ludovic Lamothe: Valses, Dances Espagnoles, Scènes de Carnaval et autres.* Edited by Antione Jean and Fernand Lamothe. Port-au-Prince: n.p.

Lassègue, Franck. 1919. *Etudes critiques sur la musique haïtienne.* 1ere serie. Port-au-Prince: Imprimerie du Sacre-Coeur.

———. 1929. *Ciselures, la musique à travers Haïti.* Albert, France: Libraire A. Crossel.

Lawless, Robert. 1992. *Haiti's Bad Press.* Rochester, Vt.: Schenkman Books.

LeBon, Gustav. 1894. *Lois psychologiques d'évolution des peuples.* Paris: Alcan.

Legendre, Franck. 1939. "La Danse sous la Tonnelle." *Les Griots* 3, no. 3: 354–60.

Léger, Jacques Nicolas. 1907/1970. *Haiti, Her History and Her Detractors.* New York and Washington: Neale Publishing Co., 1907. Reprint, Westport, Conn.: Negro Universities Press, 1970.

de Lesspinasse, Eugène. n.d. "Do-Do Méia." Unpublished manuscript. L'Ecole Sainte Trinité Collection. Port-au-Prince, Haiti.

Lévi-Strauss, Claude. 1962. *Le Totemisme aujourd'hui.* Paris: Presses universitaires de France.

Lewis, David Levering. 1993. *W. E. B. Du Bois: Biography of a Race, 1868–1919.* Vol. 1. New York: Henry Holt and Company.

Lhamon, W. T. 1998. *Raising Cain: Blackface Performance from Jim Crow to Hip Hop.* Cambridge, Mass.: Harvard University Press.

Liautaud, André. 1928/1971. "O Beaux Soirs de Kenscoff." In *Anthologie de la poésie haïtienne "Indigène,"* 29. Port-au-Prince: Revue Indigène. Reprint, Nendeln: Kraus Reprint.

Linton, Ralph. 1943. "Nativistic Movements." *American Anthropologist* 45:230–40.

List, George. 1974. "The Reliability of Transcription." *Ethnomusicology* 18, no. 3: 353–78.

Lott, Eric. 1993. *Love and Theft: Blackface Minstrelsy and the American Working Class.* Oxford and New York: Oxford University Press.

Lowney, John. 2000. "Haiti and Black Transnationalism: Remapping the Migrant Geography of *Home to Harlem.*" *African American Review* 34, no. 3: 413–29.

Lundhal, Mats. 1979. *Peasants and Poverty: A Study of Haiti.* New York: St. Martin's Press.

"M. Elie's Recital: Successful Entertainment." 1909. Clipping from unidentified Jamaican newspaper. Private collection of Simone Elie Stecher, Pétionville, Haiti.

McAlister, Elizabeth. 2002. *Rara! Vodou, Power and Performance in Haiti and Its Diaspora.* Berkeley and Los Angeles: University of California Press.

McClintock, Anne. 1996. " 'No Longer in a Future Heaven': Nationalism, Gender, and Race." In *Becoming National: A Reader,* edited by Geoff Eley and Ronald Grigor Suny, 260–85. New York: Oxford University Press.

McCrocklin, James. 1956. *Garde D'Haiti: Twenty Years of Organization and Training by the United States Marine Corps.* Annapolis, Md.: United States Naval Institute.

McGinty, Doris E. 1979. "The Washington Conservatory of Music and School of Expression." *The Black Perspective in Music* 7, no. 1: 59–71.

McKay, Claude. 1928/1987. *Home to Harlem.* New York and London: Harper and Brothers. Reprint, Boston: Northeastern University Press.

McLaren, Joseph. 1997. *Langston Hughes: Folk Dramatist in the Protest Tradition, 1921–1943.* Westport, Conn.: Greenwood Press.

Malkki, Liisa. 1995. *Purity and Exile: Violence, Memory, and National Cosmology Among Hutu Refugees in Tanzania.* Chicago: University of Chicago Press.

Mallon, Florencia E. 1995. *Peasant and Nation: The Making of Postcolonial Mexico and Peru.* Berkeley and Los Angeles: University of California Press.

Marshall, Harriet Gibbs. 1930. *The Story of Haiti: From the Discovery of the Island by Christopher Columbus to the Present Day.* Boston: Christopher Publishing House.

Matheus, John Frederick. n.d. "Ouanga: Haitian Opera." Unpublished typescript. Clarence Cameron White Collection. Schomburg Center for Research in Black Culture. New York Public Library.

———. 1929a. "Belle Mam'selle of Martinique." *Carolina Magazine.* John F. Matheus Papers, Drain-Jordan Library, West Virginia State College. Institute, West Virginia.

———. 1929b. "Cocomacaque: A Drama of Haiti." Draft ms. of libretto. Clarence Cameron White Collection. Schomburg Center for Research in Black Culture. New York Public Library.

————. 1929c. "Coulev' Endormi." *Opportunity* 7: 376–79.

————. 1930. "Ti Yette." In *Plays and Pageants from the Life of the Negro*, 77–105. Willis Richardson, compiler. Washington, D.C.: The Associated Publishers, Inc.

————. 1937. "Sallicoco." *Opportunity* 15: 236–39.

————. 1946. "The English Language Program in Haiti." Unpublished manuscript. John F. Matheus Papers. Drain-Jordan Library, West Virginia State College. Institute, West Virginia.

————. 1972. "Ouanga: My Venture in Libretto Creation." *CLA (College Language Association) Journal* 15, no. 4: 428–40.

————. 1974. "Citadelle." John F. Matheus Papers, Drain-Jordan Library. West Virginia State College. Institute, West Virginia.

Maximilien, Louis. 1945/1982. *Le Vodou Haïtien: Rites radas-canzo*. Port-au-Prince: Imprimerie de l'Etat. Reprint, Port-au-Prince: Imprimerie Henri Deschamps.

————. 1953. "Considerations sur le folklore: À propos de la musique de Werner Jaegerhuber." *Le National*, 25, 27, 28, 29, 30 April and 1 May: 3, 6, 3, 3, 5, 3. "Notes on Folklore with respect to the music of Werner Jaegerhuber." Translated by Julius Wiesel. Unpublished ms. in the collection of the Société de Recherche et Diffusion de la Musique Haïtienne, Montréal, Québec, Canada.

Melville, George. n.d. "Justin Elie Writes Notable Work." Clipping from unidentified newspaper. Private collection of Simone Elie Stecher. Pétionville, Haiti.

Michel, Rose Lherisson. 1970. *Cantiques et chansons*. Port-au-Prince: Imprimerie des Antilles.

Mintz, Sidney W. 1974. *Caribbean Transformations*. Baltimore: Johns Hopkins University Press.

————. 1985. "From Plantations to Peasantries in the Caribbean." In *Caribbean Contours*, edited by Sidney W. Mintz and Sally Price, 127–54. Baltimore: Johns Hopkins University Press.

Moore, Robin. 1997. *Nationalizing Blackness: Afrocubanismo and Artistic Revolution in Havana, 1920–1940*. Pittsburgh: University of Pittsburgh Press.

Moral, Paul. 1961. *Le Paysan Haïtien (étude sur la vie rurale en Haïti)*. Saint-Amand: G.P. Maisonneuve & Larose.

Moreau de Saint-Méry, Médéric Louis de. 1797. *Description topographique, physique, civile, politique et historique de la partie française de l'isle Saint-Domingue*. 2 vols. Philadelphia: Chez l'auteur; Paris: Chez Dupont, 1797–98.

————. 1985. *A Civilization That Perished: The Last Years of White Colonial Rule in Haiti*. A translation of *A Topographical, Physical, Civil, Political and Historical Description of the French Part of the Island of Santo Domingo, with General Observations on its Population, on the Character and Customs of its Diverse Inhabitants, on its Climate, Culture, Production, Administration, Etc.* Translated by Ivor D. Spencer. Lanham, Md.: University Press of America.

Morisseau-Leroy, Félix. 1939. "Nuits d'Haiti." *Les Griots* 3, no. 3: 361–66.

Moses, Wilson Jeremiah. 1987. *The Golden Age of Black Nationalism, 1850–1925*. New York: Oxford University Press.

Nau, Emile. 1894/1963. *Histoire des caciques d'Haiti*. 2 vols. Paris: Gustave Guerin et Cie. Reprint, Port-au-Prince: Editions Panorama.

Nettl, Bruno. 1983. *The Study of Ethnomusicology: Twenty-Nine Issues and Concepts*. Urbana: University of Illinois Press.

Niles, Blair. 1926. *Black Haiti*. New York: Putnam's Sons.

Nicholls, David. 1974a. "Ideology and Political Protest in Haiti, 1930–46." *Journal of Contemporary History* 9, no. 4: 3–26.

———. 1974b. "A Work of Combat: Mulatto Historians and the Haitian Past, 1847–1867." *Journal of Interamerican Studies and World Affairs* 16, no. 1: 15–38.

———. 1979. *From Dessalines to Duvalier: Race, Colour, and National Independence in Haiti.* Cambridge: Cambridge University Press.

———. 1985. *Haiti in Caribbean Context: Ethnicity, Economy and Revolt.* New York: St. Martin's Press.

O'Meally, Robert, and Geneviève Fabre. 1994. "Introduction." In *History and Memory in African-American Culture,* edited by Geneviève Fabre and Robert O'Meally, 3–17. New York: Oxford University Press.

Pacini-Hernandez, Deborah. 1995. *Bachata: A Social History of a Dominican Popular Music.* Philadelphia: Temple University Press.

Pamphile, Léon D. 1980. "Education in Haiti during the American Occupation." D.Ed. diss., University of Pittsburgh.

———. 2001. *Haitians and African Americans: A Heritage of Tragedy and Hope.* Gainsville: University Press of Florida.

Paquin, Lyonel. 1983. *The Haitians: Class and Color Politics.* New York: Multi-Type.

Peña, Manuel. 1999. *The Mexican-American Orquesta.* Austin: University of Texas Press.

Peterson, Carla. 1995. *"Doers of the Word": African-American Women Speakers and Writers in the North (1830–1880).* New York: Oxford University Press.

"Pianoforte Recital in Kingston." 1909. Clipping from unidentified Jamaican newspaper. Private collection of Simone Elie Stecher. Pétionville, Haiti.

"Pianoforte Recital: M. Elie's Farewell Concert." 1909. Clipping from unidentified Jamaican newspaper. Private collection of Simone Elie Stecher. Pétionville, Haiti.

Pisani, Michael V. 1998. "I'm an Indian Too: Creating Native American Identities in Nineteenth- and Twentieth-Century Music." In *The Exotic in Western Music,* edited by Jonathan Bellman, 218–57. Boston: Northeastern University Press.

Plummer, Brenda Gayle. 1981. "Race, Nationality, and Trade in the Caribbean: The Syrians in Haiti, 1903–34." *The International History Review* 3, no. 4: 23–59.

———. 1982. "The Afro-American Response to the Occupation of Haiti, 1915–1934." *Phylon* 43, no. 2: 125–43.

———. 1988. *Haiti and the Great Powers, 1902–1915.* Baton Rouge: Louisiana State University Press.

———. 1992. *Haiti and the United States: The Psychological Moment.* Athens: University of Georgia Press.

Porter, James. 2001. "'Bring Me the Head of James Macpherson': The Execution of Ossian and the Wellsprings of Folkloric Discourse." *Journal of American Folklore* 114, no. 454: 396–435.

Pradel, Seymour. 1912. "Musique et musiciens haïtiens." *Haiti Littéraire,* 20 June.

Pratt, Mary Louise. 1992. *Imperial Eyes: Travel Writing and Transculturation.* New York: Routledge.

Pressoir, Charles Fernand. 1947. *Débats sur le créole et le folklore.* Port-au-Prince: Imprimerie de l'Etat.

Price, Hannibal. 1900. *De la réhabilitation de la race noire par la république d'Haïti.* Port-au-Prince: J. Verrollot.

Price-Mars, Jean. 1912. "La reforme de l'enseignement primaire." *Haiti litteraire et scientifique,* July 5: 312–17.

———. 1919. *La Vocation de l'élite.* Port-au-Prince: Imprimerie Edmond Chenet.

———. 1928/1983. *Ainsi parla l'oncle.* Paris: Imprimerie de Compiègne. *So Spoke the Uncle.* Translated by Magdaline W. Shannon. Washington, D.C.: Three Continents Press.

———. 1929. *Une étape d'évolution haïtienne.* Port-au-Prince: Imprimerie La Presse.

———. 1932. "A propos de 'La Renaissance Nègre aux Etats-Unis.'" *La Relève* 1, no. 3: 8–14.

———. 1938. "Lemba Pétro, un culte secret, étude de sociologie religieuse." *Revue d'histoire et de géographie d'Haiti* 9, no. 28: 12–31.

"Programs for Today." 1931. *New York World Telegram.* July 27. Private collection of Simone Elie Stecher. Pétionville, Haiti.

RAM. 1993. *Aïbobo.* CinéDisc CD 12191.

Rampersad, Arnold. 2002. *The Life of Langston Hughes,* vol. 1, *1902–1941: I, Too, Sing America.* New York: Oxford University Press.

Ramsey, Kate. 2002. "Without One Ritual Note: Folklore Performance and the Haitian State, 1935–1946." *Radical History Review* 84: 7–42.

Ratner, Conrad H. 1923. "Justin Elie, and the Revival of the Music of the Natives of Latin America." Clipping from unidentified magazine. Personal collection of Simone Elie Stecher. Pétionville, Haiti.

"Le récital du compositeur White à Parisiana." 1928. Clipping from unidentified Haitian newspaper. Clarence Cameron White Papers. Schomburg Center for Research in Black Culture. New York Public Library.

Reed-Danahay, Deborah E. 1997. "Introduction." In *Auto/ethnography: Rewriting the Self and the Social,* edited by Deborah E. Reed-Danahay, 1–20. Oxford and New York: Berg.

Reily, Suzel Ana. 2001. "To Remember Captivity: The *Congados* of Southern Minas Gerais." *Latin American Music Review* 22, no. 1: 4–30.

Renda, Mary A. 2001. *Taking Haiti: Military Occupation and the Culture of U.S. Imperialism.* Chapel Hill: University of North Carolina Press.

Ricourt, Volvic. 1933. "Hommage à Justin Elie: Sonnet." *Le Temps* 2, no. 88 (30 December): 8.

Roach, Joseph. 1996. *Cities of the Dead: Circum-Atlantic Performance.* New York: Columbia University Press.

Roberts, John. 1989. *From Trickster To Badman: The Black Folk Hero in Slavery and Freedom.* Philadelphia: University of Pennsylvania Press.

Robinson, Cedric J. 1994. "W. E. B. Du Bois and Black Sovereignty." In *Imagining Home: Class, Culture and Nationalism in the African Diaspora,* edited by Sidney Lemelle and Robin D. G. Kelley, 145–57. London: Verso.

Romero, Lora. 1997. *Home Fronts: Domesticity and Its Critics in the Antebellum United States.* Durham: Duke University Press.

Roumain, Jacques. 1931. *La Montagne ensorcelèe.* Port-au-Prince: Collection Indigène "La Presse."

———. 1934. *Analyse schématique.* Port-au-Prince: Comité Central du Parti Communiste Haitien.

———. 1942. *A propos de la campagne 'anti-superstitieuse.'* Port-au-Prince: Imprimerie de l'Etat.

————. 1943. *Le Sacrifice du tambour assoto(r)*. Port-au-Prince: Bureau d'Ethnologie, no. 2.

————. 1946. *Gouverneurs de la rosée*. Paris: Les Editeurs Français Reunis.

Ryko, Jehan. n.d. "Miss Ragtime (épisode des 'Cas qu'au. . .en cas qui. . .')." Private collection, Jean-Claude Desmangles. Port-au-Prince, Haiti.

Saint-Louis, Carlos, and Maurice A. Lubin, eds. 1950. *Panorama de la poesie haïtienne*. Port-au-Prince: Editions Henri Deschamps.

Sanders, Leslie Catherine. 2002. "Introduction." In *The Collected Works of Langston Hughes*, vol. 6, *The Plays to 1942*, edited by Leslie Catherine Sanders, 1–13. Columbia: University of Missouri Press.

Saunders, James Robert. 1987. "A West Virginia Scholar in the Harlem Renaissance: The Long and Varied Career of John Frederick Matheus." *The Langston Hughes Review* 6, no. 2 (Fall): 22–28.

Savaille, Rulhière. 1979. *La Grève de 29: la première grève des étudiants haïtiens, 31 octobre 1929*. Port-au-Prince: Les Ateliers Fardin.

Savain, Roger. 1950. Untitled biography of Werner A. Jaegerhuber. In *Complaintes Haïtiennes (Haitian Folklore Songs— Canciones del Folklore Haitiana)*. 2d ed. Port-au-Prince: Compagnie Lithographique.

Schieffelin, Bambi B., and Rachelle Charlier Doucet. 1998. "The 'Real' Haitian Creole: Ideology, Metalinguistics, and Orthographic Choice." In *Language Ideologies: Practice and Theory*, edited by Bambi B. Schieffelin, Kathryn A. Woolard, and Paul V. Kroskrity. 285–316. New York: Oxford University Press.

Schmidt, Hans. 1995. *The United States Occupation of Haiti, 1915–1934*. New Brunswick: Rutgers University Press. Originally published, 1971.

Scott, James. 1990. *Domination and the Arts of Resistance: Hidden Transcripts*. New Haven: Yale University Press.

Semple, Ellen Churchill. 1911. *Influences of Geographic Environment on the Basis of Ratzel's System of Anthropo-geography*. New York and London: Henry Holt.

Seabrook, William B. 1929/1989. *The Magic Island*. New York: Harcourt Brace, 1929. Reprint, New York: Paragon House.

"Service Orchestra Is Lauded." 1931. *The Washington Post*. March 3. Private collection of Simone Elie Stecher, Pétionville, Haiti.

Shannon, Magdaline. 1996. *Jean Price-Mars, the Haitian Elite and the American Occupation, 1915–1935*. New York: St. Martin's Press.

Slonimsky, Nicolas. 1945. *Music of Latin America*. New York: Thomas Y. Crowell Co. Reprint, New York: Da Capo Press, 1972.

Smith, Catherine Parsons. 2000. *William Grant Still: A Study in Contradictions*. Berkeley and Los Angeles: University of California Press.

Somers, Lee. n.d. "Prologues and Epilogues: Novelty!" Clipping from unidentified source. Private collection of Simone Elie Stecher. Pétionville, Haiti.

Sommer, Doris. 1991. *Foundational Fictions: The National Romances of Latin America*. Berkeley and Los Angeles : University of California Press.

Spivak, Gayatri Chakravorty. 1988. "Can the Subaltern Speak?" In *Marxism and the Interpretation of Culture: Limits, Boundaries, and Frontiers*, edited by Cary Nelson and Lawrence Grossberg. Urbana: University of Illinois Press.

Statement of Purpose for Bureau d'Ethnologie. 1956. *Bulletin du Bureau d'Ethnologie* 2, no. 13: vii. Port-au-Prince: Imprimerie de l'Etat.

Stebich, Ute. 1992. *A Haitian Celebration: Art and Culture*. Milwaukee: Milwaukee Art Museum.

Stephens, Michelle A. 1998. "Black Transnationalism and the Politics of National Identity: West Indian Intellectuals in Harlem in the Age of War and Revolution." *American Quarterly* 50, no. 3: 592–608.

Still, William Grant. 1990. *Troubled Island: An Opera in Three Acts.* Libretto by Langston Hughes. Sound recording. Flagstaff, Ariz.: William Grant Still Music. The recording consists of two tape cassettes from the first (and only) three performances of the opera on March 31, April 10, and May 1, 1949 by the New York City Center Opera Company. The copyright is held by Southern Music and the Voice of America.

Still, William Grant, and Langston Hughes. 1949. "Troubled Island: An Opera in Three Acts." Photocopy of unpublished orchestra score. Center for Black Music Research, Columbia College Chicago.

"Studying Haitian Life." n.d. Editorial in the *Pittsburgh Courier.* In Scrapbook: Haiti. Clarence Cameron White Collection. Schomburg Center for Research in Black Culture. New York Public Library.

Stuempfle, Stephen. 1995. *The Steelband Movement: The Forging of a National Art in Trinidad and Tobago.* Philadelphia: University of Pennsylvania Press.

Sturken, Marita. 1997. *Tangled Memories: The Vietnam War, the AIDS Epidemic, and the Politics of Remembering.* Berkeley and Los Angeles: University of California Press.

Sylvain, Benito. 1901. *Du sort des indigènes dans les colonies d'exploitation.* Paris: Boyer.

Sylvain, Normil G. 1927. "Chronique—Programme." *La revue indigène* 1, no. 1: 1–10.

Sylvain, Suzanne. 1936. *Le Créole Haïtien, morphologie et syntaxe.* Port-au-Prince: Wettern.

Terrell, Mary Church. 1933. "Local Composer Wins Medal for Best American Opera." *Washington Star.* May 28.

Terry, William E. 1977. "The Negro Music Journal: An Appraisal." *The Black Perspective in Music* 5: 146–60.

Trouillot, Michel-Rolph. 1990. *Haiti, State against Nation: The Origins and Legacy of Duvalierism.* New York: Monthly Review Press.

———. 1995. *Silencing the Past: Power and the Production of History.* Boston: Beacon Press.

Tuohy, Sue. 2001. "The Sonic Dimensions of Nationalism in Modern China: Musical Representation and Transformation." *Ethnomusicology* 45, no. 1: 107–31.

Turino, Thomas. 1999. "Signs of Imagination, Identity, and Experience: A Peircian Semiotic Theory for Music." *Ethnomusicology* 43, no. 2: 221–55.

———. 2000. *Nationalists, Cosmopolitans, and Popular Music in Zimbabwe.* Chicago: University of Chicago Press.

Turnier, A. 1982. *Avec Mérisier Jeannis: Une tranche de vie Jacmelienne et nationale.* Port-au-Prince: Imprimerie Le Natal.

Turner, Victor. 1977. *The Ritual Process: Structure and Anti-Structure.* Ithaca: Cornell University Paperbacks.

Valdman, Albert. 1984. "The Linguistic Situation of Haiti." In *Haiti—Today and Tommorrow: An Interdisciplinary Study,* edited by Charles R. Foster and Albert Valdman, 77–100. Lanham, Md.: University Press of America.

Victor, René. 1943. *Les Voix de nos rues.* Port-au-Prince: Imprimerie de l'Etat.

Vilaire, Jean-Joseph. 1950a. "La Mort de l'Indien." In *Panorama de la poesie haïtienne,* edited by Carlos Saint-Louis and Maurice A. Lubin. 237. Port-au-Prince: Editions Henri Deschamps.

———. 1950b. "Caonabo." In *Panorama de la poesie haïtienne,* edited by Carlos Saint-Louis and Maurice A. Lubin, 237–38. Port-au-Prince: Editions Henri Deschamps.

Vincent, Sténio. 1910. *La République d'Haïti, telle qu'elle est.* Bruxelles: Société Anonyme Belge d'Imprimerie.

———. 1931. *En posant les jalons.* Port-au-Prince: Imprimerie de l'Etat.

"Le violoniste C.C. White et notre grand musicien Lamothe." n.d. Clipping from unidentified Haitian newspaper. In Scrapbook: Haiti. Clarence Cameron White Collection. Schomburg Center for Research in Black Culture. New York Public Library.

Volvic, Rémy Joseph. 1949. "A la memoire d'Occide Jeanty." *Les Griots* 2, no. 54 (4 February): 1–2.

"Voodoux at the Rendez-Vous." 1923. *Evening Telegram,* 28 July.

Wade, Peter. 2000. *Music, Race, and Nation: Música Tropical in Colombia.* Chicago: University of Chicago Press.

Washington, Booker T. 1901. *Up From Slavery: An Autobiography.* New York: Avon Books. Reprint, Garden City, N.J.: Doubleday, 1965.

———. 1915. "Haiti and the United States." *Outlook* 111 (November 17): 681.

Whisnant, David. 1983. *All That Is Native and Fine: The Politics of Culture in an American Region.* Chapel Hill: University of North Carolina Press.

White, Clarence Cameron. 1927. "The Labor Motif in Negro Music." *The Modern Quarterly* 4: 79–81.

———. 1928. Scrapbook: Haiti. Collection of photographs. Clarence Cameron White Collection. Schomburg Center for Research in Black Culture. New York Public Library.

———. 1929. "A Musical Pilgrimage to Haiti, the Island of Beauty, Mystery and Rhythm." *The Etude* 7: 505–506.

———. 1935. "History of Negro Music." Unpublished manuscript. Clarence Cameron White Papers. Schomburg Center for Research in Black Culture. New York Public Library.

White, Clarence Cameron, and John Matheus. 1932. *Ouanga! Opera in A Prologue and Three Acts Based on The Haitian Drama by John F. Matheus.* Piano/vocal score. Paris: Néocopie Musicale. Clarence Cameron White Collection. Schomburg Center for Research in Black Culture. New York Public Library.

———. 1955. *Ouanga: A Haitian Opera in Three Acts.* Piano/vocal score. New York: Sam Fox Publishing Company.

Wilcken, Lois E. 1992a. *The Drums of Vodou.* Tempe, Ariz.: White Cliffs Media Company.

———. 1992b. "Power, Ambivalence, and the Remaking of Haitian Vodoun Music in New York." *Latin American Music Review* 13, no. 1: 1–32.

Williams, Raymond. 1977. *Marxism and Literature.* New York: Oxford University Press.

Wirkus, Faustin, and Taney Dudley. 1931. *The White King of La Gonave.* Garden City, N.Y.: Garden City Publishing.

Weinstein, Brian, and Aaron Segal. 1984. *Haiti: Political Failures, Cultural Successes.* New York: Praeger.

Yano, Christine R. 2002. *Tears of Longing: Nostalgia and the Nation in Japanese Popular Song.* Harvard East Asian Monographs, no. 206. Cambridge, Mass.: Harvard University Press.

Yuval-Davis, Nina, and Floya Anthias, eds. 1989. *Women-Nation-State.* London: Macmillan.

INDEX